ONLY A
PRAYER
MEETING

Studies on Prayer Meetings
and Prayer Meeting Addresses

C. H. Spurgeon

C . H . S P U R G E O N
C L A S S I C S

FOREWORD BY MARK DEVER

HERITAGE

Scripture quotations are taken from the *King James Version*.

Contents

PART I

ADDRESSES ON PRAYER

AND

PRAYER MEETINGS

Prefatory Note

Mr. Spurgeon long ago had the intention of collecting into a volume a selection from the Addresses delivered by him at the Metropolitan Tabernacle and other Prayer-meetings, but the opportunity of carrying out that idea never came to him.

It is hoped that the publication of the forty Addresses here gathered together will be helpful to others who have the responsibility of conducting Prayer-meetings, as well as interesting to readers in general because of the variety of subjects discussed in them.

In his first volume of 'Lectures to my Students,' when speaking upon 'The Faculty of Impromptu Speech' MR. SPURGEON said:—'Ever since I have been in London, in order to get into the habit of speaking extemporaneously, I have never studied or prepared anything for the Monday evening Prayer-meeting. I have all along selected that occasion as the opportunity for offhand exhortation; but you will observe that I do not, at such times, select difficult expository topics, or abstruse themes, but restrict myself to simple homely talk about the elements of our faith. When standing up, on such occasions, one's mind makes a review, and enquires, "What subject has already taken up ny thought during the day ? What have I met with in my reading during the past week ? What is most laid upon my heart at this hour ? What is suggested by the hymns or the prayers ?"'

One of the Addresses in this volume—the exposition of Psalm lxxxi. 16—was delivered at a Prayer-meeting in New Park Street Chapel in 1857; but most of them were given in the Metropolitan Tabernacle, at those wonderful Monday-evening gatherings, concerning which MR. SPURGEON once wrote in 'The Sword and the Trowel': 'A Wesleyan minister lately said that he was never more surprised in his life than when he dropped into the Tabernacle, and found the ground-floor and part of the gallery filled at a Prayer-meeting. He believed that such a thing was almost without a parallel in London, and that it accounted for the success of the ministry. We concur in his impartial judgment. Will not all the churches try the power of prayer?'

The second chapter in this book is the only one that was not delivered as an address; but it so well sets forth Mr. Spurgeon's opinions of what Prayer-meetings should be, that it is included in order to make the volume as complete as possible.

Other of Mr.Spurgeon's Prayer-meeting addresses have been published in his volumes entitled *The Bible and the Newspaper*, *Be of Good Cheer*, *Till He come*, and *The Soul-Winner*.

1

Only a Prayer Meeting!

What a company we have here tonight! It fills my heart with gladness, and my eyes with tears of joy, to see so many hundreds of persons gathered together at what is sometimes wickedly described as 'only a prayer meeting'. It is good for us to draw nigh unto God in prayer, and specially good to make up a great congregation for such a purpose. We have attended little prayer meetings of four or five, and we have been glad to be there, for we had the promise of our Lord's presence; but our minds are grieved to see so little attention given to united prayer by many of our churches. We have longed to see great numbers of God's people coming up to pray, and we now enjoy this sight. Let us praise God that it is so. How could we expect a blessing if we were too idle to ask for it? How could we look for a Pentecost if we never met with one accord, in one place, to wait upon the Lord? Brethren, we shall never see much change for the better in our churches in general till the prayer meeting occupies a higher place in the esteem of Christians. To mix it up with the weeknight lecture, and really make an end of it, is a sad sign of declension. I wonder some two or three earnest souls in such churches do not band themselves together to restore the meeting for prayer, and bind themselves with a pledge to keep it up whether the minister will come to it or not.

But now that we have come together, how shall we pray? Let us not degenerate into formality, or we shall be dead while we think we live. Let us not waver through unbelief, or we shall pray in vain. The Lord saith to his church, 'Open thy mouth, wide, and I will fill it.' Oh, for great faith with which to offer great prayers! We have been mingling praise and prayer together as a delicious compound of spices, fit to be presented upon the altar of incense through Christ our Lord; may we not, at this time, offer some special far-reaching petition? It is suggested to me that we pray for a true and genuine revival of religion throughout the world.

I am glad of any signs of life, even if they should be feverish and transient, and I am slow to judge any well-intended movement; but yet I am very fearful that many so-called 'revivals' have, in the long run, wrought more harm than good. Places which have had the most of religious excitement are frequently the most difficult to move. Men's minds have been baked hard in the oven of fanaticism. A species of religious gambling has fascinated many men, and given them a distaste for the sober business of true godliness. But if I would nail down counterfeits upon the counter, I do not therefore undervalue true gold. Far from it. It is to be desired, beyond measure, that the Lord would send a real and lasting revival of spiritual life. We need a work of the Holy Ghost of a supernatural kind, putting power into the preaching of the Word, inspiring all believers with heavenly energy, and solemnly affecting the hearts of the careless so that they may turn to God and live. We would not be drunk with the wine of carnal excitement, but we would be filled with the Spirit; we would not leap upon the altar, and shout and cry, 'O Baal, hear us!' but we would behold the fire descending from heaven in answer to the effectual fervent prayers of righteous men. Can we not entreat the Lord our God to make bare his holy arm in the eyes of all the people in this day of declension and vanity?

We want a revival of old-fashioned doctrine. Our fear is that, if 'modern thought' proceeds much further, the fashion of our religion will be as much Mohammedan as Christian; in fact, it will be more like infidelity than either. A converted Jew, staying in London, went into a dissenting chapel which I could mention; and when he returned to the friend with whom he was staying, he enquired what the religion of the place could be, for he had heard nothing of what he had received as the Christian faith. The doctrines which are distinctive of the New Testament may not be actually denied in set terms, but they are spirited away; familiar phrases are used, but a new sense is attached to them.

Certain modern preachers talk much of Christ, and yet reject Christianity. Under cover of extolling the Teacher, they reject his teaching for theories more in accord with the spirit of the age. At first, Calvinism was too harsh, then Evangelical doctrines became too antiquated, and now the Scriptures themselves must bow to man's alteration and improvement. There is plenty of preaching in the present day in which no mention is made of the depravity of human nature, the work of the Holy Ghost, the blood of atonement or the punishment of sin. The deity of Christ is not so often assailed, but the gospel which he gave us, through his own teaching and that of the apostles, is questioned, criticised and set aside. One of the great missionary societies actually informs us, by one of its writers, that it does not send out missionaries to save the heathen from the wrath to come, but to prepare them 'for the higher realm which awaits them beyond the river of death'. I confess that I have better hopes for the future of the heathen than for the state of those who thus write concerning them. The heathen will derive but small advantage from the gospel which such triflers with the Scriptures are likely to carry them.

I know not a single doctrine which is not at this hour studiously undermined by those who ought to be its defenders; there is not a truth that is precious to the soul which is not now denied by those whose profession it is to proclaim it. The times are out of joint, and many are hoping to make them more and more so. To me, it is clear that we need a revival of old-fashioned gospel preaching like that of Whitefield and Wesley: to me, preferably that of Whitefield. We need to believe: the Scriptures must be made the infallible foundation of all teaching; the ruin, redemption and regeneration of mankind must be set forth in unmistakable terms, and that right speedily, or faith will be more rare than gold of Ophir. We must demand from our teachers that they give us a 'Thus saith the Lord'; for, at this time, they give us their own imaginations. Today, the Word of the Lord in the Book of Jeremiah is true:

> Hearken not unto the words of the prophets that prophesy unto you: they make you vain: they speak a vision of their own heart, and not out of the mouth of the LORD. They say still unto them that despise me, The LORD hath said, Ye shall have peace; and they say unto every one that walketh after the imagination of his own heart, No evil shall come upon you (Jer. 23:16, 17).

Beware of those who say that there is no hell, and who declare new ways to heaven. May the Lord have mercy upon them!

Urgently do we need a revival of personal godliness. This is, indeed, the secret of church prosperity. When individuals fall from their steadfastness, the church is tossed to and fro; when personal faith is steadfast, the church abides true to her Lord. We have in and around our own denomination many true-hearted servants of Christ, who are hardly put to it to know what to do. Their loyalty to their Lord and to his truth is greater than their love to sect or party, and they know not whether to abide in their present position and fight out the great question, or to lift the old banner and quit their apostatising associates. Do whichever they may, it is upon the truly godly and spiritual that the future of religion depends in the hand of God. Oh, for more truly holy men, quickened and filled with the Holy Spirit, consecrated to the Lord, and sanctified by his truth! What can be accomplished by worldly professors, theatre-going church-members, semi-infidel teachers and philosophical preachers? Nothing but ruin can follow from a preponderance of these. Their presence is grievous to God, and disastrous to his people. Brethren, we must each one live if the church is to be alive; we must live unto God if we expect to see the pleasure of the Lord prospering in our hands. Sanctified men are the necessity of every age, for they are the salt of society and the saviours of the race. The Lord has made a man more precious than a wedge of gold: I mean, a decided, instructed, bold, unswerving man of God.

We deeply want a revival of domestic religion. We have been saddened at the terrible accounts of the impurity of this city; but, doubtless, one cause of this state of things is the neglect of household religion among Christians, and the entire absence of common decency in many of the lodgings of the poor. The Christian family was the bulwark of godliness in the days of the Puritans; but in these evil times hundreds of families of so-called Christians have no family worship, no restraint upon growing sons, and no wholesome instruction or discipline. See how the families of many professors are as dressy, as godless as the children of the non-religious! How can we hope to see the Kingdom of our Lord advance when his own disciples do not teach his gospel to their own sons and daughters? Have we not need to repeat the lament of Jeremiah: 'Even the sea monsters draw out the breast, they give suck to their young ones: the daughter of my people is become cruel, like the ostriches in the wilderness' (Lam. 4:3). How different this from the father of the faithful, of whom the Lord said, 'I know him [Abraham], that he will command his children and his household after him, and they shall keep the way of the Lord' (Gen. 18:19).

The surest way to promote godliness abroad is to labour for it at home. The shortest method for the overthrow of priestcraft is for every man to be the priest in his own house, and to warn his sons against deceitful men. May our dear children be so well taught from infancy that they may not only escape the common vices of the age, but grow up to become patterns of holiness! This is a great difficulty to our poorer friends in this loathsome city, which is becoming as polluted as heathendom. A good sister, who lives close to this house of prayer, came up from a country town with her little boy, and she was horrified before long to hear him use profane language, being evidently unaware of its meaning. He had picked it up in the street close to his mother's door. Where are the children of working folks to run if they are not able to walk the streets? All around us, vice has become so daring that a blind man may almost be envied; but even he has ears, and will, therefore, be vexed with the filthy conversation of the wicked. Good people say to me, 'What are we to do?' I wish those who live in the breezy country village would stop there, and not come into our close streets, and lanes, and courts, which reek with blasphemy and dirty talk. Why do working men so often think it necessary, in their ordinary conversation, to use such abominable expressions, which have no useful meaning, and are simply disgusting? If ever Christian people should be pure, and should watch over their children with a holy jealousy, now is the time, and this is a worthy subject for daily prayer.

I would sooner have the doctrines of grace revived, individual piety deepened and family religion increased than I would watch a frantic crowd parading the street with noisy music, and harsh clamour. I see no special virtue in drums and tambourines. Make what noise you will to attract the careless if you afterwards give them sound instruction in the truth, and make them to know the meaning of the Word of the Lord; but if it be mere stir, and song, and swagger, what is the good of it? If gospel truth is not taught, your work will be a building of wood, hay and stubble, soon to be consumed. Quick building is seldom permanent. Gold, silver and precious stones are scarce material, not easily found; but then they endure the fire. What is the use of religion which comes up in a night, and perishes as soon? Ah, me! what empty bragging we have heard! The thing was done, but then it was never worth doing; soon things were as if it never had been done; and, moreover, this sham way of doing it made it all the harder toil for the real worker.

O Christian men and women, be thorough in what you do, and know, and teach! Hold truth as with an iron grip; let your families be trained in the fear of God, and be yourselves 'holiness unto the Lord'; so shall you stand like rocks amid the surging waves of error and ungodliness which rage around you.

We want, also, more and more, a revival of vigorous consecrated strength. I have pleaded for true piety; I now beg for one of the highest results of it. We need saints. It may be that all cannot attain unto 'the first three'; but we cannot do without champions. We need gracious minds trained to a high form of spiritual life by much converse with God in solitude. These are the standard-bearers of the army: each one is a king's son. There is an air about them, humble as they are, as of men who breathe a purer atmosphere. Such was Abraham, who, by his communion with God, acquired a more than royal bearing. The king of Sodom shrinks into insignificance in the presence of the high-minded sheik who will not take of his lawful spoils from a thread to a shoe-latchet, lest the heathen king should say, 'I have made Abraham rich.' Saints acquire nobility from their constant resort to the place where the Lord meets with them. There, also, they acquire that power in prayer which we so greatly need. Oh, that we had more men like John Knox, whose prayers were more terrible to Queen Mary than ten thousand men! Oh, that we had more Elijahs, by whose faith the windows of heaven should be shut or opened! This power comes not by a sudden effort; it is the outcome of a life devoted to the God of Israel. If our life is all in public, it will be a frothy, vapoury, ineffectual existence; but if we hold high converse with God in secret, we shall be mighty for good. The Puritans were abundant in meditation and prayer; and there were giants on the earth in those days. He that is a prince with God will take high rank with men, after the true measure of nobility.

May the Lord send us many self-contained Christians, whose godliness leans on God for itself, and is not a second-hand affair! We see too many Christian people depending upon one another, like houses 'run up' by 'jerry-builders', which are so slenderly built that, if you were to pull down the last one in the row, they would all follow. Beware of being a lean-to; endeavour to rest on your own walls of real faith in the Lord Jesus. I tremble for a church whose continuance depends upon the talent and cleverness of one man. If he is removed, the whole thing will collapse: this is a wretched business. May none of us fall into a mean, poverty-stricken dependence on man! We want among us believers like those solid, substantial family mansions which stand from generation to generation as landmarks of the country: no lath-and-plaster fabrics, but edifices solidly constructed to bear all weathers, and defy time itself. Given a host of men who are steadfast, immovable, always abounding in the work of the Lord, and then the glory of God's grace will be clearly manifested, not only in them, but in those round about them. The Lord send us a revival of consecrated strength, and heavenly energy! May the weakest among us be as David, and David as the angel of the Lord!

As for you who are not converted to God, many of you will be caught in the great wave of blessing, if God shall cause it to break over us. When saints live unto God, sinners are converted to God. 'I was converted,' said one, 'not by hearing a sermon, but by seeing one.' 'How was that?' he was asked. 'My next-door neighbour was the only man in the street who went to a place of worship; and, as I saw him go out as regularly as clockwork, I said to myself, "That man regards the Sabbath, and the God of the Sabbath, and I do not." By and by, I went into his house, and I saw that comfort and order reigned in it, while my room was wretched. I saw how his wife and children dwelt in love, and I said to myself, "This home is happy because the father fears God." I saw my neighbour calm in trouble, and patient under persecution. I knew him to be upright, true, and kind, and I said to myself, "I will find out this man's secret, and thus I was converted." ' Preach by your hands if you cannot preach by your tongues. When our church-members show the fruits of true godliness, we shall soon have enquiries for the tree which bears such a crop.

Dear friends, at our prayer meetings of late, our Lord has very graciously spoken to one and another of the unconverted among us. What a mercy that they were so far interested as to come! We have not said very much to them, but we have been praying for them; and we have talked of the joys of our holy faith, and one after another they have quietly given their hearts to God while in the prayer meeting. I feel very glad about it; it was all that we needed to make these meetings the gate of heaven. Such conversions are specially beautiful, they are so altogether of the Lord, and are so much the result of his working by the whole church that I am doubly delighted with them Oh, that every gathering of faithful men might be a lure to attract others to Jesus!

May many souls fly to him because they see others speeding in that direction! Why not? The coming together of the saints is the first part of Pentecost, and the ingathering of sinners is the second. It began with 'only a prayer-meeting', but it ended with a grand baptism of thousands of converts. Oh, that the prayers of believers may act as loadstones to sinners!

There are a few among us who are not saved, and but a few. I do not believe they will long escape the saving influence which floods these assemblies. We have made a holy ring around certain of them; and they must soon yield to our importunity, for we are pleading with God as well as with them. Their wives are praying for them, their brothers and sisters are praying for them, and others are in the devout confederacy; therefore they must be brought in. Oh, that they would come at once! Why this reluctance to be blessed? Why this hesitation to be saved? Lord, we turn from these poor foolish procrastinators to thyself, and we plead for them with thine all-wise and gracious Spirit! Lord, turn them, and they shall be turned! By their conversion, prove that a true revival has commenced tonight! Let it spread through all our households, and then run from church to church till the whole of Christendom shall be ablaze with the heaven-descended fire! Let us pray.

2

Prayer Meetings

As They Were, and As They Should Be

Among the faults, which have largely disappeared from prayer meetings as they used to be conducted in my early days, these were the principal ones. First, the excessive length of the prayers. A brother would fix himself against the table-pew, and pray for twenty minutes or half-an-hour, and then conclude by asking forgiveness for his shortcomings – a petition which was hardly sanctioned by those who had undergone the penance of endeavouring to join in his long-winded discourse. A good cure for this evil is for the minister judiciously to admonish the brother to study brevity, and if this avail not, to jog his elbow when the people are getting weary. This fault, which is the ruin of all fervency, ought to be extirpated by all means, even at the expense of the personal feelings of the offender.

Cant phrases were another evil. 'We would not rush into thy presence as the unthinking (!) horse into battle.' As if horses ever did think, and as if it were not better to exhibit the spirit and energy of the horse rather than the sluggishness and stupidity of the ass. As the verse from which we imagine this fine sentence to be derived has more to do with sinning than with praying, we are glad that the phrase is on its last legs. 'Go from heart to heart as oil from vessel to vessel.' This is probably a quotation from the nursery romance of *Ali Baba and the Forty Thieves*, but as destitute of sense, Scripture and poetry as ever sentence could be conceived to be. We are not aware that oil runs from one vessel to another in any very mysterious or wonderful manner; it is true it is rather slow in coming out, and is therefore an apt symbol of some people's earnestness; but surely it would be better to have the grace direct from heaven than to have it out of another vessel

– a Popish idea which the metaphor seems to insinuate, if indeed it has any meaning at all.

A very favourite description of the suppliant was, 'thy poor unworthy dust' – an epithet generally applied to themselves by the proudest men in the congregation, and not seldom by the most monied and grovelling, in which case the last two words are not so very inappropriate. We have heard of a good man who, in pleading for his children and grandchildren, was so completely beclouded in the binding influence of this expression that he exclaimed, 'O Lord, save thy dust, and thy dust's dust, and thy dust's dust's dust!' When Abraham said, 'I have taken upon me to speak unto the Lord, which am but dust and ashes' (Gen. 18:27), the utterance was forcible and deeply expressive; but in its misquoted, perverted and abused form, the sooner it is consigned to its own element the better. Very many other perversions of Scripture, uncouth similes and ridiculous metaphors will recall themselves to the reader; we have neither time nor patience to recapitulate them; they are a sort of spiritual slang, the offspring of unholy ignorance, unmanly imitation or graceless hypocrisy; they are at once a dishonour to those who constantly repeat them, and an intolerable nuisance to those whose ears are jaded with them. They have had the most baneful effects upon our prayer meetings, and we rejoice to assist in bringing them to their deserved and ignoble end.

Another evil was mistaking preaching for prayer. The friends who were reputed to be 'gifted' indulged themselves in public prayer with a review of their own experience, a recapitulation of their creed, an occasional running commentary upon a chapter or Psalm, or even a criticism upon the Pastor and his sermons. It was too often quite forgotten that the brother was addressing the divine Majesty, before whose wisdom a display of our knowledge is impertinence, and before whose glory an attempt at swelling words and pompous periods is little short of profanity; the harangue was evidently intended for man rather than God, and on some occasions did not contain a single petition from beginning to end. We hope that good men are leaving this unhallowed practice and are beginning to see that sermons and doctrinal disquisitions are miserable substitutes for earnest wrestling prayers, when our place is before the mercy-seat, and our engagement is intercession with the Most High.

Monotonous repetition frequently occurred, and is not yet extinct. Christian men, who object to forms of prayer, will nevertheless use the same words, the same sentences, the identical address at the commencement and the exact ascriptions at the conclusion. We have known some brethren's prayers by heart, so that we could calculate within a few seconds when they would conclude. Now this cometh of evil. All that can be said against the prayers of the Church of England, which were many of them composed by eminent Christians, and are, some of them, as beautiful as they are scriptural, must apply with tenfold force to those dreary compositions which have little virtue left, since their extempore character is clearly disproved. Oh, for warm hearts, burning with red hot desires which make a channel from the lip with glowing words, then, indeed, this complaint would never be made – 'What is the use in my going to the prayer meeting, when I know all that will be said if So-and-so is called on?' This is not an uncommon excuse for staying away; and, really, while flesh is weak, it is not so very unreasonable a plea; we have heard far worse apologies for greater offences. If our (so-called) 'praying men' drive the people away by their constant repetitions, one-half at least of the fault lies at their door.

Most of these diseases, we trust, are finding their cure; but the man would be hardy, not to say foolhardy, who should affirm that there is now no room for further improvement. 'Advance' must still be our motto, and in the matter of the prayer meeting it will be found most suitable.

Our brethren will excuse our offering them advice, and must take it only for what it is worth; but having to superintend a large church, and to conduct a prayer meeting which scarcely ever numbers less than from a thousand to twelve hundred attendants, we will simply give our own notions as to the most efficient method of promoting and sustaining these holy gatherings.

1.   Let the minister himself set a very high value upon this means of grace. Let him frequently speak of it as being dear to his own heart; and let him prove his words by throwing all his vigour into it, being absent as seldom as possible, and doing all in his power to give an interest to the meeting. If our pastors set the ill example of coming in late, of frequently staying away,

or conducting the engagements in a drowsy, formal way, we shall soon see our people despising the exercise, and forsaking the assembling of themselves together. A warm-hearted address of ten minutes, with a few lively words interposed between the prayers, will do much, with God's blessing, to foster a love for the prayer meeting.

2.   Let the brethren labour their brevity. If each person will offer the petition most laid upon his heart by the Holy Spirit, and then make room for another, the evening will be far more profitable, and the prayers incomparably more fervent than if each brother ran round the whole circle of petition without dwelling on one point. Compare the subjects of prayer to so many nails; it will be better for a petitioner to drive one nail home with repeated blows than to deal one ineffectual tap to them one after another. Let as many as possible take part in the utterance of the church's desires; the change of voice will prevent weariness, and the variety of subjects will excite attention. Better to have six pleading earnestly than two drowsily; far better for the whole meeting that the many wants should be represented experimentally by many intercessors than formally by two or three. As a general rule, meetings in which no prayer exceeds ten minutes, and the most are under five, will exhibit the most fervour and life; in fact, length is a deathblow to earnestness, and brevity is an assistant to zeal. When we have had ten prayers in the hour, varied with the singing of single verses, we have far oftener been in the Spirit than when only four persons have engaged in supplication. This is an observation confirmed by the opinion of our fellow worshippers; it might not hold good in all cases, but it is so with us, and therefore we thus witness.

3.   Persuade all the brethren to pray aloud. If the younger and less-instructed members shrink from the privilege, tell them they are not to speak to man, but to God. Assure them that it does us all good to hear their groans and ineffectual attempts at utterance. For our own part, a few breakdowns come very sweetly home; and, awakening our sympathies, constrain us to aid the brother by our more earnest wrestlings. It gives a reality and life to the whole matter, to hear those trembling lips utter thanks for new life just received, and to hear that choking voice confessing the sin from which it has just escaped. The cries of

the lambs must mingle with the bleating of the sheep, or the flock will lack much of its natural music. As Mr Beecher well says, 'Humble prayers, timid prayers, half-inaudible prayers, the utterances of uncultured lips, may cut a poor figure as a lecture-room literature; but are they to be scornfully disdained? If a child may not talk at all till it can speak fluent English, will it ever learn to speak well? There should be a process of education going on continually, by which all the members of the church shall be able to contribute of their experiences and gifts; and in such a course of development, the first hesitating, stumbling, ungrammatical prayer of a confused Christian may be worth more to the church than the best prayer of the most eloquent pastor.'

Every man, feeling that he is to take part in the meeting at some time or other, will become at once interested, and from interest may advance to love. Some of those who have now the best gifts of utterance had few enough when they began.

4.   Encourage the attendants to send in special requests for prayer as often as they feel constrained to do so. These little scraps of paper, in themselves most truly prayers, may be used as kindling to the fire in the whole assembly.

5.   Suffer neither hymn, nor chapter, nor address to supplant prayer. We remember hearing seven verses of a hymn, ending with 'he hates to put away', until we lost all relish for the service, and have hardly been reconciled to the hymn ever since. Remember that we meet for prayer; and, oh, that it may be that genuine, familiar converse with God which shall drive out the formality and pomposity which so much mar our public supplication!

6.   It is not at all amiss to let two or even three competent brethren succeed each other without pause, but this must be done judiciously; and if one of the three should become prolix, let the pause come in as soon as he has finished. Sing only one verse, or at the most two, between the prayers, and let those be such as shall not distract the mind from the subject by being alien from the spirit of the meeting. Why need to sing about the temptations of Satan just after an earnest prayer for the conversion of sinners; and when a brother has just had joyous

fellowship with Christ in intercession, why drag him down by singing,' 'Tis a point I long to know'?

Of course, we ought to have said all manner of good things about the necessity of the Holy Spirit; but upon that matter we are all agreed, knowing right well that all must be in vain without his presence. Our object has rather been to gather out the stones from the way than to speak of that divine life which alone can enable us to run therein.

3

Business Prayers

Dear friends, I think that many of these Monday evening meetings for prayer will never be forgotten by us who have been privileged to be present at them. Perhaps, even throughout eternity, we shall gratefully recall the hallowed hours that we have spent here around the throne of grace. I know that, very often, as I have gone home, I have felt that the spirit of prayer has been so manifestly poured out in our midst that we have been carried right up to the gates of heaven on the wings of believing supplication, and the sacred anointing which we have received from the Holy Spirit's gracious influences has left a blessed perfume and holy savour upon us long after we have left the assembly.

If we are to receive such a blessing tonight, and whenever we meet together in the name of Jesus, for prayer and praise, we must sincerely desire it, confidently expect it, and go straight to God and ask for it. There is no need for us to go beating about the bush, and not telling the Lord distinctly what it is that we crave at his hands. Nor will it be seemly for us to make any attempts to use fine language; but let us ask God, in the simplest and most direct manner, for just the things that we want for ourselves, or for others, or for his cause and Kingdom. Then let us remember our Lord's words, 'What things soever ye desire, when ye pray, believe that ye receive them, and ye shall have them' (Mark 11:24), and, at the close of the meeting, let us go on our way rejoicing, and thankful for what we have received.

I believe in business prayers: I mean, prayers in which you take to God one of the many precious promises which he has given us in his Word, and expect it to be fulfilled as certainly as we look for the money to be given to us when we go to the bank to cash a cheque or a note. We should not think of going there, lolling over the counter, chatting with the clerks upon every conceivable subject except the one thing for which we had gone to the bank, and then coming away without the coin we needed; but we should lay before the clerk the promise to pay the bearer a certain sum, tell him in what form we wished to take the amount, count the cash after him and then go our way to attend to other business. That is just an illustration of the method in which we should draw supplies from the Bank of Heaven. We should seek out the promise which applies to that particular case, plead it before the Lord in faith, expect to have the blessing to which it relates, and then, having received it, let us proceed to the next duty devolving upon us.

There are many requests which have been sent to us for presentation this evening. Among them is one from a venerable clergyman, who has often entreated us to remember him in prayer, and who still suffers from such deep depression of spirit that he is unable satisfactorily to discharge the duties of his sacred office. Then there are letters from friends who are in various stages of spiritual sickness and who desire us to bring their cases before the Lord in believing and sympathetic supplication.

We will pray that the mental affliction of this dear servant of Christ may be removed in God's own time and that the soul maladies of these other tried ones may also be cured by the great Physician. Verily, there is a God that heareth prayer. Do any of you doubt it? If so, you will not receive answers to your petitions, 'for he that cometh to God must believe that he is, and that he is a rewarder of them that diligently seek him' (Heb. 11:6).

I must, however, by way of warning, just mention that I have known some persons who, with altogether wrong motives, have tried to use for very improper purposes the fact that God hears prayer. They have set their hearts on something which they fancy that they want; and although they cannot reasonably expect that God will do what they ask, because there is no real need that it should be done, they keep on praying, and are sorely disappointed because they are not heard. If you were to say to your child, 'I will give you anything you like to ask for', you certainly would not be so unkind as to let him have a dose of prussic acid for breakfast, or a razor to cut his throat with, however earnestly he might plead for such things. In your promise, there is always implied the natural reservation that, if your boy asks foolishly, you will refuse to give him what he asks.

If God had ever given to me absolute power in prayer, he would practically have put the reins of the universe into my hands; and I should very soon want to kneel down, and cry, 'O Lord, wilt thou not take away from me such a dangerous weapon? If it is left in my hands, I fear that I shall be very likely to use it for that which is directly opposed to my own best interests and to thy glory.' We are not to take the place of God, or to make a god of ourselves. God will attend to the cry of his children, but he will be their Father, and will only comply with their petitions if he sees that they are right and proper.

When you tell your child that you will give him anything he asks for, it is clearly understood that his requests must be reasonable if they are to be granted. You do not mean that your boy is to be master of the family, and that his will is to rule the whole household; but you mean that you will give him anything that a loving and obedient child ought to ask for, and that his prayer must be rational, and the right kind of petition to come from the mouth of your son.

God has never given an absolutely unconditional promise to hear every prayer that may be presented to him; but, side by side with the promise, he has put other things which qualify and explain it. For instance, in one of our Lord's last addresses to his disciples, he said, 'If ye abide in me, and my words abide in you, ye shall ask what ye will, and it shall be done unto you' (John 15:7). The apostle Paul wrote to the Romans, 'Likewise the Spirit also helpeth our infirmities: for we know not what we should pray for as we ought: but the Spirit itself maketh intercession for us with groanings which cannot be uttered' (Rom. 8:26); and he teaches us how to pray, and what to pray for.

David knew enough of the will of God to be able to say: 'Trust in the LORD, and do good; so shalt thou dwell in the land, and verily thou shalt be fed. Delight thyself also in the LORD; and he shall give thee the desires of thine heart' (Ps. 37:3-4). Do not imagine that the Lord will give you the desires of your heart unless first you delight in him. If a man really, in his inmost soul, does delight in the Lord, his mind and God's mind will be in harmony, and he will ask in prayer what God will be able and willing to grant. If his delight is in God himself, and not merely in God's gifts, he will say, 'Bless his dear name, let him do what he will with me, I will still be satisfied, and will praise him both for what he bestows and what he withholds.'

If you delight more in God's gifts than in God himself, you are practically setting up another god above him, and this you must never do. Even when a man truly loves the Lord Jesus Christ, there may be within him something which is very like idolatry. There is even a danger of loving some things which are associated with Christ as much as we love Christ himself; and we must be on the watch against such a feeling as that. Love him, dear friends, even when you do not realise his presence; love him even when you do not feel his love; if you cannot walk in the light of his countenance, hide beneath the shadow of his wings; and, under all circumstances, let it be your joy still to say, 'he is worthy to be praised, he is ever to be blessed, whatever he does with me'. Ask your Lord so to teach you by his gracious Spirit that no prayer shall come from your lips, and that no desire shall be formed in your heart, except that which is in accordance with his holy will.

It would be wise for you to pray in this fashion, 'Lord, do not take the least notice of any petition of mine if I ask for anything that is not for thy glory and for my own and others' good!' The very best of us are often only like sick people, and you know how they get strange notions into their heads, and talk all manner of nonsense, and have a lot of curious and foolish whims and fancies. I would like to say to you now that if I have you for my nurse in any illness that may come upon me, and I then make strange and unreasonable requests, 'Be so good as to thwart me when I want that which would do me harm. Be so kind as to be cruel to me sometimes. Understand that this proviso of mine shall override all the petitions that I may put up when I am suffering from fever. Do not mind what I say then; do not give heed to me when I talk nonsense; but let me have only what I ask for when I am in my right senses, when I am my inmost, truest, healthiest self. Ask my physician what you should do, and believe that my wish is for you to do with me and for me exactly as he directs.'

It seems to me that such prayers as these which we are asked to present tonight may be offered. I cannot say as much as that for all the requests that I receive, for some of them are foolish, if not worse than that. When a person, who is in want of money, prays to God that I may give him a hundred pounds, I can assure him that I shall not do anything of the kind. If God tells me to give him a hundred pounds, that will be another matter. I should long ago have been in the bankruptcy court if I had granted half the demands of that sort which have been made upon me; and some other requests which I have received have not been much more reasonable. A young man comes to me, and wants to preach in the Tabernacle, because he says that the Lord has told him that he is to take my place one Lord's day morning. My reply is, 'Yes, of course I will let you preach when the Lord tells me to do so; but it is a lopsided revelation as it now stands, for the Lord has not revealed to me my share in the transaction' and the young man goes his way disappointed because his prayer is not answered! Do not any of you pray that which is manifestly nonsense; pray for something reasonable and sensible, and then you may have your prayers answered if they are according to the will of God.

I feel all the more free to speak thus to you, dear friends, because you are about as sensible a lot of people as I can ever hope to find; yet, every now and then, some poor crooked, cranky soul gets in amongst us, who sadly misreads or misapplies God's Word, and then begins to doubt God's faithfulness in fulfilling his promise. He makes the Lord seem to say what he never said, and never meant to say. Let no one act so foolishly, but let us exercise common sense concerning our prayers, and in all things submit our will to the wise will of our heavenly Father.

4

God's Willingness to Bless Saints and Sinners

We have been pleading with God. Prayer after prayer has knocked at heaven's gate, entreating for the conversion of souls, and the upbuilding of the church. I have no doubt that our prayer has been, in itself, acceptable with God, through Jesus Christ. It is in itself a form of worship to which our gracious God hath much respect. The golden vials of the elders before the throne are said to be full of odours, which are the prayers of saints. Prayer is typified by sweet incense, because God delights in it. He loves to see our desires for the accomplishment of his purposes. It is very pleasing to a father, as you who are parents can testify, to see his child in full sympathy with him, and anxious to help him in his work. Though he can do but little, and that little feebly and faultily, yet his eagerness to work with his father, and for his father, gives his father joy. Even thus does our heavenly Father take pleasure in us, and in our desires for his glory. '[T]hou didst well that it was in thine heart', said the Lord to David (1 Kings 8:18), even when he did not accept what David proposed to do; and I believe there may be glory brought to God, not only by those prayers which are manifestly answered, but by those which for wise reasons the good Lord is pleased to lay on one side. We are nothing better than children even in prayer, and therefore it is not every request that is wise; but yet we are children, and therefore the cries which come from our hearts touch the heart of our great Father in heaven. Our desires that souls may be saved, and that the church may prosper, are so much in accordance with the mind of God that they must be a sweet savour unto him. Therefore, brethren, let us pray on as long as breath remains. If prayer pleaseth God, it should always please us.

There are two things, however, which sometimes puzzle us. One is to see a child of God anxious to bring others to Christ, and perseveringly using the ordained means, and yet success is not given him, and men are not brought to Jesus; at least, they are not brought in such numbers as the eager worker desired and expected. Strange sight! Are we really more anxious to save souls than God himself is? It would be a marvellous spectacle if it were actually the case! It certainly looks so. This is the appearance upon the surface. Our earnest spirits long for the salvation of men. If we could save them, we would save them at once. If it were possible for us, when we speak, to convince and convert every sinner within hearing, it should be done. It looks, for the moment, as though we were more merciful than the All-merciful, more compassionate than he is of whom it is written, 'God is love' (1 John 4:8b).

Ah, my brethren, it only seems to be so: we humbly ask pardon for yielding to the illusion even for an instant! It is our ignorance of our own hearts which makes us think ourselves so supremely kind and loving. Somewhat of pride mingles with this fond conceit of our own goodness. I fear that, if we were weighed in the scales of the sanctuary, it would be found that we do not possess all that agonising pity which we suppose ourselves to possess. Too often our compassion shows itself in spasms, and is not a matter of fixed principle. Our zeal comes and goes; but if we felt it as intensely as we think we do, or as intensely always as we do sometimes, then we might have more reason for our complaining and wondering. For the present, we may rather blush for ourselves than complain of our God. We have not yet done all that lies in our power, and therefore we have no ground upon which to complain of our God.

If we are disappointed about our success in Christ's work, what shall we say? Shall we not first look for the cause within ourselves? From observation and experience, I have learned to look very hopefully upon dissatisfaction and anguish when they are seen in Christian workers. It gives me no sorrow to see my brethren unhappy and miserable because others are not saved. It would be a far sadder thing to see them useless and yet contented. If ever I have been satisfied with what I have done for the Lord, I have invariably found my service to prove barren. Pangs go with birth, and anguish precedes success. So far as I am able to judge, it does not seem that the Lord can wisely bless people who are satisfied with themselves, and with their own efforts. It would not be safe to trust the conceited with any large measure of success: they might be injured for life by such honour. Certainly God himself would have small honour, for the individual would steal every bit of it, and wear it himself. When you get to feel, 'I am not satisfied, for God is not blessing me as I long to be blessed, and therefore I fear something must be hindering the blessing', then you are advancing towards a right condition, a condition favourable to success.

The Lord is always willing to bless us up to the measure of our fitness to be blessed; and sometimes it is absolutely necessary that we should be distressed, brokenhearted and brought to an agony of prayer, before we can hold the choice gift of the God of grace. I am sure it is so. We are straitened in ourselves. Our own unfitness turns aside the divine benediction. The Lord will have us know the value of the blessing before he gives it to us; and he will also have us know our own inability, apart from his Holy Spirit, to perform any good work, or bring forth any holy fruit. Our God takes care always to have security that, if he works a great work by us, we shall not appropriate the glory of it to ourselves. He brings us down lower and lower in our own esteem, until we feel that we are nothing at all, and then he condescends to use us. Some trumpets are so stuffed with self that God cannot blow through them. Some pitchers are too full of their own muddy water for God to pour the water of life into them. However much we may wish for a blessing, God will not set the seal of his blessing to work which is begun and carried on in the power of self.

Besides this, the Lord wants us to be more thoroughly in sympathy with himself. He has two designs in making use of us in his service, not only to save souls, but also to bless us as the instruments of such salvation. There are always two edges to God's sword: so that, while he kills sin in the hearer, he strikes a blow at sin in the preacher also. God has a way of killing two birds with one stone, or, if I may use such an expression, of making two birds alive with one quickening word. He has a way of blessing the very channel through which the blessing comes, as well as the people who receive the blessing. It was grace to the Gentiles to be preached to; but Paul called it 'grace' to be permitted to preach the unsearchable riches of Christ. The Lord intends to educate us by non-success as well as by success, and therefore he causes us to sigh and cry until his Spirit puts forth his power.

It is a natural law in the spiritual world that joy is not born without sorrow. We must travail in birth before Christ will be formed in men's hearts. There is no reaping in joy without a previous sowing in tears. As Christ himself suffered to make us blest, so, in our measure, must we endure pain of heart in order to give men peace of mind. We must die that others may live. We must agonise that the tempted may rest. We must mourn that mourners may rejoice. It is a noble thing for a Christian man to act as a priest before the Lord, and, in a certain manner, to take upon himself the sins of the people, confessing them as though they were his own, and mourning over men's hardness of heart as though it were his own hardness of heart. We do well to take the sinner's place in prayer even as our Lord took that place in sacrifice. It is ours to lay ourselves before God, and cry out of the depths of our souls, as Moses did, 'if thou wilt forgive their sin – and if not, blot me, I pray thee, out of thy book which thou hast written' (Exod. 32:32). Moses was now in a prepared state to see the nation saved. Some try to make out that Moses did not mean what he said; but he did mean it, and the Lord did not rebuke him for excess of zeal or unguardedness of speech. Remember that, for speaking unadvisedly with his lips on another occasion, Moses was shut out of the land of promise, yet for this language he received no check whatever, but prevailed with the Lord to turn away his anger from Israel. He felt, in the compassion of his soul, much more than could be justified by reasoning in cool blood, even as Paul did when he wrote, 'For I could wish that myself were accursed from Christ for my brethren, my kinsmen according to the flesh' (Rom. 9:3).

If you ever reach such a stage of compassion, you will feel ready, if it were possible, as it were, to put your own soul in pawn for the souls of others; and you will express yourself in words which others may call fanatical. When it comes to that pass with you, the Lord will hear you. If you cannot live without a blessing, you shall not live without it. He who weeps for souls shall before long weep for joy. When we live, men will live; when we are quickened to fullness of life, the living waters shall flow out of us. Perhaps we have to reach a higher point of grace and love before we shall receive the fullness of the blessing. At any rate, I put the case very strongly, on purpose that you may see the wrongfulness of the supposition that the fault of our non-success lies with the Lord. It cannot be that God is less willing for men to be saved than we are; it cannot be that we have outrun love itself on its own ground. We cry, 'Arm of the Lord, awake!' and he replies, 'Awake, awake, O Zion!' The slumber is with us, and not with him. We must not think that the Lord has set a barrier in the way of our efforts, but we must be encouraged to feel that, if we love the souls of men, the Lord must love them more; and that, if we would do anything and everything in our power to secure their salvation, we may depend upon it that the Lord is not slack in grace.

A second matter equally causes a difficulty in people's minds, and that is to see sinners more willing to be saved than God is to save them. I have often seen this to be the case apparently. Apparently, I say, for it could never be really so. According to the statement of the anxious, it is the case; but their statements are born of confusion, and not of the truth. It cannot be that a sinner should be eager for reconciliation, and the Lord be hard to bring to terms. Did you ever hear of a flock of sheep in the Highlands travelling all over the hills, and roaming down the glens, trying to find their shepherd? Have you seen reports in the newspapers of the efforts made by the lost sheep to discover their shepherd, when he has been buried in the snow, and needed to be dug out? You smile, but the parable is to the point. I have observed several singular facts in natural history, but I have never heard of anything so remarkable as sheep seeking out their shepherd, and tracking his wandering footsteps in the cloudy and dark day. Yet this is what we might expect if it be true that sinners seek after the Lord Jesus, and cannot find him. They say, 'I have sought the Lord, and he has not been found of me; I have cried to him in prayer, and he has not regarded me. Alas, I have hungered and thirsted for Christ, but he is not willing that I should enjoy him!' What singular spectacles! A sheep seeking its straying shepherd! A piece of money searching for its mistress! A prodigal son rejoicing over his lost father! The supposition is altogether too absurd. Is it not? Can it be that, in this race of love, you, a poor, dead sinner, have outstripped the living Saviour? We sometimes sing:

> No sinner can be beforehand with thee, thy grace is most sovereign, most rich, and most free;

and I believe it. If I were to see a needle running across a table all by itself, I should know that under the table a magnet was at work out of sight. When I see a sinner running after Christ, I feel certain that divine love is drawing him: the cords may be invisible, but we are quite sure that they are there. If you are seeking Christ, it is because he is seeking you. The desire for grace is caused by the very grace which we desire. You must not dare to charge the Lord

Jesus with unwillingness to save, seeing he has laid down his life to prove his eagerness to redeem. No, it is not possible that there can be any backwardness with the Saviour; the backwardness lies with you. Get rid of the unbelieving and dishonouring notion that Jesus is unwilling to forgive, and at once throw yourself into his arms. He thirsts to bless men; it is his meat and his drink in this respect to do the will of him that sent him. You are being drawn by his loving hands; those warm desires for salvation are created in you by his Holy Spirit: believe this, and thus recognise the bond which unites you to the Lord; by faith, that bond will become consciously stronger from day to day. Trust wholly in Jesus, and the work is done. Trust him simply, trust him solely, trust him without hesitation and you are saved.

It is remarkable that, very often, the most commonplace things that we say in our preaching strike attention and convey blessing. An evangelist, some time ago, while he was explaining faith, took up a book, and handed it to a friend. 'Now,' said he to his friend, 'suppose this to be salvation; I freely present it to you. Have you got it?' 'Yes, I have it.' 'How did you get it? Did you buy it? Did you work for it? Did you make it?' 'No, you gave it to me, and I took it.' 'I gave it to you, and you took it'; and that is how we receive salvation from the Lord. He gives it to us freely, and we take it by faith; that is all. Did the friend wash his hands, or put on kid gloves, before he took the book? No. If he had done so, he would not more surely have received the book; his hand did very well just as it was. It is just so with the gift of God.

If a very poor man asks you to help him, and you offer him a shilling, he does not say, 'Please, sir, I cannot accept your money, for I am not dressed in good enough clothes.' He is not so foolish; he asks no questions, but gladly takes what is freely given. Even so, let us accept Christ as the gift of God. The worse we are, the more we need Jesus; and the more unprepared for Christ we seem, the more prepared we are for him, in the unquestionable sense that need is the best preparation for receiving charity. When the housewife looks at the linen for the laundry, she does not say, 'This garment is too dirty to be washed.' No, no. As she looks over the household linen, there may be a piece or two so little soiled that she questions whether she shall send them to be washed; but if one piece is worse than the rest, she is quite sure that it is fit to go, and she puts it without a question into the bag.

O my sinful friend, your sinfulness is the reason why you should go to Christ for cleansing! Did you ever know a man stop away from dinner because he was hungry? Did you ever say, 'I must not drink because I am thirsty'? Do men say, 'When I am not quite so thirsty, then I will drink; when I am not quite so faint, then I will eat'? Does any sick man say, 'I am so ill that I shall not send for a doctor till I am better'? We do not talk in this fashion about other matters; then why do we talk so about our souls? Jesus Christ asks nothing of us except that we will receive him; and he presents himself to us freely. We say, 'There is nothing freer than a gift', so there is nothing freer than the grace of God. '[T]his is the record, that God hath given to us eternal life, and this life is in his Son' (1 John 5:11). 'God so loved the world, that he gave his only begotten Son, that whosoever believeth in him should not perish, but have everlasting life' (John 3:16).

Jesus and his salvation are matters of pure gift; then why will you not have them? Do you say, 'Oh, that we might receive them'? Do you still say that you are more willing to receive than God is to give, when God has already given, and you have not received? You know the message of the king who had invited many guests to his son's wedding feast, 'Behold, I have prepared my dinner: my oxen and my fatlings are killed, and all things are ready: come unto the marriage' (Matt. 22:4). It was pitiful that everything should be prepared, and yet the guests should not come. My good sister, how would you feel if you had invited your friends to see you, and then, when everything was ready, you found that nobody came to partake of your feast? Would you not cry, 'What am I to do? Here is everything ready, but no one to eat it!' One thing, however, would be clear, nobody could say that you were unwilling that they should come. All things are ready, and everything will be spoiled if there are no guests: the hostess longs to see every seat at the table filled.

Jesus himself, that great provision of God, will be of no use if sinners do not come to him to be saved: the substitutionary sacrifice will be an eternal waste if men are not redeemed thereby: the provisions of atoning love will be a superfluity if the guilty do not come and partake of them. 'My oxen and my fatlings are killed. Then, if nobody comes to the wedding, all my preparations will be in vain.' The king must have guests for his feast, and therefore he said to his servant, 'Go out quickly into the streets and lanes of the city, and bring in hither the poor, and the maimed, and the halt, and the blind.' When this was done, and there was still room, he said to his servant, 'Go out into the highways and hedges, and compel them to come in, that my house may be filled.' A mingled company sat down to the feast. You fancy that they appeared very odd and out of place. Poor people, picked from the streets, how would they appear at a royal table feasting upon dainties?

Ah, you make a great mistake if you imagine that they looked to be a motley crew! The spectacle was magnificent; they were all dressed as ladies and gentlemen, for they had put on wedding-garments furnished by the giver of the banquet. As they sat at the table, they looked like courtiers, for they were all dressed in robes worthy of the great occasion. They hardly knew themselves, or one another. One of them would look across the table to a man who used to be his companion in poverty, and he would say, 'Is that you?' And the other would reply, 'It is, and it is not. I have undergone a great change. I have put off my rags, and I am covered with beauty.' If you came to Christ, the poorest of you shall be made to sit among princes. You, who are covered with leprosy and pollution, may come just as you are, and the Lord will welcome you, will heal you and bid you be at home at his table, where fat things full of marrow prove the splendour of his love. Come to Jesus, and see if it be not so.

Some of you seem to me like the poor dogs that go about muzzled; if there is a bone, they cannot get at it. It seems as if the devil has muzzled some of you, so that you dare not take the good things of the gospel to yourselves. O Lord, be pleased to take the muzzles off these poor dogs! Oh, that they could but get a taste of what the Lord has prepared for them that love him! You may have any and every gospel blessing if you dare to take it. Make a dash for it. Believe that Jesus Christ is able to save you. Trust him, and he has saved you.

Do you say that you will not now believe, but will wait till your own heart is better, and you feel more inward encouragement? How foolish! You will wait in vain. Did you ever hear of the deaf man who waited to hear the ticking of a sundial? He was as wise a man as you are. Cease to look within, and begin to look up. Jesus saves all those who trust him to save them. End all questions and delays, and be saved at once.

5

Confession of Sin

(An address delivered at Mentone, during the week of universal Prayer, in connection with the Evangelical Alliance, in January, 1886.)

Dear friends, according to the printed programme, the subject for this morning is humiliation on account of national, social and personal sins. The very fact that there is such a thing as sin should humble us in the very dust. Sins against God our Creator! How can creatures dare to rebel against the Almighty Lord who made them? Sins against so good a God! Why, and wherefore do they exist? Sins so wilful, so wanton, so injurious to ourselves! What madness! If there could be conceived to be the slightest speck of good resulting from sin, it might be urged in its favour; but it is evil, only evil, and that continually. It dishonours God, and it also destroys ourselves. What do we want with sin? There is variety enough in that which is permitted us – abundant exercise that would yield us pleasure and joy, and would allow full and healthy play to our whole being – yet we must needs break down all restraint, and go after sin. We have left the clear, cool, flowing streams from Lebanon to go and drink of the polluted pools of Sodom. We have turned away from that which was sweet, and safe, and satisfactory; and we have gone to that which is bitter upon the palate even now, and will be far more bitter in the bowels in the world to come. At the remembrance of the very fact of sin, we should lie in the dust before God.

Is there one of us who knows thoroughly what the evil of sin is? I do not think there is. If any one of us were to see the depravity of his own heart, he would lose his reason. Concealed within sin there lurks a measureless world of mischief; who can know it? Were it not that the infinite satisfaction resulting from the atoning sacrifice of our Lord Jesus Christ is ever present before the eye of the great God, he would at once ease him of his adversaries, and sweep both sin and sinners out of the world.

I am asked to speak concerning national sins; but this is a work too delicate for me, and I fear it would do but little good even if executed to perfection. We are of many nationalities, and each man is jealous for his country. Let each nationality confess its own sin by one of its own representatives; and perhaps this were better done apart: who cares to expose in public the faults of his own family? Moreover, general descriptions of a people must necessarily be in a great measure incorrect. Little is done for the benefit of anybody by *American Notes*, which hold a nation up to ridicule, or by descriptions of English manners, which are only regarded as true where caricature is accepted as portrait! Patriotism repents for its beloved land in secret; but it is wounded by unqualified and sweeping censures. The fact is that all nations are of one blood, and display the same faults; but there is a considerable variety as to the proportion in which the evil ingredients are mixed. Sin is neither an English, nor a French, nor a German weed; it grows wherever there is an inch of human soil. If I spoke of drunkenness as an English sin, I should be quite correct; for it is so to a terrible extent. May God help every friend of Britain to protest against the intemperance of his country! But since I have been in this town, I am less able to speak of the superior sobriety of France; and it is to be feared that the serpent, which lurks in the cup of red wine, biteth like an adder in all lands. Let this evil be confessed by all who lament it, and let it be fought against with every lawful weapon within reach. To confess it, and then to countenance it, will be to make our day of humiliation a day of hypocrisy.

This much I must say of national sins, that, wherever great powers have interfered with smaller and inoffensive nationalities, for the sake of increasing their territory, or their influence, they are verily guilty; and wherein nations have shown a feverish irritability, or a readiness for war, they are also to be censured. Is not war always a conglomerate of crimes? Wherein our civilised races have oppressed and degraded aboriginal tribes, the sin cries out before high heaven. I blush to own the part of my own country in the enormous infamy of the opium traffic. May God forgive this great wickedness, and deliver us from it! But enough of this, lest I should awaken difference of opinion where I would excite a common repentance. Let each nationality humble itself apart, and cry, in the language of Daniel: 'O Lord, to us belongeth confusion of face, to our kings, to our princes, and to our fathers, because we have sinned against thee' (Dan. 9:8).

Neither will I dwell at any length upon social sins. Ah, me! How have both our ears been made to tingle during the past year! I could wish that I had never heard nor read of those things which are done of the infamous in secret. Henceforth, for tales of horror men will turn, not to the writer of fiction, but to the discoverer of fact. Ah, God! What a world we live in! Our fine boulevards, our pleasant streets, our noble mansions, these make a goodly show. These people, dressed in their Sunday garments, are pleasant to look upon. Alas, this is but a film! Our cities reek with the crimes of Sodom. It is of no use for us to mince matters, or delude ourselves as to the sad facts of the case. We have festering within the body politic the foul diseases of the vilest ages. We talk of Christian lands; as yet the earth has not seen such prodigies. Countries are labelled 'Christian' to the dishonour of the sacred name of our divine Lord. Social iniquity, like a troubled sea, which cannot rest, is constantly casting up mire and dirt; and I fear there is not a family which has not found this black sea encroaching upon it. In very deed, the world still lieth in the bosom of the wicked one. Do not let Christian people imagine that, in order to reach the heathen, they must travel thousands of miles; the heathen are all around us, perishing in their sins. The sooner we recognise that we are to be lights in the midst of darkness, and salt in the midst of putrefaction, the better for the accomplishment of our life-work. If we believe that the world has become cleansed and sanctified into a church, we shall live in a fool's paradise, we shall help to sustain a huge hypocrisy, and we shall miss the purpose for which a church is continued in the midst of the world.

Amongst social sins, I feel inclined to lay most stress upon the widespread social atheism of the present time. It is not that many are avowed infidels, but that so many are so, and have not the honesty to avow it. Men forget God; he is not in all their thoughts, or ways, or estimates. Attempts are made to remove the idea of God from science, from trade, from politics, and from education. There is not so much even of external religion as there used to be; many are casting off outward respect for it. And can we wonder? Certain of our theologians have questioned the inspiration of the Scriptures, and cast doubt upon even the historical facts therein narrated. The teachings of our Lord and of his apostles have been assailed by their pretended defenders, and the doctrines of our holy faith have, one by one, been betrayed into the hands of enemies. Of course, the people deny when their ministers doubt. Unbelief is in the air; scepticism has become the fashion of the period. All this must be preparing calamity for a coming day. People do not deny the Lord who made them without heaping up wrath against the day of wrath.

I prefer, however, dear friends, to spend the few minutes remaining to me in recalling to our minds our own personal sins. These are the sins for which our penitence is most required, and for which it is most effectual. We cannot vanquish widespread social sins, but by God's grace we can overcome our own. It may be idle for an obscure individual to lift the lash against a nation, but the least of us may scourge his own home-born sin, and hope for a good result from the chastisement.

Let us personally prostrate ourselves at the feet of our Lord Jesus. Let us recollect that many of us may be much more guilty than may appear from our outward lives. Our secret sins, our heart sins, our sins of omission must be taken into account. It may have been impossible for some of us to have sinned as others have done; let us not take credit to ourselves on that account. The dog is not to be praised for not straying if it has been chained up. If we have done evil as we could, we need not glory that we have not done that which was impossible to us. Sins of thought, of desire and of word are also to be put down in our statement, together with all our ingratitude to God, and want of love to our neighbour, and our pride, and self-seeking, and discontent.

Let no one of us ever think of compounding for sins which he has committed by the reflection that he has not fallen so grievously as others. We may be very respectable people, and yet we may, in some respects, exceed in sin those who appear to be greater sinners. What if I am not unchaste, yet Pharisaic pride may make me quite as obnoxious to Almighty God. What if I am not a gambler, yet a malicious mind will as surely shut me out of heaven. What if I am not a blasphemer, yet the carnal mind is enmity against God; and if my nature is not changed, I am not reconciled to God. Therefore it becomes each one to look narrowly within, by hearty self-examination; and, after doing so, it will be the wisdom of each one to cry, with penitent David: 'Have mercy upon me, O God, according to thy lovingkindness: according unto the multitude of thy tender mercies blot out my transgressions' (Ps. 51:1).

Since I am a believer in the Lord Jesus Christ, I know assuredly, at this moment, that all my sins are forgiven me. As to the pardon of every true believer, there can be no doubt, if we believe the testimony of Holy Scripture. But yet we never dare to quit the place of the publican, who cried, 'God be merciful to me a sinner!' We acknowledge that we need continually to receive that pardon which we already enjoy. To congratulate ourselves upon a fancied perfection is a folly in which we ought never to indulge. Though we know we are forgiven, our grief for our transgressions is increased. Sin becomes in our esteem more exceeding sinful because of the love which pardons it. It laid on thee, O Lord, so heavy a burden that, when we think of all thine exceeding sorrows, we are ashamed and confounded, and feel that we never can open our mouths again with so much as the semblance of self-congratulation! 'To us belongeth shame and confusion of face', and it is the only heritage that we have earned by our own merits.

Our sins, dear friends, ought to be viewed very much in relation to our privileges. The sin of those who know more than others is marked with a special emphasis. Those who sin against a tender and enlightened conscience, and against holy examples and influences, sin with a tenfold guilt. Some men have to do violence to their better selves in order to do wrong; many amiable women have to harden themselves ere they can unite in the follies of others. Ever remember that light increases our guilt if we sin against it.

Forget not, also, that even in making confession of sin we may sin. A confession of sin which comes not from the heart, and does not affect the afterlife, is in itself a sin. Confession, in which there is no faith in Jesus, is an additional transgression, in so far as it is the language of unbelief. I am not sure that it is not a sin for a child of God to confess sin which has been forgiven, as if it were not forgiven. Though we are all to confess our sins, no 'General Confession' can suit all men alike. Be it ever remembered that there is a wide difference between men and men; some are unforgiven, and others have been washed from their iniquities through the blood of Jesus. For the unforgiven to confess their sin as unforgiven is truthful and right; but for a child of God, who is, forgiven, to speak of his sin as though it had never been put away, is to dishonour that glorious sacrifice by which the Lord Jesus has finished transgression, and made an end of sin. Shall we make the wondrous death on Calvary to be of none effect? Never let us so transgress. Do not, therefore, you who are trusting in Christ, come with your confession in the spirit of bondage, much less of despair. Own your sins with your heads in your Father's bosom, weeping because of the great love which has forgiven you.

With all this upon our minds, let us return to the sorrowful remembrance of our shortcomings as members of the church of Christ. How far have we been partakers in the widespread worldliness of professing Christians? It is a sad thing that the church and the world are so much alike in these days. A clear division should be manifest between the two. The world was once destroyed by a flood, and what was the cause of it? It was because 'the sons of God saw the daughters of men that they were fair; and they took them wives of all which they chose' (Gen. 6:2). When thus the church and the world were confused, destruction was at hand. It is neither for the good of the world nor for the good of the church that the lines of demarcation should grow dim. There is an eternal difference between him that feareth God and him that feareth him not; and when professing Christians cannot be distinguished from worldly men, it is because the salt has lost its savour.

Another greatly prevailing sin is the sad indifference concerning the souls of our fellow men. Certain doctrines have been introduced which tend to make men feel easy as to the future of the impenitent: a condition which naturally leads to indifference as to whether they are led to faith in Jesus, or are allowed to remain in their sins. We are all sufficiently callous without these modern soporifics. I dread any form of teaching which would diminish my horror of a man's dying without God and without hope. It is no work of ours to buoy up men with a hope for which there is no scriptural warrant. We would fain deliver souls from going down into the pit; we leave others to speculate upon their coming out if once they fall into it. In any case, may we never grow unmindful of the souls of our fellow men; but, wherever we are found, may we watch for opportunities of warning men of the wrath to come, and wooing them to the Saviour's love!

Brethren in Christ, may we not have sinned in looking too exclusively to our own work, and forgetting the labours of our brethren in other parts of the field? How few of us can rejoice when the Lord blesses others more than he does ourselves!

Is there not sin, also, in the disunion which exists among professing Christians? Shall we never come together? Could we not all revise our opinions by the Word of God? This Holy Book is acknowledged by us all to be our guide; should we not be agreed with one another if we were all agreed with the Bible? It seems to me an axiom that persons who are agreed with the same rule must be agreed with one another. If this suffices not, will we not labour to be one with each other by being one with Christ? If we are all united to *him*, must we not be united to one another?

My dear brethren, I dare not omit mention of that sin of sins, our wretched unbelief. Do we believe anything as we ought to believe it? Have we a firm grip of eternal certainties? Do we not act towards God as if he were a shadow, instead of resting upon him as the Rock of ages? We do not half believe the divine promises, nor rely upon the immutable goodness and faithfulness of our heavenly Father. We are alive unto God; but, alas! that life beats feebly within our bosom. Where is our confidence in the gospel? Where is our glory in the cross? We are trembling followers of a Master who deserves the unwavering faith of everyone who has the honour to be his disciple.

Only a minute remains in which to acknowledge our shortcomings as to private prayer. Where are the men mighty in supplication? Do not our closets cry out against us? Where are our united pleadings with the Lord? Do not many forget meetings for prayer? Are not many altogether unaware of what they are like?

Have we not been lacking in meditation, in communion, in walking with God? Where are the saints now? We have a superabundance of professors, but where are the truly eminent Christians? I believe that the strength of the church lies in that inner circle of champions which is composed of the thoroughly consecrated, the men who are favoured of the Lord. Holy Bernard was the light of his age, and passing on from age to age we see men who blazed with the light of God; but we ought each one of us to seek to be saints in the highest sense of the word. We must aim at being the holiest of men and women. Let it be ours to be like the mountain-tops that catch first the beams of the rising sun, and reflect the light upon the lowlands. If we are not such, we ought to be; and wherein we are not all that we ought to be, we sin.

Let us now lay bare our hearts before God, and ask him to search us so that our guilt may be perfectly removed, and we may

6

I Pray You to Fasten Your Grips

be clean in his sight, and so enter with joyous hearts into the New Year. May the Holy Spirit pour upon us the spirit of grace and of supplications! Amen.

This sentence I met with in one of those marvellous letters which Samuel Rutherford left as a priceless legacy to the church of God in all ages. Truly, he hath dust of gold. I thought it would make a capital text for a prayer meeting address, so I jotted it down. It gripped me, and so I gripped it, in the hope that it might grip you, and lead you 'to fasten your grips'.

But do not imagine that I have taken a text from Rutherford because I could not find one in the Bible, for there are many passages of Scripture which teach the same lesson. As for instance, that exhortation, 'lay hold on eternal life' (1 Tim. 6:12), or that other, 'Hold that fast which thou hast' (Rev. 3:11), or that other, 'Hold fast the form of sound words' (2 Tim. 1:13). The things of God are not to be trifled with, 'lest at any time we should let them slip' (Heb. 2:1). They are to be grasped, as Jacob seized the angel, crying, 'I will not let thee go' (Gen. 32:26). Faith is first the eye of the soul, wherewith it sees the invisible things of God; and then it becomes the hand of the soul, with which it gets a grip of the substance of 'the things not seen as yet'. A man has two hands and I would urge you to take a double hold upon those things which Satan will try to steal from you. Take hold of them as the limpet takes hold upon the rock, or as the magnet takes hold of steel. Give a life grip: a death grip: 'I pray you to fasten your grips.'

And, first, do this with regard to the Lord Jesus Christ. Cling to his cross as the sole hope of your soul. You, who already hold him by faith, I would stir up to hold fast the beginning of your confidence even to the end. Hold to him more intelligently and more decidedly than ever. Let everything else go, but keep your hand upon him as Joab held to the horns of the altar. Should Jesus ask you, 'Will ye also go away?' Answer at once, 'Lord, to whom shall we go? thou hast the words of eternal life' (John 6:67-8). As he holds you by his grace, so hold him by the grace which he has wrought in you. You must not ever have to think, as that Swedish sailor did, of whom Mr Faithfull told us that he said, 'he once had Christ, and had lost him'. 'I pray you to fasten your grips' so firmly that no such awful thought shall ever darken your minds. 'I held him,' said the spouse in the Canticles, 'and would not let him go, until I had brought him into my mother's house, and into the chamber of her that conceived me' (Song 3:4). You cannot bring Jesus to others if you do not hold him fast yourselves. Never dream of letting him go who is your hope, your joy, your all. He is yours to have and to hold when death shall part you from all beside.

If any of you have never taken hold upon Christ Jesus, 'I pray you to fasten your grips' on him tonight. Oh, that the Holy Spirit may teach you, lead you and enable you to do so at this moment! Christ is no shadow; you can lay hold of him, there is something to lay hold upon. Grasp him now as a drowning man would seize a lifebuoy, as a man dying of hunger would clutch at a bit of bread. Jesus will not try to get away from you. He did not withdraw his garment from the woman who touched it for healing; he never denied himself to a seeking soul. Hold him, then, with a daring grasp. Make bold with our good Lord, for he loves a daring faith. Hath he not said, '[H]im that cometh to me I will in no wise cast out' (John 6:37)? Grasp him, for he puts himself in your way at this good hour. Men are eager enough to snatch at the shadows of this poor fleeting world; why are you so slow to 'fasten your grips' upon him who is grace and truth? What life, what salvation, what everlasting joy shall come streaming out of him into you, if you are now moved to lay hold on him, and take him as your own! Think it no robbery. He is God's unspeakable gift, freely bestowed on needy sinners.

In the next place, 'I pray you to fasten your grips' on the doctrines of the gospel. You do believe them, dear friends, or you would not rally around the preacher. If there are any of you who do not believe them, and yet are members of this church, you can scarcely remain so with a clear conscience, for our Confession of Faith is most explicit on those points. When any cease to hold the grand doctrines of a free grace gospel, they generally clear out within a very short time, for they are weary of the constant preaching of them. My ministry is a flail which parts the chaff from the wheat, and a fan which drives the chaff away; and I desire it to be so. I aim at separating the chaff from the wheat. If I hear that somebody has been offended because of the truth which I have preached, I remember that many were offended at that infinitely greater Preacher who, on one occasion, found that many went back, and walked no more with him, for he had uttered a hard saying, 'Who could hear it?' Doth this offend you? You will be more offended yet, as we further and further dive into the truth of sovereign, distinguishing grace.

But you, dear friends, have taken hold of the doctrines of grace, and 'I pray you to fasten your grips.' These are times when everything will be snatched away from you unless you hold it fast. Some years ago, I was highly flattered by a neighbour of rather advanced views, who said that the region of South London was difficult to work in, because the people were infected with a kind of teaching which it was impossible to destroy; for when people once got hold of it, they obstinately refused to let it go. I am rejoiced that this is the case. The doctrines of a gracious gospel are so scriptural, so comforting, so self-evidencing, so satisfying that men will not readily quit them when once they know their virtue. 'Free grace and dying love' are such old wine that no man desireth new. Gospel truths saturate a believer right through, and remain in the grain of the cloth like the old red of soldiers' coats. The gospel is like some perfumes which never leave the boxes in which they have once lain. The love of free grace dwells in the core of our heart. It has not only reached our bone, but it has impregnated the marrow; you cannot get it out of us, even if you kill us. I judge how it is with you by what I know of myself; I could be ground into atoms so small that you could not see them without a powerful microscope, but every atom would sparkle with belief in the atoning sacrifice, and the eternal love which gave it.

'I pray you to fasten your grips' upon the revealed truths of God's Word, so that you shall never flinch from avowing and defending them, whatever ridicule your adherence to them may cost you. I told an American friend, yesterday, that I could claim no credit for preaching a free grace gospel, because I did not know any other, and would not know any other if I could. 'I determined not to know anything among you save Jesus Christ, and him crucified' (1 Cor. 2:2). I will be an agnostic to all but my Lord and his infallible Word. Once, when I had been preaching in Wales, an old lady told me that she had been very pleased with what I had said, but I was inferior to Christmas Evans, because he had only one eye, while I had two. I hope I have only one eye, however, in the higher sense. When a man gets a single eye for God's glory, and preaches nothing else but the doctrine of the Word, he will take good aim, and hit a glorious mark. I pray that I may myself 'fasten my grips' more and more upon the one and only gospel, and that all of you may do the same, without a single exception. We will not let go a particle of that perfect system of revealed truth of which Christ is the centre, and grace is the circumference.

Thirdly, dear friends, for your own comfort, 'I pray you to fasten your grips' on the promises of God. In days to come, the younger ones amongst us may see the wisdom of this advice. I will tell you what will help you to fasten your grips: a sharp touch of rheumatism, if grace goes with it. I do not want you to have the rheumatism, or any other trial; but if you do, I trust you will have grace given to lay hold upon precious promises suitable to your condition. Sanctified afflictions will help you to fasten your grips. If you have a very dear one long lying ill, or if your property is melting away, or if your jubilant spirits are sinking in depression, you will want the promises, and you will feel the necessity of fastening your grips. A grip of a promise of God is better than a grasp of a bag of gold. A grip of such a promise as this, 'I will never leave thee, nor forsake thee', will enable you to understand the exhortation which Paul saddles upon it, 'Let your conversation be without covetousness; and be content with such things as ye have: for he hath said, I will never leave thee, nor forsake thee' (Heb. 13:5). If you are afraid of trouble, if you are doubting and fearing, 'I pray you to fasten your grips' on the everlasting covenant. You have an anchor, within the veil, which will never give way; but mind that your cable is firmly held on board your vessel, for it is to this end of it that your care must be given; and, therefore, 'I pray you to fasten your grips.'

'I pray you to fasten your grips', also, on the service which God has given you to do. You who conduct Bible classes and missions, you who teach in the Sunday school, you who visit the kitchens of the lodging-houses, you who go round with those brown-covered sermons, and leave them from door to door, you who labour for your gracious Lord in any way: did you say that you thought of giving up your work? What are you at? 'I pray you to fasten your grips.' I heard, the other day, of a place of worship from which the congregation has gradually migrated, till very, very few remain. On looking over it, I said to one of the deacons, 'This place might do for me when I give up the Tabernacle, because of my general weakness and failure of health.' He gave me no verbal answer, but he laughed, as if he could not contain himself, and that was all he said. I did not ask him to explain what he meant by laughing at my remarks. The laughter said more than words. I see you are laughing, too. Well, you are going to give up your class, are you? Shall I laugh? I would if it would be interpreted by you as I interpreted my deacon's laugh.

It does seem ridiculous for anyone who has a work to do for Christ to talk of giving it up, unless there is a sheer inability to go on. I could rather weep than laugh, for it is even more sad than absurd. Here you are highly honoured by having the opportunity of doing good, and winning souls, and you talk of giving up? 'I pray you to fasten your grips.' Of course, when you cannot do the work because of age and infirmity, it will be your wisdom to stand out of the way, and let somebody else do it better; but as long as you can do it, 'I pray you to fasten your grips.' Some old men of my acquaintance carried on Sunday-school work till they died, and some aged ministers have been useful to the very last. One good point in the chapter from the Acts, which we read yesterday morning, was the fine fidelity of the Roman soldiers. The Sadducees and the high priest, little can be said in their praise; but the soldiers stood at the door of the prison in the morning, though an angel had set the apostles free. They stood as sentries where they were bidden to stand; and you, who are good soldiers of Jesus Christ, must stand where your Lord and Master has placed you: sentries fixed like statues till recalled.

I have heard that, on one occasion, Sir Henry Havelock was going over London Bridge with his son, and that he said, 'Stop here, Harry, until I come back.' He forgot all about his boy, finished his business in the city and went home. His wife said to him, 'Where is Harry?' 'Bless me,' he replied, 'he is on London Bridge; I told him to stop there until I returned, and I am sure he will do so.' He hastened to the spot, and there was young Harry. 'What, Harry, are you still here?' 'Yes, father; you told me to stop here until you came back, and I have done so.' A soldier's son could do no otherwise; and you are sons of the great Captain of our salvation, even the Lord of hosts. Keep your places, whatever happens; and work on whatever occurs. Having done all, still stand; and you have not done all yet. Blessed shall that servant be whom his Lord at his coming shall find watching and working. To desert your posts will be too shameful. Are you weary? Rest in your Lord. Are you discouraged? Let patience have her perfect work. No, no, my beloved, we will not one of us think of retiring. 'I pray you to fasten your grips.'

Now here is a harder bit. 'I pray you to fasten your grips' upon the cross. I mean, the cross which you are to bear after Jesus. You see, you are bound to carry it, for all believers in the Crucified must be cross-bearers. The cross of Christ has saved you, and now there is a cross of your own which the Lord has prepared for your shoulders, which you are to carry because you are saved. On affliction, loss, reproach for Christ's sake, 'I pray you to fasten your grips.' This cross you must take up. You are not to wait to have it forced upon unwilling shoulders. Your Lord's command is, '[T]ake up thy [his] cross, and follow me' (Matt. 16:24). Stoop down to it, grasp it and bear it. Let your hand embrace it for Christ's sake. Do not shun that which is the badge of true saints, and at once their burden and their blessing. Is it reproach? Count it greater riches than all the treasures of Egypt. Is it loss for the sake of holiness? Espouse it, as your joyful bride. Is it any form of persecution? Rejoice and be exceeding glad that you are counted worthy to suffer for your Lord's sake. Is it any other form of sorrow which attaches to the life of the godly? Do not rebel against it, but 'take it up', and bear cheerfully the sacred load. Sanctified afflictions are spiritual promotions.

Even if your cross grows heavier as you carry it, welcome it, and follow on in the footsteps of the Well-beloved, as one of an elect train, chosen in the furnace of affliction. Some day, you will come to see the excellent uses of your crosses, and then you will praise God for them. By faith and patience you may even fall in love with the cross, till you would not even wish to part with it. Submission is the near road to comfort, and cheerful acquiescence finds the cross on the back to be like wings to the shoulders. '[W]e glory in tribulations also' (Rom. 5:3). 'I pray you to fasten your grips' upon your cross, and hold it fast as a treasure rather than an infliction. What I say unto you, I say also to myself. I owe more than I can ever tell you to pain, and weakness, and other forms of my Lord's dear cross. It is not an iron cross, as I once thought it, it is only a wooden one; and he himself always bears the heavier end. I could almost sing, 'sweet affliction'; surely its bitterness is soon over.

'I pray you to fasten your grips' in a practical manner upon one another. Brethren, let us love one another, for love is of God. We are heartily joined together in one spirit: let us remain so. Let our love increase exceedingly, as we are pressed together by surrounding opposition. Let all those who are one in the common faith get together; and cheer each other. I will not venture upon shaking hands at this moment with Mr Faithfull, the brother who labours in Marseilles, because example is very contagious, and he has told us that the sailors give him awful grips when they shake hands. A very little while ago, I could not even hold a pen, and I dare not run the risk of a sailor's grip with this most excellent friend; but spiritually, if not corporeally, let us all give each other one of those sailor grips with our hearts, if not with our hands. Brethren, you are very, very dear to me, and you return that love. Be of like mind among yourselves. Are you out at elbows with one another? Are there even two women who cannot agree? Remember how our apostle said, 'I beseech Euodias, and beseech Syntyche, that they be of the same mind in the Lord' (Phil. 4:2). They were only two private members, but Paul could not let them fall out. Put an end to discord at once. 'I pray you to fasten your grips.' Be not cold and distant towards your fellow members, but let love reign supreme everywhere.

> Tis a shameful sight,
> When children of one family
> Fall out, and chide, and fight

Get to know each other better. 'Bear ye one another's burdens, and so fulfil the law of Christ' (Gal. 6:2). Bear and forbear, feeling that you are not yourselves perfect. Let us live in hearty love, first to our adorable Lord, and then with all our fellow servants, and so we shall become strong in the Lord, and the Lord will command his blessing to fall like the dew of Hermon where he sees brotherly love abounding. I speak not thus because you fail in this respect, but I speak the more freely because I trust you excel in it. Oh, that all churches were abodes of love! What do we see in many places? No contending earnestly for the faith, but much contending as to who shall be the greatest. I heard, the other day, of a church which has come to nothing, and one told me that the reason was that 'everybody wanted to be boss'. You know what the word means; I think it is of American origin, and includes a good deal. Diotrephes is a dreadful mischief-maker. Let us not imitate him, but let us be ready to wash the saints' feet.

'I pray you to fasten your grips' on all God's chosen in every place, on all God's church throughout the whole world; let us pray for all the Lord's people. Let us grip our brethren in America, who have sent so many gracious representatives among us. Let us do the same with the churches on the Continent, for whom our brother Faithful has spoken. God bless France, and save her! Our evangelist, Mr. Harmer, has just touched the coast of Africa, and his presence makes us think of the Congo and the Cape. With both hands, and with all our hearts we salute all the people of God throughout the world, rejoicing that we are one body in Christ Jesus. In this holy love, 'I pray you to fasten your grips.' Amen.

PART 2

Expositions of Scripture

7

The First Public Worship in the World

[T]hen began men to call upon the name of the LORD
(Gen. 4:26).

Before we join in prayer again, and I hope we shall spend the greater part of our time tonight in that most delightful and most profitable exercise, I should like to make just a few remarks upon the last verse of the fourth chapter of the book of Genesis. To Adam and Eve there was born a son instead of Abel, namely, Seth; and to Seth himself there was also born a son, whom he named Enos. After the record of his birth, we are told:

> *[T]hen began men to call upon the name of the* LORD.

I suppose that, by this expression, it is meant that they began to have set assemblies for the worship of Jehovah, and that they came together for what we generally speak of now as public worship; for men had, doubtless, called upon the name of the Lord, each one by himself, from the very first. We cannot doubt that our father Adam and our mother Eve were, by divine grace, led to repent of their great sin, and to cry for mercy and pardon; and if they did so, we are quite sure that they never neglected to pray both separately and together. There was Abel, too; he 'brought of the firstlings of his flock' in sacrifice to God, 'And the LORD had respect unto Abel and to his offering'. His was the offering of a believer, and therefore his sacrifice was accepted. I suppose that, often, as a solitary man, he would go forth privately to worship God on his own account.

But, after Abel's death, and the birth of Seth and Enos, there were two families in which the fear of the Lord manifested, the family of Adam and the family of his son Seth. When Enos was born, as the first of a long succession of descendants that has continued to this day, men began to meet together in assemblies for the worship of Jehovah; they were very, very few: but yet, from that time, they 'began to call upon the name of the Lord'. So, if there should be two of your families who find yourselves in some back settlement of Canada, if there should be only your two families in the whole region, mind that you get together on the Sabbath day, and worship the Lord as best you can. Let this be your example; there were at the first only two families that feared Jehovah, yet 'Then began men to call upon the name of the Lord.'

It is not essential to the constitution of a congregation, nor is it essential to the formation of a Christian church, that there should be large numbers; it is neither necessary to the devotion nor to the acceptance of it with God that there should be a crowd of people; for, when there were but twos and threes, only two families, or perhaps three, upon the face of the whole earth, 'Then began men to call upon the name of the Lord.' Some of you may not always have the privilege of living where so many of us meet together to worship God. It is a very joyous thing to gather with the multitude to keep holy-day – the more the merrier, in our Lord's service, I am sure – but if you should find yourselves in some remote part of your own country, or far away from the assemblies of God's people in other lands, do not let that hinder you from meeting together as a Christian church, and observing the ordinances of the Christian religion. Remember that our Lord Jesus said, 'Where two or three are gathered together in my name, there am I in the midst of them'; and you may be sure that, if he is in the assembly, however few may be present, they make up a valid, lawful congregation, and a real church in the New Testament meaning of that term. Whether the company is large or small, Charles Wesley's hymn is always in season:

> Meet and right it is to sing,
> In every time and place,
> Glory to our heavenly King,
> The God of truth and grace.

Join we then with sweet accord,
All in one thanksgiving join!
Holy, Holy, Holy Lord,
Eternal praise be thine.

Father, God, thy love we praise,
Which gave thy Son to die;
Jesus, full of truth and grace,
Alike we glorify:
Spirit, Comforter divine,
Praise by all to thee be given,
Till we in full chorus join,
And earth is turn'd to heaven.

There was also, at the time mentioned in this passage, a special reason why the godly ones should call upon the name of the Lord, for there was an opposition element in the world. Cain, as well as Seth, was the founder of a family. There were, henceforth, two lines of generation in the world, the line of grace that seemed to keep largely to the family of Seth, and the line of sin, the line of rebellion, and the line of darkness and death which kept mainly to the family of Cain. Cain's descendants multiplied; I do not know what religion they had, or professed to have, but whatever they had, it was not the religion of grace, and they went continually further and further away from the light, always with their backs to the sun. Consequently, the people of God, pained and grieved to find that there was another family in the world, the seed of the serpent multiplying among them, thought it their duty, as well as their privilege, to set up a standard, and make it known to all that they were believers, that they feared Jehovah, the one living and true God. '[T]hen began men to call upon the name of the LORD.'

And, brethren, if anything should make us come out boldly in our worship of God, it is the publicity of the sin of the ungodly; if anything should make us band together, it is the presence of sin in so many of our fellow creatures; if anything should make us pray, it is the prevalence of iniquity all around us; if anything should make us feel that we who love the Lord must unite to serve him, and throw our whole heart and soul into united prayer to the Most High, and united adoration of God over all, blessed forevermore, it is when we hear the blasphemies of men and see their rebellion against the Lord. '[T]hen began men to call upon the name of the LORD' when others turned aside from his ways; and thus, dear friends, should it be with you who are his loyal subjects. The more you are surrounded by enemies of the truth, the more you see of the prevalence of sin in the world, the more necessity is there for frequent attendance at public worship, the scriptural observance of all the ordinances of the Lord's house, and the more earnest and resolute contention for the faith once for all delivered to the saints. We live in such times as these, and therefore we need to hear and to heed the stirring summons:

> Stand up! Stand up for Jesus!
> The trumpet-call obey;
> Forth to the mighty conflict,
> In this his glorious day;
> Ye that are men, now serve him,
> Against unnumbered foes;
> Your courage rise with danger,
> And strength to strength oppose.

Another thought strikes me. This public worship was a very small affair at the beginning, yet it has lasted to this day; and if ever the church of God in any place grows exceedingly small and feeble, let us not despair of it, but remember what it was at its commencement. It was a tiny rill when first the stream of public worship leaped into life; it was a small assembly, that first church of God, that first separated congregation that met together to declare that Jehovah was their Lord; yet the little one has become many a thousand, and the small one a strong nation. It has often declined, but it has as frequently revived; it has been sometimes hidden, but by-and-by it has been again revealed; it has been almost crushed out in some countries, but, in due time, through the power of God's mighty grace, it has been made to flourish again. Well did Wesley sing of his Saviour:

> When he first the work begun,
> Small and feeble was his day:
> Now the Word doth swiftly run,
> Now it wins its widening way:
> More and more it spreads and grows,
> Ever mighty to prevail;
> Sin's strongholds it now o'erthrows,

Shakes the trembling gates of hell.
Saw ye not the cloud arise,
Little as a human hand?
Now it spreads along the skies
Hangs o'er all the thirsty land:
Lo, the promise of a shower,
Drops already from above;
But the Lord will shortly pour
All the Spirit of his love.

Men still continue 'to call upon the name of the LORD', or, as the marginal reading puts it, 'to call themselves by the name of the LORD'. May the Lord multiply these assemblies, and grant grace to many more of our fellow creatures to meet together with us in the name of the Lord, and to call themselves by his sacred name! Thus shall be fulfilled that gracious promise of the Lord to his ancient people, 'I will pour water upon him that is thirsty, and floods upon the dry ground: I will pour my Spirit upon thy seed, and my blessing upon thine offspring: and they shall spring up as among the grass, as willows by the water courses. One shall say, I am the Lord's; and another shall call himself by the name of Jacob; and another shall subscribe with his hand unto the Lord, and surname himself by the name of Israel.'

As of old, men met to call upon the name of the Lord, so still do we gather together to call upon his name in prayer, in praise and in the preaching of his Word, and especially to call upon his name in the New Testament sense of repentance towards God and faith in our Lord Jesus Christ. In this sense, 'whosoever shall call upon the name of the Lord shall be saved'. Thus early, and thus late, have men called upon the name of the Lord; and if the days should grow darker even than they are at present, and the number of the faithful should get fewer and yet fewer still, there will always be some left to call upon his name, until 'he shall come to be glorified in his saints, and to be admired in all them that believe ... Wherefore also we pray always for you, that our God would count you worthy of this calling, and fulfil all the good pleasure of his goodness, and the work of faith with power: that the name of our Lord Jesus Christ may be glorified in you, and ye in him, according to the grace of our God and the Lord Jesus Christ.' Amen.

8

Concerning the Dropping of Honeycombs

*Fear not, Abram: I am thy shield, and thy
exceeding great reward* (Gen. 15:1).

Turn to the nineteenth Psalm, and the tenth verse, and there read,
in our version, 'sweeter also than honey and the honeycomb'.
This is applied to 'the judgments of the LORD,' which are 'true and
righteous altogether'. The expression sets forth David's esteem
of the law of God, and we may fitly apply it to Holy Scripture.
The Hebrew hath it, 'sweeter than the dropping of honeycombs'.
Whereupon good Mr Brooks observes, 'It is sweeter than that
which drops immediately and naturally without any force or art,
which is counted the purest and the sweetest honey.'

There are texts of Scripture which are exceedingly sweet, and
marvellously free in the giving forth of their sweetness, needing
little study or meditation. Children have their drops, and their
little candies, which melt away in their mouths; and, even so,
certain Scriptures are prepared for the Lord's little children;
they have only to receive them by the mouth of faith, and their
enjoyment is great. Some words of the Lord are as nuts that need
cracking, or grapes that need treading in the winepress, for their
meaning lieth not upon the surface; but those to which I refer are
ready for use: they are simple sweetnesses, prepared pleasures
– in fact, drops of delight. To enjoy these, one does not need to
be a theologian or a grammarian, much less a philosopher or
a mystic. The honey of the meaning flows out of the comb of the
words as fluid consolation, liquid love, pure joy and perfect truth.
The student does not need to pore over his book, or the preacher
to consult his library, or the hearer to collect his knowledge;

the dainty comfort offers itself to the palate, and goeth down sweetly, spreading its savour over the whole inner man without effort.

I should like, as the Holy Spirit opens up the Word to me, to give my friends, every now and then, a drop of honey out of the rock, by dwelling upon certain easy texts as they yield themselves to my heart. I would not so much think as enjoy, and then give to you that which has been precious to my own heart. There are some preachers, whose main business seems to be to lead people among the thorns, where they are torn with perplexities; it is mine, on this occasion, to run by way of the plain, along the level road of evident teaching. On the Sabbath, it is well to rest the mind as well as the body. We do not so much want deep problems to make our heads ache as holy consolations to quiet our hearts. Those who use such long words that they cannot be understood without a dictionary go very near to breaking the Sabbath themselves, and compelling their hearers to do the same. At any rate, on these occasions, I shall neither perplex my readers, nor cause them any mental labour. Honey-drops are for pleasure, not for labour; and they are for children rather than for students. Many a sweet truth in God's Word is so very simple that it does not need excogitating so much as enjoying. When you get a honey-drop, you just put it in your mouth, and let it lie there, or turn it round with your tongue till it dissolves. Let us do this, as occasion offers, with several simple passages: and just now with these words from the book of Genesis, fifteenth chapter, and first verse. Bees, and their hives and combs, are very plentiful in Palestine, and here we have good store of sweetness. The one sentence which I have pitched upon is full, and rich, and simple, and we will try to enjoy it. It is God's word to his servant Abraham:

> *Fear not, Abram: I am thy shield, and thy exceeding great reward.*

'Fear not, Abram'. Alas! fear is an ague which haunts these marsh-lands. When shall we get to higher ground, and dwell above? Fear is a complaint common among the Lord's people; we might be sure that it was so when we learned that Abram suffered from it, for he was the most vigorous of believers. Does Abram need a 'fear not'? Then we may be pretty sure that we require it, too. I am afraid that, wherever there is faith, there will also be a measure of fear; though the less of it there is, the better will it be. How tenderly the Lord quiets the fears of his children! 'Fear not, Abram'. As much as if he had said, 'You are all alone; but fear not, for I am with you. You are in much labour; but fear not, I will help you. You have no portion in this strange land; but fear not, for I am your God. Do not fear in the present; do not fear in the future. Fear neither the failure of friends nor the fury of foes. Be brave, calm, hopeful, trustful, joyful. "Fear not, Abram". You have just been fighting the kings; you felt yourself to be a man of peace, and not accustomed to the deadly strife; but I have given the plunderers, like driven stubble, to your bow, and you have brought back Lot and all his train of servants that were taken prisoners. You need not even fear for your relatives; I will bless them for your sake. Beside that, you have not touched a thread or a shoe-latchet of the King of Sodom's goods, but you have borne yourself in a right royal manner; therefore, fear not to enjoy your success, you shall be safe from all attacks, and you shall live in the respect of the great ones around you.' This blessed 'Fear not' was a quietus to every form of alarm which might come near the man of God.

But the Lord seemed to think that, after his conflict and his victory, Abram might begin to sink. It is often so with bold men; it was so even with Elias, the prophet of fire. Men are not afraid when the battle rages, their spirit is equal to the danger and the struggle; but when all is over, then a reaction comes, and they greatly need the Lord's 'Fear not'. Have you never felt yourself strangely supported under the direst afflictions, so that they seemed not to be afflictions at all? And yet, when pressure has been removed, you have been ready to faint, like Samson after he had slain the Philistines. Fear is apt to be greatest when the reason for it is smallest.

We are often quiet in a storm, and distracted in a calm. We are singular beings, mysteries to ourselves, and riddles to our neighbours. Our constitution and disposition are made up of odds and ends, and gatherings from all manner of beasts, and birds, and fishes, and no one can understand us except the Lord; but, blessed be his name, he knows us altogether, and therefore he brings forth the right consolation at the right mo-

ment, saying, 'Fear not', in the instant wherein we are most
likely to fear.

'Fear not, Abram'. Were there not two things about which
the patriarch might have feared? First, about his own safety. This
was met by the assurance, 'Fear not, Abram: I am thy shield'.
When he had no other guard, Abraham was shielded by his God.
He was like a sheep in the midst of wolves, a lone stranger surrounded by hostile nations; but a spell was upon the Canaan-
ites, for the Lord had said, 'Touch not Mine anointed, and do my
prophets no harm.' The protected of the Lord needed not to wear
armour, nor bear a sword, for Jehovah had said, 'I am thy shield'.
Abraham possessed no fortress, he commanded no army; he did
not even dwell in a house, and yet he was safe enough. His tents
were no defence, and yet no one ever broke into them, or dared
to threaten those who dwelt within: no assassin waylaid him, no
marauder attacked him; he dwelt at ease behind the broad shield
of the Almighty. He was as safe as if he had been enclosed within
walls that reached to heaven. The armour of God covered him
from head to foot.

So, dear friends, when we seem to have nothing visible to protect us, what a blessing it is to know that we are guarded by the invisible and omnipotent God! The visible must always of necessity
be finite, but the invisible God is infinite, there is no searching of
his understanding. You are infinitely safe if you are a believer in the
living God, your beginnings and your endings, your wakings and
your sleepings, your journeyings and your restings, your sufferings
and your doings, your slander or your honour, your poverty or your
wealth, your all for ever and ever is most secure when the Lord is
your Keeper, and your shield upon your right hand. Be it ours to
leave our cares, and give our hearts up to the repose of faith. Come,
sing with me that verse of the beloved Toplady:

Inspirer and Hearer of prayer,
Thou Shepherd and Guardian of thine,
my all to thy covenant care
I sleeping and waking resign.
If thou art my shield and my sun,
The night is no darkness to me;
And fast as my moments roll on,
They bring me but nearer to thee.

We are safe if God be with us. We may be in the midst of cruel adversaries, but no weapon that is formed against us can prosper if God be our shield. Please notice that the Lord does not say, 'I will shield you'; but, 'I, the Almighty, am your shield; it is not alone my power, my wisdom, my love, which will protect you, but I myself will be your shield.'

Then Abram may have thought, 'I shall be protected; but, after all, shall I not spend my life in vain?' He might have feared for his success. He had led the life of a gypsy, roaming through a land in which he owned no foot of ground; therefore the Lord added, 'I am thy reward.' He does not say, 'I will reward you'; but he says, 'I am thy reward.' Dear brother-ministers, if souls are saved, they are a form of reward to you; but, nevertheless, rejoice not in them, but rather rejoice that your names are written in heaven. I have quoted an old text, first spoken to chosen men who had healed the sick and cast out devils in Christ's name. Yes, dear brethren, if many receive our word, it is our joy that they have received it; but, still, we may be disappointed in our estimate of conversions; and, at the best, our success will not equal our desires.

The only reward that a Christian can fully rejoice in, without any reservation, is this assurance of the Lord, 'I am thy reward.' Did not the father, in the parable, say to the elder son, when he grumbled and growled at the reception given to his brother, 'Son, thou art ever with me, and all that I have is thine'? That was reward enough, was it not? It is wealth enough to a believer to possess his God, honour enough to please his God, happiness enough to enjoy his God. My heart's best treasure lies here: 'This God is our God for ever and ever; he will be our Guide even unto death.'

'Oh, but people have been so ungrateful to me!' True, but your God does not forget your work of faith and labour of love. 'Ah, sir, I am dreadfully poor!' Yet you have God All-sufficient; and all things are yours. 'Alas! I am so ill.' But Jehovah Rophi is the Lord that healeth thee. 'Alas! I have no friends left to me.' Yet the best of friends changes not, and dies not. Is he not better to you than a host of other friends? How great is your God? He filleth all things. Then, what more can you seek? Would you have two persons occupying the same place? If God fills all, where is there room for another? Is not God's grace sufficient for you? Do you bemoan a cup of water which has been spilled at your feet? A well is near. Did I hear you cry, 'I have not a drop in my bucket'? A river flows hard by: the river of God, which is full of water. O mournful soul, why art thou disquieted? What aileth thee that thou shouldst fret thy life into rags?

Very fitly does the Lord say to Abram, 'I am thy exceeding great reward.' He is infinitely more as a reward than we could ever have deserved, desired or expected. There is no measuring such a reward as God himself. If we were to pine away in poverty, it would be joy enough to know that God gives himself over to us to be our portion. The tried people of God will tell you that, in their sharpest sorrows, their joys have reached floodtide when they have known and felt that the Lord is their Covenant God, their Father, their all. Our cup runs over when faith receives Jehovah himself as the crown of the race, the wages of the service. What more can even God bestow than himself?

Now you see what I meant at the beginning, by honey-drops. I have not strained after novel thoughts or choice words, but have persuaded you to taste the natural sweetness of the Scripture. Receive it as God gives it; and go your way, and let the flavour of it fill your mouths all through the week. Fear not, Mary; fear not, William; fear not, Sarah; fear not, John. The Lord saith to thee, even as to Abraham, 'I am thy shield, and thy exceeding great reward.' No Scripture is of private interpretation; you may take out the name of Abram, and put your own name into the promise if you are of Abraham's spiritual seed, and do not stagger at the promise through unbelief. 'If children, then heirs', applies to all the spiritual family. The ground whereon thou liest, the Lord thy God has given thee; if thou canst rest on this Word, it is thine to rest upon. The Lord is thy Defender and Rewarder, and by the double title he shuts out all fear, making thy rest to be doubly sure. Wherefore, cease thou from all anxiety. Rest in the Lord, and wait patiently for him. This day he bids thee dwell at ease, and delight thyself in HIM.

9

'Do Not Sin Against the Child'

(An Address at a Prayer Meeting for Sabbath Schools)

And Reuben answered them, saying, Spake I not unto you, saying, Do not sin against the child; and ye would not hear? therefore, behold, also his blood is required (Gen. 42:22).

You know how Joseph's brethren, through envy, sold him into Egypt, and how, ultimately, they were themselves compelled to go down into Egypt to buy corn. When they were treated roughly by the governor of that country, whom they did not know to be their brother, their consciences smote them, and they said one to another, 'We are verily guilty concerning our brother, in that we saw the anguish of his soul, when he besought us, and we would not hear; therefore is this distress come upon us.' While their consciences were thus accusing them, the voice of their elder brother chimed in, saying, 'Spake I not unto you, saying, Do not sin against the child'. From which I gather that, if we commit sin after being warned, the voice of conscience will be all the more condemning, for it will be supported by the memory of disregarded admonitions, which will revive again, and with solemn voices say to us, 'Said we not unto you, Do not sin against the child?' We who know what is due to children will be far more guilty than others if we sin against their souls. Wiser views as to the needs and hopes of the little ones are now abroad in the world than those which ruled the public mind fifty years ago, and we shall be doubly criminal if now we bring evil upon the little ones.

The advice of Reuben may well be given to all grown-up persons: 'Do not sin against the child'. Thus would I speak to every parent, to every elder brother or sister, to every schoolmaster, to every employer, to every man and woman, whether they have families or not, 'Do not sin against the child': neither against your own child, nor against anybody's child, nor against the poor waif of the street whom they call 'nobody's child'. If you sin against adults, 'Do not sin against the child'. If a man must be profane, let him have too much reverence for a child to pollute its little ear with blasphemy. If a man must drink, let him have too much respect for childhood to entice his boy to sip at the intoxicating cup. If there be aught of lewdness or coarseness on foot, screen the young child from the sight and hearing of it. O ye parents, do not follow trades which will ruin your children, do not select houses where they will be cast into evil society, do not bring depraved persons within your doors to defile them! For a man to lead others like himself into temptation is bad enough; but to sow the vile seed of vice in hearts that are as yet untainted by any gross, actual sin, is a hideous piece of wickedness. Do not commit spiritual infanticide. For God's sake, in the name of common humanity, I pray you, if you have any sort of feeling left, do not play the Herod by morally murdering the innocents. I have heard that when, in the cruel sack of a city, a soldier was about to kill a child, his hand was stayed by the little one's crying out, 'O sir, please don't kill me; I am so little!' The feebleness and littleness of childhood should appeal to the worst of men, and restrain them from sinning against the child.

According to the story of Joseph, there are three ways of sinning against the child. The first was contained in the proposition of the envious brothers, 'Let us slay him, and we shall see what will become of his dreams.' 'Shed no blood', said Reuben, who had reasons of his own for wishing to save Joseph's life. There is such a thing as morally and spiritually slaying boys and girls, and here even the Reubens unite with us; even those, who are not so good as they should be, will join in the earnest protest, 'Do not sin against the child', do not train him in dishonesty, lying, drunkenness and vice. No one among us would wish to do so, yet it is continually being done by evil example. Many sons are ruined by their fathers. Those who gave them birth give them their death. They brought them into the world of sin, and they seem intent to bring them into the world of punishment, and will succeed in the fearful attempt unless the grace of God shall interfere. Many are doing all they can, by their own conduct at home and abroad, to educate their offspring into pests of society and plagues to their country.

When I see the number of juvenile criminals, I cannot help asking, 'Who slew all these?' and it is sad to have for an answer, 'These are mostly the victims of their parents' sin.' The fiercest beasts of prey will not destroy their own young; but sin makes men unnatural, so that they destroy their offspring's souls without thought. To teach a child a lascivious song is unutterably wicked; to introduce him to the wine cup is evil. To take children to places of amusement where everything is polluting; where the quick-witted boy soon spies out vice, and learns to be precocious in it; where the girl, while sitting to see the play, has kindled within her passions which need no fuel: to do this is to act the tempter's part. Would you poison young hearts, and do them lifelong mischief? I wish that the guardians of public morals would put down all open impurity; but if that cannot be, at least let the young be shielded. He who instructs a youth in the vices of the world is a despicable wretch, a panderer to the devil, for whom contempt is a feeling too lenient. No, even though thou be of all men most hardened, there can be no need to worry the lambs, and offer the babes before the shrine of Moloch.

The same evil may be committed by indoctrinating children with evil teachings. They learn so soon that it is a sad thing to teach them error. It is a dreadful thing when the infidel father sneers at the cross of Christ in the presence of his boy, when he utters horrible things against our blessed Lord in the hearing of tender youth. It is sad, to the last degree, that those who have been singing holy hymns in the Sabbath school should go home to hear God blasphemed, and to see holy things spit upon and despised. To the very worst unbeliever, we might well say, 'Do not thus ruin your child's immortal soul; if you are resolved to perish yourself, do not drag your child downward, too.'

But there is a second way of sinning against the child, of which Reuben's own proposition may serve as an illustration. Though not with a bad motive, Reuben said, 'Cast him into this pit that is in the wilderness, and lay no hand upon him.' The idea of many is to leave the child as a child, and then look him up in after days, and seek to deliver him from destruction. Do not kill him, but leave him alone till riper years. Do not kill him, that would be wicked murder; but leave him in the wilderness till a more convenient season, when, like Reuben, you hope to come to his rescue. Upon this point, I shall touch many more than upon the first. Many professing Christians ignore the multitudes of children around them, and act as if there were no such living beings. They may go to Sunday school or not; they do not know, and do not care. At any rate, these good people cannot trouble themselves with teaching children. I would earnestly say, 'Do not sin against the child by such neglect.' 'No,' says Reuben, 'we will look after him when he is a man. He is in the pit now, but we are in hopes of getting him out afterwards.'

That is the common notion – that the children are to grow up unconverted, and that they are to be saved in afterlife. They are to be left in the pit now, and to be drawn out by-and-by. This pernicious notion is sinning against the child. No word of Holy Scripture gives countenance to such a policy of delay and neglect. Neither nature nor grace pleads for it. It was the complaint of Jeremiah, 'Even the sea monsters draw out the breast, they give suck to their young ones: the daughter of my people is become cruel, like the ostriches in the wilderness.' Let not such a charge lie against any one of us. Our design and object should be that our children, while they are yet children, should be brought to Christ; and I ask those dear brothers and sisters here present who love the Lord not to doubt about the conversion of their little ones, but to seek it at once with all their hearts. Why should our Josephs remain in the pit of nature's corruption? Let us pray the Lord at once to take them up out of the horrible pit, and save them with a great salvation.

There is yet a third way of sinning against the child, which plan was actually tried upon Joseph; they sold him: sold him to the Ishmaelites. The merchantmen came by, and they offered so many pieces of silver for him, and his brothers readily handed him over for a reward. I am afraid that some are half inclined to do the same now. It is imagined that now we have school boards we shall not want Sabbath schools so much, but may give over the young to the Secularists. Because the children are to be taught the multiplication table, they will not need to be taught the fear

of the Lord! Strange reasoning this! Can geography teach them
the way to heaven, or arithmetic remove their countless sins?
The more of secular knowledge our juveniles acquire, the more
will they need to be taught in the fear of the Lord. To leave our
youthful population in the hands of secular teachers will be to
sell them to the Ishmaelites. Nor is it less perilous to leave them
to the seductive arts of Ritualists and Papists. We who love the
gospel must not let the children slip through our hands into the
power of those who would enslave their minds by superstitious
dogmas. We sin against the child if we hand it over to teachers
of error.

The same selling of the young Josephs can be effected by
looking only to their worldly interests, and forgetting their
souls. A great many parents sell their children by putting them
out as apprentices to men of no character, or by placing them
in situations where ungodliness is the paramount influence.
Frequently, the father does not ask where the boy can go on
the Sabbath-day, and the mother does not enquire whether her
girl can hear the gospel when she gets out; but good wages are
looked after, and not much else. They count themselves very
staunch if they draw a line at Roman Catholics, but worldliness
and even profligacy are not reckoned as barriers in many cases.
How many there are of those who call themselves Christians
who sell their daughters in marriage to rich men! The men have
no religion whatever, but 'it is a splendid match', because they
move in high society. Young men and women are put into the
matrimonial market, and disposed of to the highest bidder: God
is not thought of in the matter. Thus the rich depart from the
Lord, and curse their children quite as much as the poor. I am
sure you would not literally sell your offspring for slaves, and
yet to sell their souls is by no means less abominable. 'Do not
sin against the child'. Do not sell him to the Ishmaelites. 'Ah!'
say you, 'the money is always handy.' Will you take the price of
blood? Shall the blood of your children's souls be on your skirts?
I pray you, pause awhile ere you commit this great crime.

Sometimes, a child may be sinned against because he is dis-
liked.

The excuse for undue harshness and severity is, 'he is such
a strange child!' You have heard of the cygnet that was hatched
in a duck's nest. Neither duck, nor drake, nor ducklings could

make anything out of the ugly bird; and yet, in truth, it was superior to all the rest. Joseph was the swan in Jacob's nest, and his brothers and even his father did not understand him. His father rebuked him, and said, 'Shall I and thy mother and thy brethren indeed come to bow down ourselves to thee to the earth?' He was not understood by his own kin. I should fancy he was a most uncomfortable boy to live with; for when his elder brothers transgressed, he felt bound to bring to his father the report of their evil deeds. I doubt not that they called him 'a little sneak', though, indeed, he was a gracious child. His dreams also were very odd, and considerably provoking, for he was always the hero of them. His brothers called him 'this dreamer', and evidently thought him to be a mere fool. He was his father's pet boy, and this made him even more obnoxious to the other sons. Yet that very child, who was so despised by his brothers, was the Joseph among them. History repeats itself; and the difference in your child, which now causes him to be pecked at, may perhaps arise from a superiority which as yet has not found its sphere; at any rate, 'Do not sin against the child' because he is singular, for he may rise to special distinction. Do not, of course, show him partiality, and make him a coat of many colours; because, if you do, his brothers will have some excuse for their envy; but, on the other hand, do not suffer him to be snubbed, and do not allow his spirit to be crushed.

I have known some who, when they have met with a little Joseph, have sinned against him by foolish flattery. The boy has said something rather good, and then they have set him upon the table so that everybody might see him, and admire what he had to say, while he was coaxed into repeating his sage observations. Thus the child was made self-conceited, forward and pert. Children who are much exhibited are usually spoiled in the operation. I think I hear the proud parent say, 'Now do see – do see what a wonderful boy my Harry is!' Yes, I do see; I do see what a wonderful stupid his mother is. I do see how unwise his father is to expose his boy to such peril. Do not sin against the child by fostering his pride, which, as it is an ill weed, will grow apace of itself.

In many cases, the sin is of quite the opposite character. Contemptuous sneers have chilled many a good desire, and ridicule has nipped in the bud many a sincere purpose. Beware of checking youthful enthusiasm for good things. God forbid that you or I should quench one tiny spark of grace in a lad's heart, or destroy a single bud of promise! We believe in the piety of children; let us never speak, or act, or look as if we despised it.

'Do not sin against the child', whoever you may be. Whether you are teacher or parent, take care that, if there is any trace of the little Joseph in your child, even though it be but in his dreams, you do not sin against him by attempting to repress the noble flame which God may be kindling in his soul. I cannot just now mention the many, many ways in which we may be offending against one of the Lord's little ones; but I would have you recollect that, if the Lord's love should light upon your boy, and he should grow up to be a distinguished servant of the Lord, your conscience will prick you, and a voice will say in your soul, 'Spake I not unto you ... Do not sin against the child'? And if, on the other hand, your child should not become a Joseph, but an Absalom, it will be a horrible thing to be compelled to mingle with your lamentations the overwhelming consciousness that you led your child into the sin by which he became the dishonour of your family. If I see my child perish, and know that he becomes a reprobate through my ill teaching and example, I shall have to wring my hands with dread remorse, and cry, 'I slew my child! I slew my child! and when I did it, I knew better; but I disregarded the voice which said to me, "Do not sin against the child".'

Now, dear Sunday school teachers, I will mention one or two matters which concern you. 'Do not sin against the child' by coming to your class with a chilly heart. Why should you make your children cold towards divine things? Do not sin against them by coming too late, for that will make them think that punctuality is not a virtue, and that the Sunday school is of no very great importance. 'Do not sin against the child' by coming irregularly, and absenting yourself on the smallest pretence, for that is distinctly saying to the child, 'You can neglect to serve God when you please, for you see I do.' 'Do not sin against the child' by merely going through class routine, without really teaching and instructing. That is the shadow of Sunday school teaching, and not the substance, and it is in some respects worse than nothing. 'Do not sin against the child' by merely telling him a number of stories without setting forth the Saviour; for that will be giving him a stone instead of bread. 'Do not sin against the child' by aiming at anything short of his conversion to God through Jesus Christ the Saviour.

And then, you parents, 'Do not sin against the child' by being so very soon angry. I have frequently heard grown-up people repeat that verse, 'Children, obey your parents in all things.' It is a very proper text; a very proper text, and boys and girls should carefully attend to it. I like to hear fathers and mothers preach from it; but there is that other one, you know, which is quite as fully inspired, 'Fathers, provoke not your children to anger, lest they be discouraged.' Do not pick up every little thing against a good child, and throw it in his or her teeth, and say, 'Ah, if you were a Christian child, you would not do this, and you would not do that!' I am not so sure. You who are heads of families do a great many wrong things yourselves, and yet I hope you are Christians; and if your Father in heaven were sometimes to be as severe with you as you are with the sincere little ones when you are out of temper, I am afraid it would go very hard with you. Be gentle, and kind, and tender, and loving.

At the same time, do not sin against any child by over-indulgence. Spoiled children are like spoiled fruit; the less we see of them, the better. In some families, the master of the house is the youngest boy, though he is not yet big enough to wear knickerbockers. He manages his mother, and his mother, of course, manages his father, and so, in that way, he rules the whole house. This is unwise, unnatural and highly perilous to the pampered child. Keep boys and girls in proper subjection, for they cannot be happy themselves, nor can you be so, unless they are in their places. Do not water your young plants either with vinegar or with syrup. Neither use too much nor too little of rebuke. Seek wisdom of the Lord, and keep the middle of the way.

In a word, 'Do not sin against the child', but train it in the way it should go, and bring it to Jesus that he may bless it. Cease not to pray for the child till his young heart is given to the Lord. May the Holy Spirit make you wise to deal with these young immortals! Like plastic clay, they are on the wheel. Oh, that he would teach us to mould and fashion their characters! Above all, may he put his own hand to the work, and then it will be done indeed.

10

Fighting and Praying

Then came Amalek, and fought with Israel in Rephidim.
And Moses said unto Joshua, Choose us out men, and
go out, fight with Amalek: to morrow I will stand on
the top of the hill with the rod of God in mine hand
(Exod. 17:8, 9).

'Then came Amalek'; that is, after the manna had fallen, after the rock had been smitten. First food, then conflict. God spared his people all battles in their early days. For awhile, their adversaries were as still as a stone. But when everything was arranged, and the commissariat of the camp was provided for, '[T]hen came Amalek'. Brethren, in our march to heaven, it may happen that one part of the way is free from conflict; but let no man wonder if things change. One of these days, we shall read this despatch from the seat of war, 'Then came Amalek, and fought with Israel'. Do not court attack, nor even desire it. When you hear the older folk talk about their inward conflicts, do not lament if your chronicle of wars is a short one. There is a time when kings go forth to battle, and that time will come to you soon enough. It has often been the Lord's way to give his people space for refreshment before trying them.

The same truth holds good as to service for the Lord. In the case before us, warfare was service. Some newborn converts rush to the service of God before their knowledge or their strength has fitted them for it. I want to speak very guardedly, for I have great sympathy with their zeal; but I wish to show unto them a more excellent way. Few begin work for God too soon. Ah, me! Some professors have not begun yet, after years of profession. What shall we do with old sluggards, who have been lying in bed for thirty years? Are they worth the trouble of waking? I fear not. May the Lord be gracious to them, and save them! We cannot work for God too soon; yet it is possible to go to work before you have sharpened your tools. There is a time for every purpose; and each thing is good in its season. Learn, and then teach. I would have you serve the Lord successfully: wherefore, as God gave to Israel manna and water before he sent them to fight with Amalek, so should every believer first feed on the truth himself, and then go forth to teach others also. Feed that you may work, and work because you have been fed.

After the manna and after the smitten rock came the fight: 'Then came Amalek'. He was a descendant of Esau, full of his father's hate. This tribe fell upon Israel without proclamation of war, in a cowardly manner, and slew the hindmost of them, when they were not expecting an attack. They were the first of the nations that dared enter the lists against Jehovah. The others had been cowed by the wonders of the Red Sea; but Amalek was daring and presumptuous. According to the Hebrew, Amalek laid his hand upon the throne of God, and dared to molest his people.

Note well that, in this battle of the Lord, there were two kinds of fighting. The first was the Joshua-service; and that was done in the plain by the fighting men. The second was the Moses-service; and this was done upon the side of the hill, by the men of God, who communed with heaven. We need both modes of warfare.

I. To begin with, we want much of THE JOSHUA-SERVICE. This is the service of many. Moses said to Joshua, 'Choose us out men, and go out, fight with Amalek.' We have a battle against sin, error, pride, self and everything that is contrary to God and to his Christ; and in the Joshua-service many can be employed. As the Holy Spirit has given diversities of gifts, so are there varieties of agencies for battling for the truth. Every believer should be a soldier in Christ's own army of salvation. We must not join a church with the main design of our own edification: our chief point in life is far higher than the most spiritual form of self-interest. We must live to battle for Christ Jesus our Lord in all manner of ways. To feed on the manna of heaven, and then to wrestle with the evils of earth, is a healthy combination. We need, all of us, to stand up for Jesus in these evil days: the enemies are many and powerful, and no man, redeemed by Christ, must keep back from the conflict. Friend, what part will you take?

In this Joshua-service, all the combatants were under due command. 'Joshua did as Moses had said to him', and the people did as Joshua commanded them. In all holy service, willingness to be led is a great point. Certain workers may be very good personally; but they will never combine with others to make a conquering band. They work very well alone, or as fore-horses in the team; but they cannot trot in double harness. We most of all need men and women who can keep rank, who can do their work quietly and perseveringly, and are ready to follow the direction of those whom God may call to be leaders. A general can do nothing without such soldiers; and they feel that they can do little without him. Soldiers without discipline become a mob, and not an army. May the Lord send us troops of disciplined warriors prepared to chase the Amalekites! All at it, and always at it, and all for the love of Jesus: this makes a fine motto. Friend, will you be one of the steady workers?

In Joshua-work, courage was required. 'Go out fight with Amalek.' The Amalekites were fierce, cruel, strong. They are said to have been the chief among the nations: by which I understand, first among the plunderers of the desert. The soldiers under Joshua had courage, and faced their wolfish foes. Saints need courage for Jesus in these days. May God, in his mercy, make his people bold against scepticism, superstition and open wickedness! In these days, boldness is a jewel, for men are not sure about anything, or they speak as if they were not; and when men are not sure themselves, they can never convince others. A modern-thought gentleman said in a paper, the other day, 'We are not all so cocksure as Mr. Spurgeon.' No; and the more's the pity. If ministers are not absolutely certain of what they preach, they are not likely to convince others. If you doubt a thing, let it alone till your doubt is solved one way or the other. He that doubts creates doubters. Only he that believes will make believers. In this age of unbelief, if you are to win victories, you must have convictions, and you must have the courage of those convictions, and refuse to bow down before the infidelity of the age. We are called, not to flirt with error, but to fight with it; therefore, let us be brave, and push on the conflict.

Those fighting under Joshua did not grow weary. Moses had the more spiritual work, and his hands grew heavy: we sooner tire in private devotion than in public service. Joshua and his men were not weary: never let us be weary in well-doing. Do you ever grow weary in one peculiar way of serving God? It may be useful to try something else. 'You mean, drop what I am doing?' No; I do not. I mean, do something extra. It often happens that a man cannot do one thing, but he can do two things. Do you think the observation strange? It is true. Variety of labour serves for recreation. In the service of God, it is a relief to turn from one consecrated effort to another; and so rest one set of faculties by exercising others. Throw your whole soul into the heavenly crusade, and weary not through your fight with Amalek from dawn to set of sun. Friend, will you be unwearied in the heavenly war?

In the Joshua-service, they were successful, for 'they discomfited Amalek and his people with the edge of the sword'. Beloved workers for the Lord, may he grant you like success against evil! The devil goes to be beaten, and he shall be beaten. If we have but courage and faith in God, and can use the edge of the sword, we shall yet defeat the powers of darkness. Many evils are deeply entrenched in modern society: the drunkenness, the scepticism, the superstition and the vice around us are a tremendous force; but the gospel of our Lord Jesus Christ is equal to the emergency. If all professedly Christian men were actuated by the spirit of the gospel, many evils would be greatly diminished. If we also believed in the power of the gospel, so as to tell it out to our fellows with joyful confidence, in the power of the Spirit of God, we should soon see the wickedness and worldliness of the age put to the rout. Alas, brethren! the fault of many workers is that they do not use the edge of the sword. One does not like to think of the edge of a sword; but nothing else will serve in battle. One gentleman has preached a magnificent sermon, everybody admired it. Yes, that was the richly adorned hilt of the sword; but nobody was wounded. Another man, in rough tones, boldly stated a naked truth, and pressed it home on the conscience, and that truth has pricked his hearer in the heart.

The edge of the sword means business, and people know it.

They are not amused, but are made to mourn and repent. What cares the evil heart of man for the scabbard of our sword? It needs the edge, and must have it. In talking to people, are we not often afraid of using the edge of the sword? 'Well,' says one, 'I try to bring in the gospel gradually.' Quite right; but the best way to bring in the edge of the sword gradually is to cut with it at once. We are such a long while parading and parleying that we do not come to the point, and tell men that they are lost in sin, and must immediately fly to Christ for refuge, or they will perish. We must bring forth the truth clearly and boldly, if any good is to be done. 'Joshua discomfited Amalek with the edge of the sword.' We must use the Word of God, which is the sword of the Spirit, and force it home upon the attention and the conscience of all we can reach. Give the people plenty of instruction as to the central truth of salvation through the blood of Jesus. We may do as we like about flags and drums; I mean, preaching about this or that minor point, but we must come to the edge of the sword: the wrath to come for the ungodly, and salvation in Christ for believers. Give men plenty of that sacred command, 'Believe on the Lord Jesus Christ, and thou shalt be saved.' Strike home in the name of the Lord, and command all men everywhere to repent. Quote Scripture; quote it continually. Bring out the doctrines of grace, which are the burden of the inspired Book. It is the Word of God that saves souls, not our comment upon it. Smite them with the edge of the sword.

Thus I have spoken about the Joshua-work, wishing with my whole soul that every member of the visible church would enter the ranks, and use the sword with his whole heart. Oh, that those who are marching to the promised rest may serve the Lord valiantly while they are on the road thither! If you are saved yourselves, may the Lord employ you in his army, and glorify himself in you!

II. The second part of the subject is full of interest. It is THE MOSES-SERVICE: the service of Moses and his comrades. These did not go down to the battlefield themselves, but they climbed the mountainside, where they could see the warriors in the conflict; and there Moses lifted up the rod of God.

Note that the Moses-service was essential to the battle; for when Moses held up his hand, Israel prevailed; and when he let down his hand, Amalek prevailed. The scales of the conflict were in the hand of Moses, and they turned as his prayer and testimony failed or continued. It was quite as necessary that Moses should be on the hill as that Joshua should be in the plain. This part of church-work is often overlooked; but it is quite as necessary as the activity of the many. We need the secret prevalence of chosen servants of the Lord, whose business is not so much with men for God as with God for men.

This holy work was of a very special character. Only three were able to enter into it. I believe that, in every church, the deeply spiritual, who prevalently commune with God, and bring down the blessing upon the work of the rest, are comparatively few: I might almost say, are absolutely few. God lays, his own hand upon one here, and another there, and causes them to approach unto him. 'Would God that all the Lord's servants were prophets!' But it is not so. The Lord uses many in his working service, who, nevertheless, are not among his intimates. They do not hold high rank among the intercessors who have power with God. This service is peculiar; but the more widely it is exercised, the better for the cause of God. We want many who can draw down power from God, as well as many who can use that power against the enemy.

This Moses-service lay in very close communion with God. Moses, and Aaron, and Hur were called to rise above the people, and to get alone, apart from the company. They climbed the hill as a symbol, and in retirement they silently communed with God. That rod of God in Moses' hand meant this: God is here with these pleading ones on the mount; and by his powerful presence he is smiting the enemy. How blessed it is for a people to be led by those whom the Lord has honoured in former times, and with whom he still holds fellowship!

In this sacred engagement, there was a terrible strain upon the one man who led the others in it. In the process of bringing down the divine power upon the people, the vehicle of communication was sorely tried. 'Moses' hands were heavy.' Beloved, if God gives you spiritual power to lead in Christian work you will soon find out that the condition of such leadership is a costly one. Your case requires a deeper humility, a steadier watchfulness, a higher consecration and a closer communion with God than that of others; and these things will try you, and, in many ways, put a heavy strain upon you. You will be like Elias, who, at one time, could run like a giant, and at another could faint and fly. The burden of the Lord is no featherweight.

In this hallowed service, help is very precious. When Moses' hands began to drop down, and he himself was faint, Aaron and Hur gave him substantial aid. They fetched a stone, and put it under him, and they made him sit thereon, with his hands still lifted high, and his eyes towards heaven. When he was all in a sweat, because of his anxious prayer, and the muscles of his arms grew weary, his brethren stood by him, each one holding up an arm lest the rod should drop; for if it did, the cause of Israel dropped also. Are you a worker? Have you a leader fit to lead you? Bring a stone, and put it under him: cheer his heart with some gracious promise from the Lord's Word, or with some happy sign from the work itself. Cheer the good man as much as possible. Do not throw a stone at him, as I have known some workers do; but put a stone under him, that he may sit down, and not be overcome. Copy Aaron and Hur, by staying up his hands, the one on the one side, and the other on the other side, so that his hands may be steady until the going down of the sun. Happy men, thus to sustain their leader! The sacred power with God, which brings down victory for others, is given to some, and they use it; but flesh is weak, and they faint. Let others of like grace gather to their help, and hold up their hands, one in one way, and one in another way, as Aaron and Hur held up the hands of Moses. Let spiritual men earnestly help those whom God calls into spiritual communion with himself, that so the name of the Lord may be glorified, and victory may follow the banners of his people.

This is the pith of my address. The prayer meeting is, after all, that spiritual power on the mountainside which makes the workers strong. Do not let the praying work flag; and even if it seems to do so, let Aaron and Hur come to the rescue. Come, and help, with all your might, to keep the rod of the Lord still steady, that the battle of the Lord may be fought out victoriously. Go on, Joshua, and use the edge of the sword: the Amalekites need it. But take heed, you who are on the mountainside, that your service does not cease. Humble men and women, unknown to fame, you may be called by God, like Moses, to hold up his rod, and bring down the blessing. If any of you grow faint, I pray that others may come forward, and keep the rod of God in its place.

The prayer meeting must be maintained at all cost. The communion of the church with God must never be broken. If you visit a factory, you may see thousands of wheels revolving, and a host of hands employed. It is a wonderful sight. Where is the power that keeps all this running? Look at that slated shed! Come into this grimy place, smelling of oil. What is it? It is the engine-house. You do not think much of it, but that is the centre of power. If you stop that engine, every wheel will stand still. Some good people say, 'I am not going out tonight. It is only a prayer meeting.' Just so. It is only the engine, but that is everything. Go on board a great ocean steamer, bound for New York. You say, 'I have been in the saloon. I have seen the wonderful luxuries provided for the passengers. It is a marvellous vessel.' Did you look at her engines? 'What! go down that ladder? I saw some black fellows below, stoking great fires; but I did not care for that.' Talk not so. If it were not for those sooty stokers, the grand saloon and the fine decks would be of no use. Prayer is the engine of the church; it supplies the force. I like to see the engines going; praying, praying, praying, praying! Then the hidden screw, down under water, drives the huge ship, and causes it to speed towards the appointed haven. Keep the Moses part of the work going; and let not the Joshua-work be slack.

Beloved in the Lord, let us hearten one another in our warfare. Let us each stand in his office, and do the part to which the Lord has called us. Let us take courage. We are sure of victory. In the margin of our Bibles we read, 'Because Amalek had laid his hand upon the throne of Jehovah, the Lord will have war with Amalek from generation to generation.' Sin lays its traitorous hand upon the very throne of God. Will he allow it? The unbelief of the age has laid its hand upon the holy sacrifice of Christ. Will the Lord be quiet concerning this? Scepticism has dared to assail the inspired Word. Will the Lord endure it? Is not the time of his coming hastening on when men grow bolder in sin? May we not, from the very infamy of the age, gather that it is coming to its climax? The iniquity of the Amalekites is filling up. The Lord will surely smite the evil of the age with the edge of the sword. Let us not be afraid.

My firm conviction is that the gospel is as powerful as ever. If we could but get it out of the sheath of so-called culture, and education, and progress, and questioning, and could use the bare, two-edged sword of the old-fashioned gospel upon the hearts of men, we should again hear shouts of victory. We have heard with our ears, O God, and our fathers have told us, what work thou didst in their days, and in the old time before them; and if we can get back the courage of the old times, and the gospel of the old times, and the spirit of the old times, we shall see a renewal of those wondrous deeds. We must exert ourselves; for Joshua did so. We must lean upon the strength of God; for Moses did so. The two together – active warfare and prayerful dependence – will bring the blessing. We are more than ever forced into this fight today. Thirty years ago, things were very different from what they are now. It was easy to gather a congregation then, compared with what it is now; the spirit of hearing is departing from our cities. Cavillers and questioners are today far more numerous than they were thirty years ago. One finds among Christian professors shoals of infidels. Ministers are, in large numbers, sowers of doubt. One who is reputed to preach evangelically told his young men, the other day, that a page of Huxley was worth all that Moses had written in Genesis. Many ministers are more at home in undermining the gospel than in the conversion of souls. Let us, therefore, look well to our weapons, and be in earnest to defend the truth of God. I charge you, each one, to do his part, and play the man in this evil day.

Though myself only fit to be numbered with the least of my Master's servants, yet I am called to lead a great work, and therefore I beg my comrades to help me. My brethren, hold up my hands! Send up your continual prayer on my behalf. If the standard-bearer falls, what will the weaklings do? I am feeble in body, and sorely pressed with anxious care; spare me what care you can by your brotherly aid, and specially by your loving words of comfort, and your pleadings in prayer. To the best of my ability, I have held the fort, and kept the faith. Though, as yet, my protest seems unavailing, and Amalek prevails by reason of scientific unbelief, yet the Lord on high is greater than the noise of many waters. Truth must yet prevail, and error must be routed. In the name of the Lord, let us set up our banners once again. Renewing the pledges of our brotherly covenant, let nothing but death divide us. Let us be one in this great conflict for the Lord and for his throne. Amen.

11

Another Spiritual Honey-Drop

*And he said, 'My presence shall go with thee,
and I will give thee rest'* (Exod. 33:14).

This is another of our choicest honey-drops* about which I will speak without premeditation, simply allowing the sweetness to flow forth of itself. It is God's word to his servant Moses.

It was not a pleasure-trip that Moses was taking; it was a journey through the wilderness, on most important business, with a great pressure on his own heart. He took his case before his God, and he said unto Jehovah, 'See, thou sayest unto me, Bring up this people: and thou hast not let me know whom thou wilt send with me. Yet thou hast said, I know thee by name, and thou hast also found grace in my sight. Now therefore, I pray thee, if I have found grace in thy sight, shew me now thy way, that I may know thee, that I may find grace in thy sight: and consider that this nation is thy people.' It is very beautiful to notice the argument that Moses uses. He says, 'Lord, thou hast set me to take care of this people. How can I do it? But they are thy people.' Therefore he gives an eye to Jehovah himself for assistance. 'Thou hast not let me know whom thou wilt send with me', is his complaint; but he seems to have an eye to the fact that HE, whose people they were, who had put him into commission to guide them, and to bear all their provocations, must intend to give him some very superior help. The answer to that is, 'my presence shall go with thee, and I will give thee rest'.

What more could Moses want than that, and what more can we want? We are so foolish that we look about for strength away from God, but there is none except in him. Dear Brother Varley, you are going to preach the gospel in the lands beyond the sea; this is the assurance that you want in going forth: 'my presence shall go with thee, and I will give thee rest'. You will want much help in journeying from place to place; and that help lies in the constant fellowship of your heart with the Lord, the continual presence of God consciously enjoyed. You have a great burden of souls lying upon you, dear friend; your strength to bear that burden lies in the realisation of God's presence with yourself. It may not appear to some that the quarter of an hour in the morning spent in looking into the face of God, with ecstatic joy, can fill us with strength; but we know, from blessed experience, that there is no strength like it. We are only strong as we are over-shadowed by the Eternal. Then Omnipotence comes streaming into us; Jehovah, in infinite, condescending liberality gives forth his might to us.

Now, notice, that Moses was not informed that God would send Hobab, his father-in-law, to go with him; he was not told that Joshua, his successor, should accompany him; nothing was said to him about the seventy elders who were to share the burden of responsibility with him. Moses was to have their presence and help, but his true power was to lie in this, 'my presence shall go with thee'. He is about to start on a journey of great importance, a journey of great trial, a journey of great provocation, a journey that is to last for forty years; but this is all the provender that he needs, and God himself could not give him more.

And then the Lord adds, 'and I will give thee rest'. The most important thing to a Christian worker, as it was to Moses, is to have rest. 'I do not expect any rest,' says one, 'while I am here.' Do you not? Then you will not do much work for the Lord. They who work most must rest most; and if they work with their mind, they cannot do it well, indeed they cannot do it at all, unless they have plenty of rest. You will notice how people that get greatly excited often talk nonsense, and people who are very fretful and fearful do not speak or act as they should. The man who is to move others must have both his own feet fixed firmly; there is nothing like having a good grip of the ground, then you can fling the fellow with whom you are wrestling, but he cannot fling you.

'Do you think Moses had this rest?' someone asks. I am sure he had, because of the meekness of his spirit. You remember how the Lord Jesus said, 'Take my yoke upon you, and learn of me; for I am meek and lowly in heart; and ye shall find rest unto your souls.' It is true that meekness of heart produces rest; but still, at the bottom, rest of heart produces meekness. You can very well afford to be quiet with your fellow men when you yourself are perfectly restful in the living God. I remember a man being run over in the street one day. Somebody rushed off, posthaste, for the nearest doctor; and when the medical man heard of the accident, he went quietly into his surgery, turned over his case of instruments, selected those that he thought he might want, and then leisurely walked to the spot where the poor man lay. The messenger tried to hurry him, but it was no use. 'Be quick, doctor,' he cried, 'the man's leg is broken, every moment is precious.' Now, the surgeon knew that he was doing the very best thing that he could do, and he was far wiser than he would have been if he had rushed off in wild haste, perhaps forgetting the very instrument he most needed, and arriving out of breath, and quite unfit for the delicate duty required of him. The doctor's composure was not the result of coldness of heart, but the result of the resolution to do the best possible thing in the best possible way. If you are conscious of the Lord's presence, you will do the best thing possible by being very calm, deliberate and quiet in his service. 'He that believeth,' in that sense, 'shall not make haste '; but he shall go about his Lord's business in a restful spirit.

Mark the kind of rest that is here mentioned. 'I will give thee rest.' All the rest that God gives us, we may safely take. No man ever rested too long upon the bosom of Jesus. I believe that many Christian workers would be better if they enjoyed more rest. I was speaking to the ministers at the Conference upon this matter, my subject being the Saviour asleep during the storm on the Sea of Galilee. He knew there was a storm coming on, but he felt so happy and restful in his Father's love and care that he went into the hinder part of the ship, the best place for sleeping, deliberately took a pillow, lay down, and went to sleep. It was the very best thing he could do. He had been busy all day, teaching and feeding the multitudes, and he felt that it was his duty to go to sleep that he might be ready for the next day's toil. When you get very weary, and perhaps worried as well, the best thing you can do is to go to sleep. Go to bed, brother, and go to sleep. It is astonishing what a difference a night's rest makes with our troubles. I would say this literally to fidgety, worrying people, like myself, 'Go to bed, brother, go to bed.' But I would also say it spiritually to all sorts of people; when you are feeling weak, and disturbed, and you do not know what to do for the best, 'Go into the presence of God, and there get rest.' 'My presence shall go with thee, and I will give thee rest.'

I will give you a little bit of worldly wisdom; it is this: whenever you do not know what to do, do not do it. But some people, when they do not know what to do, go and do it directly; and get themselves into all sorts of trouble. Many of us, like Moses, need rest. Moses has to bear two millions of people on his heart; he needs rest. He has to put up with them for forty years; he needs rest. Never had another man such a family as that, never was another man so likely to be fluttered and worried; and he was a meek-spirited man, too, who could not make a dash, as others might have done. This is his strength, that he dwells in the divine presence, and therefore is restful, calm and strong. It is only now and then that he lets the human meekness be for a moment clouded. Thus he was enabled to march along, like a king in Jeshurun, as he was; and his soul dwelt in the eternity of God, singing ever amidst ten thousand graves, for he had forty of his people dying every day, 'Lord, thou hast been our dwelling-place in all generations.'

12

The Three 'Thens' of Leviticus 26

In the twenty-sixth chapter of the book of Leviticus, there are three 'THENs', which will afford us instruction if the Spirit of God will shine upon them. Turn to the passage, and read for yourselves.

We have first the THEN of promise and threatening repeated several times. The children of Israel were not to make any graven images, nor to set up any images made by others, nor to bow to those already set up, but to keep clear of idolatry in every shape, and worship only their great invisible God, Jehovah, whose Sabbaths they were to keep, and whose precepts they were to obey; and then the Lord says, 'Then I will give you rain in due season, and the land shall yield her increase, and the trees of the field shall yield their fruit ... And I will give peace in the land, and ye shall lie down, and none shall make you afraid: and I will rid evil beasts out of the land, neither shall the sword go through your land ... And I will walk among you, and will be your God, and ye shall be my people.' Very rich are the blessings which the Lord lavishes upon an obedient people; peace and plenty, conquest and communion are the portion of believers whose hearts are chaste towards the Lord.

But should Israel refuse to hearken to the Lord, the chastening would be terrible indeed. Listen to these verses from the fifteenth to the eighteenth: 'And if ye shall despise my statutes, or if your soul abhor my judgments, so that ye will not do all my commandments, but that ye break my covenant: I also will do this unto you; I will even appoint over you terror, consumption, and the burning ague, that shall consume the eyes, and cause sorrow of heart: and ye shall sow your seed in vain, for your enemies shall eat it. And I will set my face against you, and ye shall be slain before your enemies: they that hate you shall reign over you; and ye shall flee when none pursueth you. And if ye will not yet for all this hearken unto me, then I will punish you seven times more for your sins.'

Is not this first 'then' a very terrible one? But this is not all; more sorrows are added if their sins be multiplied. Read verses 23 and 24: 'And if ye will not be reformed by me by these things, but will walk contrary unto me; Then will I also walk contrary unto you, and will punish you yet seven times for your sins.' Here we have stroke upon stroke to break a hard heart. Nor even there does the judgement rest. Hear again the word of the Lord: 'And if ye will not for all this hearken unto me, but walk contrary unto me; Then I will walk contrary unto you also in fury; and I, even I, will chastise you seven times for your sins.'

Brethren, read these words with holy trembling: they are written not for strangers, but for the seed of Israel, and for us also who are grafted in unto the true olive. Those who are written in the eternal covenant will find it a hard thing to sin against the Lord their God. The utterly ungodly often go unpunished in this life, for their punishment is reserved for the world to come, where the due reward of their deeds shall be meted out to them for ever and ever; but the Lord dealeth far otherwise with his own, whose transgressions he hath blotted out. These are absolved in their relation to him as a Judge, but as children they come under his fatherly discipline, and out of love to them he causes them in this life to smart for their sins if they break the law of his house. As our covenant God, the Lord is jealous. He is no Eli who ruins his sons by indulgence, but he scourgeth every son whom he receiveth.

Very heavily has the Lord chastised some of his children. I ask you not to judge of one case by another, nor suppose that all the family must needs be scourged in the same measure. The Lord speaks of the church as having compassion, and making a difference, and he in mercy makes differences in discipline, because real differences of character exist. Certain of the Lord's beloved ones were happily led to Christ in their early days, and therefore know nothing of those sins which are the torment of others; when these are kept by divine grace from all inconsistency, the rod is little needed, and few clouds darken their path; but there are others, of rougher mould and sadder experience, who smarted much at their first conversion, and having wandered again, are brought back with heavy chastisements, and waters of a full cup are wrung out to them. The Lord may be dealing in discipline with some among you; and if so, you will smart indeed, for our heavenly Father never plays with the rod, but uses it in real earnest. It may be that sorrow of heart consumes your eyes, and your strength is spent in vain: a blight from the Lord seems to have fallen upon you both in temporal and in spiritual things; you sow, but you do not reap; you labour, and obtain not. A faintness is in your head, so that the sound of a shaken leaf doth chase you, and you have no power to stand before your enemies. Sin and Satan, doubt and desolation triumph over you, and you flee when no man pursueth. To you it has happened according to the threatening in the nineteenth verse, 'I will break the pride of your power', for now you find no spiritual power within you, even power in prayer is gone, and all around you is barren; God hath made your heaven as iron, and your earth as brass. Ah, me! you are in, a woeful plight, for your strength is spent in vain, and your plagues are multiplied according to your sins.

It comes to this, my dear brother, that you are to be driven from your sins. God is 'avenging the quarrel of his covenant,' as he solemnly says in verse twenty-five. Read that word, and mark it. It is an awful thing to have God walking contrary to you; and yet he told you that he would do so if you walked contrary to him. What else could you expect? If you are his dear child, he will be much grieved if he sees you act like a traitor; if you have leaned upon his bosom as a favoured friend, he has a greater interest in you than in others; and he cannot therefore endure to see you polluted. The dearer you are to God, the more angry will he be with you when you sin. The more he loves you, the more determined will he be to drive out the evil, and rid you of the abominable thing which his soul hateth.

A judge, when he is sitting upon the bench, may feel a great indignation against a robber, or a murderer; yet he does not show it, but calmly condemns him to suffer the penalty of the law. See that judge without his robes, acting as a father at home: his child has transgressed, and now he is really angry, and shows far more sharpness towards his child than towards the offender. He who spoke in cold measured tones to the gross criminal now speaks severely, and with heat of spirit to his own offending boy. You all understand why he feels and acts thus; his wrath is of that kind which grows out of the truest love, a love which cannot suffer evil in its darling object. The child does not think his father loves him much when he makes him tingle and smart beneath his strokes, but we who are wiser understand that 'here in is love'.

When God chastens you, my brother, yield at once, and yield completely. If you do not, you may take warning from this chapter, for the Lord puts his threatening before you three times over: 'And if ye will not be reformed by me by these things, but will walk contrary unto me; Then will I also walk contrary unto you, and will punish you yet seven times for your sins.' The old Roman judges, when they passed along the streets, were attended by lictors; and those lictors carried an axe bound up in a bundle of rods, to signify this, that offenders should first be beaten with rods, but if these rods were of no use, they should be slain with the axe. I beseech every soul that is under the striving influences of the Spirit, or suffering from the trials of Providence, to hear at once the warning voice of the rod; for those who will not hear the rod must feel the axe.

The Lord useth great discretion and deliberation, for he doth not afflict willingly: when little will suffice, he will smite but little. If men humble themselves under his mighty hand, he will exalt them in due time; but, if they refuse and rebel, he will smite them more and more, till he has chastened them seven times for their sins. 'Then I will walk contrary unto you also in fury; and I, even I, will chastise you seven times for your sins.' We have known some men lose all their goods before they have turned to their God. Diseases, accidents, sicknesses have followed each other in quick succession, and hardly would they repent when they were all wounds, and bruises, and putrefying sores. Death has rent away their darlings; lovely children have been followed to the grave by their yet more precious mother; and hardly then has the proud spirit broken down. It has seemed as if Pharaoh was alive again, and the plagues were being repeated. Alas! in some cases, there has even been a hardening as the result of affliction; the man has accused God of harshness, and has refused to turn to the chastening hand. Ah, me! what sorrows such are preparing for themselves! Those whom the Lord means to bless he will go on smiting till they bow before him, and make a full surrender. Then, when they continue to rebel; then, when they still harden their neck; then, when they will not hear the rod; then, when they cleave to their idols, and depart from the Most High; then, he will make them to pine away in their iniquity, and will set his face against them.

We are glad to come to the second *then* of wise and penitent action. In the fortieth verse of this chapter we read, 'If they shall confess their iniquity, and the iniquity of their fathers, with their trespass which they trespassed against me, and that also they have walked contrary unto me; And that I also have walked contrary unto them, and have brought them into the land of their enemies; if then their uncircumcised hearts be humbled, and they then accept of the punishment of their iniquity: Then will I remember my covenant with Jacob, and also my covenant with Isaac, and also my covenant with Abraham will I remember; and I will remember the land.' They were brought very low: they were even driven out of their land to perish among the heathen; and God seemed utterly to have cast them off, but he declares that even then he would remember his covenant, and restore them, if they would turn from their iniquities; their turning from iniquity would be the turning-point of their affairs: the end of woe, and the dawn of hope.

I beg you to listen to this call of mercy, and to note when judgement would stay its hand. They were first to 'confess their iniquity', and then would come the mercy, but not till then. O you chastened ones, are you prepared to acknowledge your transgressions, and your doings which are not good? They were to confess their trespass, their own peculiar trespass, whatever that might be; their hearts were to search out sin, confess it and mourn over it; then would forgiveness come, there can be no pardon till this is done. We must take sin to ourselves before God can put it away from us.

Next, their heart was to be humbled; see the forty-first verse: 'ff then their uncircumcised hearts be humbled'. Proud sinners cannot be pardoned sinners. If we are not submissive, there are more plagues in store for us. They were to be lowly, and then they would be cleansed from sin. Humility dates the hour of comfort. Observe, also, the peculiar point that they were to accept the punishment of their iniquity, by which, I suppose, is meant that they must see their sorrow to be the result of their sin, and must own that it was a just infliction, a natural fruit of their own conduct. We are to have no quarrel with God, but to own that we deserve all that he has put upon us, and confess that, if he should cast us into hell itself, he would be just: then, may we look for grace. If a child should say, 'Father, you do well to punish me, for I deserve it', the father would put up the rod, for it would have wrought its end; and when a soul has been sore broken, till it sobs out in its agony, 'I deserve thy rod; I deserve thine eternal wrath, O God', then, then, then it is that the Lord accepts the repentance, and looks with an eye of mercy upon the contrite one.

The third THEN will be observed in the forty-second verse: 'Then will I remember my covenant with Jacob, and also my covenant with Isaac, and also my covenant with Abraham will I remember; and I will remember the land. The land also shall be left of them, and shall enjoy her sabbaths, while she lieth desolate without them: and they shall accept of the punishment of their iniquity: because, even because they despised my judgments, and because their soul abhorred my statutes.' '[Y]et for all that,' he mentions all their sins, and he says in the forty-fourth verse, 'when they be in the land of their enemies, I will not cast them away, neither will I abhor them, to destroy them utterly, and to break my covenant with them: for I am the LORD their God. But I will for their sakes remember the covenant of their ancestors, whom I brought forth out of the land of Egypt in the sight of the heathen, that I might be their God: I am the LORD.'

Now, fellow sinner, when the Lord has brought you down to accept the punishment which he has laid upon you, then will he remember his covenant, that old and glorious covenant of grace which was made with faithful Abraham, which, better still, is made with every believer in the person of the Lord Jesus. Abraham was the father of the faithful, and the covenant is made with all the faithful, with all the trusters, and God will remember it towards them. What is the tenor of it? 'I will be merciful to their unrighteousness, and their sins and their iniquities will I remember no more.' 'A new heart also will I give you, and a new spirit will I put within you.' This is the covenant of grace; and, oh! it is a blessed thing when God remembers it on our behalf, for then he remembers no more the iniquities of his people. Poor sinner, though he has hunted you down, and pursued you in his fierce anger; though conviction has broken you as a lion tears its prey; though you fear that the Lord has cast you away from all hope of grace, and outlawed you from all hope: yet, if you accept your punishment, then you, even you, shall sing of pardon bought with blood.

'Then', when you are proud, he will smite you; 'then', when he has smitten you, you are to accept your punishment; 'then', when you have accepted your punishment, and confessed your sin, the Lord will remember his covenant, and forgive all your iniquity. Observe well the three steps: chastisement when you are wrapped up in your iniquities; genuine submission when you feel the chastisement; and full covenant blessing when your submission is fully made. If any of us are now smarting, may we hasten there and then to full confession, and may we then receive restoration and comfort! God is very punctual; may he never find us procrastinating!

God grant that we may be kept from sin, or if we fall into it, may he deliver us from its power; and if one of these then happens to us, may the others follow in merciful succession! Amen.

13

An Address for Sad Times

[W]hen my heart is overwhelmed: lead me to the rock that is higher than I (Ps. 61:2).

David's prayer is a very wise and appropriate one. He is in great sorrow, and asks that he may be enabled to rise above it; he has great faith, and therefore is sure that there is a safe refuge for him; and he is conscious of great weakness, for he does not speak of climbing the rock of safety by himself, but implores divine leading that he may come to it. His prayer will well befit the lips of men like ourselves who dwell where troubles rage and toss their waves on high.

By many forces the heart may be overwhelmed. A sense of guilt may do it. Carelessness and indifference are swept away when the Holy Ghost works conviction of sin upon the conscience, reveals the justice of God and leads a man to see that he is in danger of the wrath to come: then heart and flesh fail, courage and hope depart, and the man is overwhelmed. Such a season is the fittest time for crying, 'lead me to the rock that is higher than I.' If you can but find shelter in the rifts of the Rock of ages, what security will be yours! The rock of atoning sacrifice rises higher than your sin, and upon it the most guilty may stand far above the surging billows of vengeance. Led by the divine hand to cling to the great Redeemer and Substitute, the utterly shipwrecked soul is safely landed, and may sing because of his escape.

Sometimes, however, believers in Jesus, though quite secure from divine wrath, are, nevertheless, overwhelmed with trouble. They should not be so; for, if their faith acted as it ought, no fear would fasten upon them; but through the infirmity of the flesh, and, partly, also through inbred sin, unbelief comes in like a flood, and drenches and deluges the anxious heart. At times also, the trials of life roll onward like enormous Atlantic billows, and toss our poor bark till we reel to and fro, and stagger like a drunken man. The ship becomes waterlogged, and does not answer to the helm of reason; she drifts with the adverse current whithersoever it pleases to hurry her, and eternal shipwreck seems near at hand. It is good for a Christian then to cry, 'lead me to the rock that is higher than I'; for, though a rock is to be avoided in a natural storm, yet in our spiritual tempests there is a high rock which is to be sought unto as our shelter and haven. Truly, that rock is higher than we are, and its very height is our comfort. God, the infinitely high and glorious, is not troubled nor dismayed. His purposes are far above and out of our sight, and they are also far beyond the operation of evil; hence, by confidence in God, we leave the storm beneath us, and smile at the hurly-burly down below.

To me, my brethren, the most overwhelming thoughts do not come to my heart from my own personal sin, for I know it is forgiven, not from worldly trouble, for I am persuaded that all things work for my good; but I am deeply distressed by the present condition of the church of God. Men, who are called of God to care for his flock, are grievously bowed down when the signs of the times are dark and lowering. Moses carried the whole people of Israel in his bosom in the wilderness, and they were sometimes a heavy load to him; and thus each true minister bears the church upon his heart, and is often sorely burdened. At this moment, I can sorrowfully cry, with Jeremiah, 'my bowels, my bowels! I am pained at my very heart. I cannot hold my peace.'

It is overwhelming to my spirit to see the growing worldliness of the visible church. Many professed Christians – the Lord alone knows whether they are true believers or no – give us grave cause for apprehension. We see them tolerating practices which would not have been endured by their fathers; my blood chills when I think of how far some fashionable professors go astray. There are families in connection with our churches in which there is no household prayer, but much luxurious eating, and drinking, and extravagance. I have my suspicions that there are, among professors, a considerable number who attend the theatre, spend their evenings in card-playing, read the most frivolous and foolish of books, and yet come to the Lord's table. If they differ from the world, it is hard to see how or where. Neither in their dress, nor in their speech, nor in their mode of trading, nor in their habits at home, are they at all superior to the unconverted. Is not this an evil under the sun? When the church descends to the world's level, her power is gone. Yet we cannot root up these suspected tares; we are even forbidden to do so, lest we root up the wheat with them. If false professors were more open in their conduct, we should know them; but their evil is secret, and therefore we are obliged to let them grow together with the wheat; yet, sometimes, the sorrowful husbandman goes to the great Owner of the farm, and cries, 'Didst thou not sow good seed in thy ground? From whence, then, hath it tares?' The answer is that 'an enemy hath done this', and we are overwhelmed in spirit because we fear that our sleeping gave the enemy the opportunity.

I look again, and see numbers of professors apostatising altogether. In this great London, many persons, who were members of churches in the country, fall into the habits of their neighbours, and absent themselves altogether from the means of grace; or treat the worship of God on the Lord's day as if it were optional; and when they attend to it, they go tripping from one place of worship to another, and forget the duties of Christian fellowship. Many others are content to hear noted preachers; not because they preach the gospel, but because they are reputed to be 'clever men'. Once, ministers were esteemed for soundness, unction and experience; but, now, men crave after popularity and cleverness.

Some, who call themselves Christians, make fine music their grand requisite. If they need that gratification, why do they not content themselves with a weekday concert in the proper place for such displays? God's house was never meant to be made into a hall where tweedle-dee and tweedle-dum may vie with each other in pleasing man's ears. Not a few choose their Sunday resort because the 'church' is an imposing structure, and the congregation is composed of 'very respectable people'. If they seek society, let them go where the elite may fitly gather, and keep themselves select; but, in the worship of God, 'the rich and poor meet together, and the Lord is the Maker of them all'. It is an ill sign when God's poor saints are despised; but so it is in this day. If tradesmen save a little money, they grow too great for the assembly in which they were once at home, and must needs make part of a more fashionable congregation. These things also cause my spirit to be overwhelmed: not because, in one single instance, it has happened to members of my own church, but because the fact is open to the view of all, and is the subject of general remark.

Equally grievous to the heart is it to see the spread of superstition. You can hardly go down a street but you will pass some Popish joss house, called an Episcopal church, where self-styled 'priests' entice silly women to the confessional, and amuse them with masses and processions. Vile impostors! Clergy of an avowedly Protestant church, and supported by this nation, they are yet ravenous to eat out the very vitals of Protestantism. Fools enough are found to believe in these priests, and bow before their crucifixes, and their stations of the cross, and the like rubbish, and the abomination evidently spreads like the leaven among the meal as described by our blessed Lord. Heaven alone knows where this England of ours is going, and he who loves his country feels his spirit overwhelmed within him.

Nor do I think this to be the worst sign of the times. All around us there is growing up in tangled masses the ill weed of 'modern thought', which is nothing better than an infidelity too cowardly to wear its proper name. There are preachers, in Christian pulpits, who deny the authenticity of various books of the Bible, and reject plenary inspiration altogether. There is not a doctrine of the gospel which is not denied by some 'thinker' or other, and even the existence of a personal God is by the more advanced regarded as a moot point; yet the churches bear with them, and allow them to pollute the pulpits once occupied by godly preachers of Christ. After having denied the faith, and plunged their daggers into the heart of vital doctrines as best they can, they still claim to be ministers of the gospel, and ask to be received into union on the ground of some peculiar inward virtue which exists in them apart from all doctrinal belief. Men, who might justly be prosecuted for obtaining property under false pretences by violating the trust deeds of our churches, may well wish to abolish creeds and articles of faith, because these are perpetual witnesses against their knavery. I would not care what became of the pelf if the churches were saved from error. I see this leaven of unbelief working in all directions, and many are tainted with it, in one point or another; it eateth like a cancer into the very soul of the churches. God deliver us from it!

It is hard to know what to do, for no one wishes to suspect his fellow, and yet a pest seems to be in the very air, so that it penetrates into the best-guarded chambers. We hear of this man and then of another broaching strange notions, and those who were thought to be pillars suddenly become rolling stones. Who will go next? And what will happen next? In the midst of this confusion, our heart is apt to be overwhelmed within us. Is there not a cause? It is not our household, it is not our estate, it is not our bodily health which is in danger, or we would bow in silence, and bear it; but it is the household of God, it is the estate and Kingdom of Christ, it is the church of God on earth which is thus suffering; and well may those, who love the Lord, and his Christ, and his truth, tremble for the ark, and feel a holy jealousy burning within them. At such a time, the prayer of David is priceless, 'lead me to the rock that is higher than I.' Let us see how this petition meets the case.

First, let us remember that God lives. Glorious thought! 'The Lord sitteth upon the flood; yea, the Lord sitteth King for ever.' 'The Lord reigneth; let the earth rejoice.' Still he effects his purposes and accomplishes his will. It would be very childish if we were afraid for the moon because dogs bay her when she walks in her splendour, it would be very absurd to fear for the eternal mountains because the winds blow upon their granite peaks, and it would be equally idle to tremble for the truth of God. The stable things will stand, and those which cannot stand are better gone. God liveth, and everything that is of God liveth in his life. On this rock let us rest.

> Error must die, and they who love her most,
> And suck the poison from her venomed lips,
> Will find her vaunted strength an empty boast,
> And share the horrors of her last eclipse.
> But truth is strong, and worthy of our trust,
> And truth shall stand when time no more shall be,
> And man is levelled to his native dust
> For God is truth to all eternity.

Next, let us remember that God's truth is still the same. It does not matter whether fifty thousand espouse its cause, or only five, or only one. Truth does not reign by the ballot box, or by the counting of heads: it abideth for ever. All the tongues of men and angels cannot make truth more true; and all the howlings of dev-ils and doubters cannot transform it into a lie. Glory be to God for this! Jesus Christ is the same yesterday, today and forever. The eternal verity holds its deniers in derision, for they are as the chaff which the wind driveth away. 'Where is the wise? Where is the scribe? Where is the disputer of this world? Hath not God made foolish the wisdom of this world?'

Another rock may also afford us shelter, namely, the high doctrine that the Lord will save his own. The much-despised truth of election stands us in good stead in troublous times. We sigh, and cry, because so many worship the deity of the hour; but the Lord answereth, 'Yet have I reserved unto myself seven thousand men who have not bowed the knee to Baal. Even so then at this present time also there is a remnant according to the election of grace.' The words of the apostle are true at this moment, 'The election hath obtained it, and the rest were blinded, according as it is written, God hath given them the spirit of slumber, eyes that they should not see, and ears that they should not hear, unto this day.' I bow before the awful sovereignty of God, and the clamour of the people comes not into mine ears. Jehovah's purpose shall stand, and he will do all his pleasure. No drop of the redeeming blood shall be spent in vain, no line of the everlasting covenant shall be erased, no decree of the Eternal shall be disannulled. This angers the adversary, but in its divine truth we find our consolation while the heathen rage, and the people imagine a vain thing.

A rock that is higher than I may be useful, not only for shel-ter, but for elevation. If you stand upon high ground, though you may be a dwarf, you can see farther than the tallest man who remains below; and now, standing upon the high rock of God's Word, what do we see? Look! Clear your eyes of doubt and mist, and look! Forget the present for awhile, and gaze through the telescope of faith. What do we see? Systems of error broken in pieces, superstitions given to the moles and to the bats, the clouds vanishing, the darkness of night disappearing, and the beasts going back to their dens, for the Sun of righteousness arises with healing beneath his wings. The day of the triumph of the truth must dawn.

If it shall not come before the advent of our Lord, it shall come then to the confusion of his adversaries, and to the delight of his saints, and there shall be 'new heavens and a new earth wherein dwelleth righteousness'. If this old earth will still reject the truth, and the old heavens still look down on a reign of error, they shall be utterly consumed with fire; and on this very earth, on which we stand, renewed and purified, there shall be placed a throne as glorious and terrible as the cross of Christ was ignominious and shameful. The blood of Jesus has fallen on this world, and guaranteed its redemption from the curse; and, one day, when he has delivered the subject creation, our Lord will dwell here, and reign amongst his ancients gloriously.

We can afford to wait, for eternity is on our side. We can afford to see the ranks of the Lord's army pushed back for awhile; we can afford to see the standard fluttered by the rough winds; we can afford to hear the 'Aha! Aha!' of the Philistines; for when the Prince cometh, they shall know his name, and the power of his might. If they will not yield to him now, and kiss his sceptre silvered with love, they shall bow before him when they see the naked iron of his rod breaking them in pieces like potters' vessels. Oh, to be on God's side! The whole root of the matter lies there. If a man knows that his heart and soul are given to the cause of God and truth, he is entrenched within an impregnable fortress, and he shall find in the eternal verities munitions of stupendous rock. He shall be steadfast 'though the earth be removed, and though the mountains be carried into the midst of the sea; though the waters thereof roar and be troubled, though the mountains shake with the swelling thereof'.

What, then, are we to do? We are to give all diligence to make our calling and election sure. See to that, for, though some denounce such holy care as selfishness, our Lord and Master knows best, and he charged his servants not so much to rejoice in their power over devils as in the fact that their names were written in heaven. Watch over your own spirit, and cast not away your confidence.

Then, zealously, in dependence upon God, do the little you can do; do it well, and keep on doing it. You and I are not called upon to regulate the world nor to stay the raging sea of human sin. Let us not attempt to wield the divine sceptre; it befits us not. Naturally, you would like to set all people right, and make all preachers orthodox. But, my brother, the task is beyond you. Be careful to be right yourself in your own life, and be resolute to bear your complete, honest, obedient testimony to all the truth you know; and there leave the business, for you are not responsible beyond your possibilities.

No one of us is much more than an emmet on its little hill. Now, if yon tiny ant were to indulge in serious reflections upon the state of London, and forget to assist in the labours of the insect commonwealth, it would be a foolish creature; but if it will let those great matters alone, and go on doing its antwork, as an ant, it will fill its little sphere, and answer the purpose of its Maker. A mother teaching her little ones, and doing all she can to bring them up in the fear of God; a humble village pastor with his score or two of people around him; a teacher with her dozen children; a quiet Christian woman in her domestic circle bearing her godly testimony; a young man speaking for Jesus to other young men – there is nothing very ambitious about the sphere of any one of these, but they are wise in the sight of the Lord. Leave the reins of the universe in the hand of the Maker of the universe, and then do what he has given you to do, in his fear, and by his Spirit, and more will come of it than you dare to hope.

We are like coral insects building each one his minute portion of a structure far down in the deeps of obscurity. We cannot as yet war with those vaunted ironclads which sweep the ocean, and hurl destruction upon cities; and yet – who knows? we may build and build until we pile up a reef upon which the proudest navies may be wrecked. By the steady, simple, honest, Christian upbuilding of holiness and truth – defying no one, attacking no one – we may nevertheless create a situation which will be eminently perilous to the boastful craft of falsehood and scepticism. A holy, earnest, gospel church is a grand wrecker of superstition and of infidelity. The life of God in man, patience in suffering, perseverance in well-doing, faithfulness to truth, prayer in the Holy Ghost, supreme zeal for the divine glory and unstaggering faith in the unseen God, these are our battle-axe and weapons of war; and, by the aid of the Holy Ghost, we shall win the battle ere the day comes to its close. Till then, O Lord, when our heart is overwhelmed, lead us to the rock which is higher than we are!

14

'Honey out of the Rock'

He should have fed them also with the finest of the wheat:
and with honey out of the rock should I have satisfied thee
(Ps. 81:16).

If you have not read what Thomas Wilcocks wrote, on *A Choice Drop of Honey from the Rock Christ*, I recommend you to get it, and read it prayerfully, and it will do you good. Let me give you a taste, to set you longing for more. Our old author well says: 'A Christian never lacks comfort but by breaking the order and method of the gospel, looking on his own attainments, and looking off Christ's perfect righteousness, which is, to choose rather to live by candlelight than by the light of the sun. The honey that you suck from your own righteousness will turn into perfect gall; and the light that you take from that to walk in, will turn into black night upon the soul. Satan is tempting thee to plod about thy own grace, to get comfort from that; then the Father comes, and points thee to Christ's grace, as rich, glorious, infinitely pleasing to him, and biddeth thee study Christ's righteousness; and his biddings are enablings; that is a blessed motion, a sweet whispering, checking thy unbelief. Follow the least hint closely with much prayer; prize it as an invaluable jewel, it is an earnest of more to come.'

So, dear friend, keep thine eye steadily fixed upon the Lord Jesus Christ, and thou shalt be 'fed with the finest of the wheat'. As thou lookest unto Jesus only, thou shalt be satisfied 'with honey out of the rock'. The sweetness of true religion is found in the Rock Christ Jesus: not in thy mere performance of certain duties, or in thine own poor promises of amendment. The sweetness is in the Rock, the Rock of ages cleft for thee.

Some of the 'honey out of the rock' is a sweet sense of our security in Christ. The believer can confidently exclaim, 'Let what will happen to me, I know that I am secure in Jesus. He is my Rock. Let me bury my only friend, let me see the last stick of my earthly possessions burned, yet I have a living, loving Saviour; I have an inheritance in reversion, a crown laid up in heaven, a kingdom entailed, which cannot be taken away from me.'

> I have a heritage of joy
> That yet I must not see :
> The hand that bled to make it mine,
> Is keeping it for me.
>
> And a 'new song' is in my mouth,
> To long-loved music set;
> Glory to thee for all the grace
> I have not tasted yet.

'I know whom I have believed, and am persuaded that he is able to keep that which I have committed unto him against that day.' 'I know that my Redeemer liveth, and that he shall stand at the latter day upon the earth: and though after my skin worms destroy this body, yet in my flesh shall I see God: whom I shall see for myself, and mine eyes shall behold, and not another; though my reins be consumed within me.' I shall one day be like Jesus for I shall see him as he is; and even now I know that I am a son of God. It is a sweet drop of 'honey out of the rock' to have a personal sense of our own individual security in Christ Jesus the Lord.

Another drop of 'honey out of the rock' is to know my perfection in Christ. The child of God, though vile and black in himself, can look to Jesus, and see himself arrayed in the spotless robe of his Saviour's righteousness, and then he can exclaim, 'In his righteousness I am perfect, I am complete in him.' Truly does Kent sing:

> In thy Surety thou art free,
> his dear hands were pierced for thee;
> With his spotless vesture on,
> Holy as the Holy One.

Saints dejected, cease to mourn,
Faith shall soon to vision turn;
Ye the Kingdom shall obtain
And with Christ exalted reign:

Ah, beloved, we only need to get the taste of unbelief out of our mouths, to enable us to enjoy the sweetness of these precious truths!

Once again, the saint's acceptance in Jesus is a sweet drop of 'honey out of the rock'. To know myself 'accepted in the Beloved' is one of the choicest things that I can learn this side of heaven. Yet another drop of 'honey out of the rock' is the fullness which the believer has from Jesus: 'And of his fullness have all we received, and grace for grace.' You cannot know the luscious sweetness of this drop of 'honey out of the rock' until you have learned that, in yourself, you are a poor sinner and nothing at all, and have taken Jesus Christ as your All-in-all.

'Oh!' says one, 'I do not have much honey out of the Rock; I wish I could taste of this sweetness.' You may do so, you shall do so, if you will only live near the Rock Christ Jesus. We must not expect the honey to come leaping out of the Rock ever so far, because we are living at a distance from the Rock. If you want 'honey out of the rock', you must live close to the Rock. If you are satisfied with the mere outside of religion, you must be content without much honey. The sweetness of religion is in the marrow; and you cannot get at that if you dwell on the outside. If you do not get 'honey out of the rock', it may be because you do not live high enough. You must have higher and more exalted thoughts concerning Jesus. Low thoughts of Christ Jesus yield us no honey; but high thoughts of Jesus bring the honey down to us. Love Jesus, admire Jesus, extol Jesus and you will find him to be a precious Saviour.

Child of God, if you want 'honey out of the rock', view Jesus in the garden, sweating 'as it were great drops of blood falling down to the ground' (Luke 22:44). He is sweating drops of honey for you. View his thorn-crowned head, and you will see every thorn sparkling and opening a fissure to let out the honey for you. Think much of Jesus, live close to him: then will you get 'honey out of the rock'. Do not have the devil's christ; he is a dwarf. THE CHRISTIAN'S CHRIST plants his foot where man lives, but his head is in the land where angels dwell. The devil would make you imagine that Christ is a weak, powerless being; do not believe any of his lies. Think highly of Christ, think lofty thoughts of Jesus. I defy you to think too much of him. You may soar upward with an eagle's wing, but you will not reach those locks that are 'bushy, and black as a raven' (Song 5 :11). You may expand your faith as far as you please, but you shall never know the full extent of his grace. With the spouse you may say, 'My Beloved is white and ruddy, the chiefest among ten thousand ... His mouth is most sweet: yea, he is altogether lovely.'

How did the honey get out of the rock? The rock of ages was cleft for me. Ah, beloved, neither you nor I would ever have had 'honey out of the rock' if Jesus had not died! The Rock of ages was riven for sinners! It was when Christ's side was pierced that the honey flowed from his heart. The wounds of Jesus stream forth with precious sweets for his beloved ones. Again I say, live near to Jesus, and with 'honey out of the rock' he will satisfy you.

> Thou shalt taste the stream that flows
> From thine eternal Rock.

15

The Prevalence of Evil an Argument in Prayer

*It is time for thee, Lord, to work: for they have
made void thy law* (Ps. 119:126).

There are many ways of pleading for the same thing when we draw near to God in prayer. In one condition of heart, one form of argument will rise to the lip; while, at another season, our circumstances may suggest quite a different way of pleading with God. I was noticing, while reading in the one hundred and nineteenth Psalm, the plea which the psalmist urges with the Most High while entreating him graciously to work among men. He says, 'IT IS TIME FOR THEE, LORD, TO WORK: FOR THEY HAVE MADE VOID THY LAW' (emphasis added). We might urge, as reasons for the Lord's working, the sorrows of mankind, the terrors of the world to come, the glory of God and the merits of the Saviour. We might plead the promises, the covenant, the prophecies and the long weary time of waiting before they are fulfilled; but it is a bright use of a gloomy fact when we can turn even the infidelity, the superstition and the rebellion of man into an argument for the Lord's interference: 'It is time for thee, Lord, to work: for they have made void thy law.' Thus we set our sail so as to use an adverse wind. We extract a reason for grace out of the reeking of iniquity.

We observe that many men now deny the inspiration of the Scriptures, and that is making void the law of the Lord. Of what use is the Bible to us if it be not infallibly inspired of the Holy Spirit? An erring guide is as bad as none at all when a step may lead to ruin. If we have not the very mind of God in these pages, their essence, their authority, their life and their power are gone.

Yet certain ministers, ay, ministers of Nonconformist churches, speak of the Bible as though it were in considerable portions of it blurred with mistakes, and by no means to be relied upon. They talk of 'essential parts of the Old Testament', as if other parts might be laid aside; and some of them set up the Gospels above the Epistles, as if the one Spirit had not dictated all the Word. It is grievous to hear divines undermining the foundations of the faith which they are supposed to preach. 'O Lord, we turn from these thine unfaithful servants to thyself, and cry, "Do thou prove the truth of the Scriptures, fulfil the promises, and put power into the teaching of the cross, so that men may be compelled to own that thy law is not void, but that the Scripture cannot be broken."'

Thirty years ago or more, John Angell James said, 'Infidelity was never more subtle, more hurtful, more plausible, perhaps more successful, than in the day in which we live. It has left the low grounds of vulgarity, and coarseness, and ribaldry, and entrenched itself upon the lofty heights of criticism, philology, and even science itself. It pervades to a fearful extent our popular literature; it has invested itself with the charms of poetry, to throw its spell over the public mind; it has endeavoured to enweave itself with science; and he must be little acquainted with the state of opinion in this land, who does not know that it is espoused by a large portion of the cultivated mind of this generation. "It is time for thee, LORD, to work". The statement is even more true at this hour, for still 'not many wise men after the flesh, not many mighty, not many noble, are called'. Let our prayers increase in fervour as we implore that 'philosophy, falsely so-called', may not be allowed to poison the springs of gospel teaching.

Certain bold spirits make void the law of God, in a very dreadful way, by teaching a code of morals and a system of ethics contrary to the Word of God. Laws as to property are freely assailed, as if the Lord had never said, 'Thou shalt not covet.' Killing is thought to be no murder if it is performed upon an enormous scale. The sacred chastities which give stability to family institutions are abused, and an attempt is made to exalt lust into the place which is due only to conjugal affection; indeed, there are filthy pens which dare to write of the marriage bond as if it were a chain and a curse. Lewd tongues attack all laws by which the social fabric is held together; the Sabbath is ridiculed, and the honouring of parents is considered out of date. Images are set up in places of worship, and material objects are publicly adored, as if this had not been most positively forbidden by the Lord of all. If it were not that the Lord of hosts has left unto us a small remnant, we should long ere this have been as Sodom, and been made like unto Gomorrah. Politically, we should before now have shot over our national Niagara into anarchy and abomination; and we should have seen in London all the horrors of the French Revolution if it had not been for the godly who leaven the mass.

How dreadful it must have been to have lived in Paris when all the foundations of society were loosed; when religion was debased into the worship of the goddess of reason; when virtue was regarded as vice, and vice as virtue! Ere it comes to that dreadful pass, be it ours to cry out unto the Lord, 'It is time for thee to work'. Surely it is now needful for the Lord to vindicate his holy law when loudmouthed blasphemers criticise the Saviour, censure their God and propose to overturn from its base the pillar of society. They not only make their own lives void of morality, but they labour to make void the 'law itself, that no one may regard it. As Caryl says, they act 'as if they would not only sin against the law, but sin away the law; not only withdraw themselves from the obedience of it, but drive it out of the world; they would make void and repeal the holy acts of God, that their own wicked acts might not be questioned; and lest the law should have a power to punish them, they will deny it a power to rule them'.

Men of another order are active and earnest in attacking the law of God, from another side, by multiplying rites, and exalting ceremonies into a place which they should never usurp. Of these, I may say for the most part, 'Father, forgive them, for they know not what they do.' 'They have a zeal of God, but not according to knowledge.' They make void the law of God through their traditions. Being in all things too superstitious, they destroy the worship of God by their will-worship. To support their own invented rites and ceremonies, they give us interpretations which becloud the gospel, and afford cover for priestcraft, monkery, Mariolatry and image worship. Sometimes, these persons are called Papists, at other times, Ritualists; and, in many cases, it is extremely difficult to see the slightest distinction between them; they are two apples from the same tree.

Remember that to worship God otherwise than he has ordained is a sin which makes void his law. We are not really serving God at all if we presume to do it in our way rather than in his way. To present to God 'the unbloody sacrifice of the mass', is to dishonour the one sacrifice of our Lord Jesus. To worship Mary is to offend Jehovah. To bow before a crucifix is to commit idolatry under pretence of reverence. Superstition is as real an adversary to the truth as scepticism itself, and it ultimately leads to irreligion. Idolatry conducts men to atheism, and superstition lands them in infidelity. Now that we see Anglican Popery covering our land with its altars, we may well cry, 'It is time for thee, Lord, to work: for they have made void thy law.' Plead with God, whenever you meet with either Rationalism or Ritualism, that he would graciously stretch out his hand, and get to his pure Word the victory.

I find that, upon the passage before us, I have written in my 'Treasury of David' as follows: 'It is time for thee, Lord, to work: for they have made void thy law.' David was a servant, and therefore it was always his time to work; but being oppressed by a sight of man's ungodly behaviour, he feels that his Master's hand is wanted, and therefore he appeals to him to work against the working of evil. Men make void the law of God by denying it to be his law, by promulgating commands and doctrines in opposition to it, by setting up tradition in its place, or by utterly disregarding and scorning the authority of the Lawgiver. When sin becomes fashionable, a holy walk is regarded as a contemptible Puritanism; vice is styled pleasure, and vanity bears the bell. Then the saints sigh for the presence and power of their God. Oh, for an hour of the King upon his throne, wielding the rod of iron! Oh, for another Pentecost, with all its wonders, to reveal the energy of God to gainsayers, and make them see that there is a God in Israel! Man's extremity, whether of need or of sin, is God's opportunity. When the earth was without form and void, the Spirit came, and moved upon the face of the waters: should he not come when society is returning to a like chaos? When Israel in Egypt was reduced to the lowest point, and it seemed that the covenant would be void, then Moses appeared, and wrought mighty miracles; so, too, when the church of God is trampled down, and her message is derided, we may expect to see the hand of the Lord stretched out for the revival of religion, the defence of the truth and the glorifying of the divine name. The Lord can work either by judgements, which hurl down the ramparts of the foe, or by revivals, which build up the walls of his own Jerusalem. How heartily may we pray the Lord to raise up new evangelists, to quicken those we already have, to set his whole church on fire and to bring the world to his feet.

Thus, dear friends, you see how the prominence of evil can be made to quicken us in supplication. Every sin may be used as a plea in prayer. If we were in a right state of mind, every time we heard a man swear in the street we should at once pray, 'It is time for thee, LORD, to work: for they have made void thy law.' Every time we took up a newspaper, and our eye glanced upon a police case, we should pray in like manner. Every time we saw sin in our neighbours, or in our families, or felt its working in ourselves, we should cry out to God, 'Lord, sin is at work, be thou also at work! Sin is hardening, sin is defiling; come, Lord, and work with all the softening and quickening processes of thy blessed Spirit, with all the purifying power of the water and of the blood, and so undo the evil working of the world, the flesh, and the devil! O Lord, meet energy with energy, meet fire with fire; and let thy Son, the seed of the woman, meet the seed of the serpent, and destroy all the works of the devil!'

Thus, you see that good arguments for prayer may be raked up among the stubble of sin. As the Greenlanders find their wood washed up by the sea, so let us find fuel for the fire of our earnestness borne to us by the troubled sea of human wickedness. Brethren, let us wrestle in prayer, using this plea. Before we do so, let us distil a song from it, and sing a part of one of Isaac Watts' hymns (Hymn 1146: 5-7):

> Lord, when iniquities abound,
> And blasphemy grows bold,
> When faith is hardly to be found,
> And love is waxing cold;
> 'Is not thy chariot hastening on?
> Hast thou not given this sign?
> May we not trust and live upon
> A promise so divine?
> "Yes," saith the Lord, "now will I rise,
> And make oppressors flee;
> I shall appear to their surprise.
> And set my servants free."'

16

The Three 'Thens' of Isaiah's Temple Vision

In the year that king Uzziah died I saw also the Lord sitting upon a throne, high and lifted up, and his train filled the temple. Above it stood the seraphims: each one had six wings; with twain he covered his face, and with twain he covered his feet, and with twain he did fly. And one cried unto another, and said, Holy, holy, holy, is the LORD of hosts: the whole earth is full of his glory. And the posts of the door moved at the voice of him that cried, and the house was filled with smoke. THEN said I, Woe is me! for I am undone; because I am a man of unclean lips, and I dwell in the midst of a people of unclean lips: for mine eyes have seen the King, the LORD of hosts. THEN flew one of the seraphims unto me, having a live coal in his hand, which he had taken with the tongs from off the altar: And he laid it upon my mouth, and said, Lo, this hath touched thy lips; and thine iniquity is taken away, and thy sin purged. Also I heard the voice of the Lord, saying, Whom shall I send, and who will go for us? THEN said I, Here am I; send me (Isa. 6: 1-8, emphasis added).

In this passage, we have the record of a vision granted to the favoured prophet Isaiah; a vision of so grand a character, and exercising so great an influence over its beholder, that he records the exact date of it – 'In the year that king Uzziah died'. Such transcendently glorious manifestations come not every day, and therefore it is well to note their occurrence with a red letter. Perhaps the date was better fixed on his memory by a thought of contrast: Judah's king was dead, and then the prophet saw the living King sitting upon his throne. That dead king had intruded into the temple; but the eternal King reigns there, and fills the holy place with his train.

Our one point just now is to mark the three 'THENS'. The prophet commences his narrative by a note of time, and he makes his time-bell ring again, and again, and again: striking then, then, THEN.

The first 'THEN' occurs thus: the prophet was led to feel his own uncleanness, and the uncleanness of those among whom he dwelt. When was that? For it is important for us to feel the same conviction, and we may do so by the same means. Was it when he had been looking into his own heart, and seeing its dire deceitfulness, and the black streams of actual transgression which welled up from that inward fountain of depravity? He might certainly have said, 'Woe is me!' if he had been looking there; but he was not doing so on this occasion.

Had he been considering the law of God, had he observed how exceeding broad it is, how it touches the thoughts and intents of the heart, and condemns us because we do not meet its demands of perfect 'obedience? Assuredly, if he had been looking into that pure and holy law, he might well have bewailed his guilt, for by the law is the knowledge of sin.

Or had he been turning over the pages of memory, and noting his own shortcomings, and the sins of his fellows? Had he noted his own failures in prayer, or in service, or in patience? Had he watched himself in private and in public, and did the record of the past bring a consciousness of sin upon him? If so, he might well enough have lamented before the Lord, and cried, 'Woe is me! for I am undone'. I might even say, had he been carrying out self-examination for a single day of his life, and had that day been the Sabbath, and had he been acting as the preacher, or had he been sitting under the most stirring ministry, and had he been at the holy feasts of the Lord, he might have found reason for confession. I will not judge all of my brethren, but I will make this confession for myself, that if I examine the best day I have ever spent, and the holiest hour I have ever lived, I can see, even with my poor, weak eyes, enough of sin in my holiest things to make me cry, 'Woe is me! for I am undone'. The best sermon I have ever preached is a sure proof to me that my lips are unclean; for, when I come to examine it with care, I discover in it a thousand defects.

But none of these things are mentioned here as the occasion for Isaiah's humbling cry. When was it then that he had such an overpowering sense of his own unworthiness, and of the sinfulness of the people among whom he dwelt? It was 'THEN' when he had seen the Lord. He had been permitted, in vision, to gaze upon the great King upon his throne; he had seen him in his infinite sovereignty; he had beheld his glory filling the temple, till the house was filled with smoke to veil the matchless splendour; he had heard, in vision, those sinless beings, the seraphim, using their lips to cry in ecstasy, 'Holy, holy, holy, is the LORD of hosts'; and he had carefully observed that, when they drew near to the awful majesty, each one of them used his wings as a fourfold veil with which to hide himself: 'with twain he covered his face, and with twain he covered his feet'. Even they did not dare to look upon God's glory, or to stand before him without a covering. What with their cry of 'Holy, holy, holy, is the LORD of hosts: the whole earth is full of his glory', and their lowly posture while adoring, the prophet was humbled by their reverence, and wondered how or in what language he should ever speak with God. John, in his Gospel, tells us that Isaiah saw the glory of God in the person of the Lord Jesus. The posts of the door moved and trembled at the presence of the Lord of the whole earth, under the stress of those adoring cries which rose from an innumerable company of angels, of whom the seraphim may be regarded as representatives. It was the sight of the thrice-holy God which made the prophet say, 'Woe is me! for I am undone; because I am a man of unclean lips'.

O my dear brethren and sisters, if you have never seen God, if you have never had a faith's view of him, you have not really seen yourselves! You will never know how black you are till you have seen how bright he is; and inasmuch as you will never know all his brightness, so you will never know all your own blackness. Learn, however, this lesson, that for you to turn your face away from God in order to repent of sin is a great mistake; it is a sight of God in Christ Jesus which will breed humiliation and lowly confession of sin. Dream not that you are to stay away from Christ till you sufficiently lament your sin; it is a grave error and a grievous folly, for nothing makes sin to appear so exceeding sinful as a view of the glory of God in Christ Jesus. No, your face must be towards your Father's house, and you must hopefully resolve to arise and go to your Father, or you will never cry, 'Father, I have sinned against heaven, and in thy sight.' Yes, and I will venture to say that the nearer the prodigal came to his father, the more he repented; and when his face was hidden in his father's bosom, and kiss after kiss saluted him, then his repentance was deepest of all. O poor hearts, if you cannot come to Christ with repentance, come to him for repentance! If you want to feel, 'Woe is me!' come and see the glory of Jesus, and the holiness of the great God; and then will your knee bow, and your heart tremble. There is no road to repentance so short and sure as to remember your God, and enter spiritually into his presence. 'I saw the Lord sitting upon a throne, high and lifted up ..... THEN said I, Woe is me!'

Now, is there any man here who says, 'I have had intimate communion with God'? Brother, we will listen to your speech, and judge of your pretensions. Did I hear you say, 'I am a man who lives very near to God. I walk in the light as God is in the light, and enjoy a higher life than other Christians'? Brother, your speech is as sounding brass and as a tinkling cymbal, for no man, who has come fresh from God, ever speaks in tones of self-congratulation. What said Job? 'Behold I am vile; what shall I answer thee? I have heard of thee by the hearing of the ear: but now mine eye seeth thee. Wherefore I abhor myself, and repent in dust and ashes' (Job 40:4; 42:5, 6). This was the experience of a perfect and an upright man, one that feared God, and eschewed evil; and if you have really entered into communion with the Lord, the same humble emotions will fill your breast. No man has seen the Lord, high and lifted up, if he exalts himself. When we are favoured to know the Lord, we are humbled then, and not till then.

You see the prophet trembling: in himself unclean, and conscious of it, and surrounded by a people as unclean as himself, and it is while he stands in that condition that we meet with our second 'THEN'. 'Then flew one of the seraphims unto me, having a live coal in his hand, which he had taken with the tongs from off the altar: And he laid it upon my mouth, and said, Lo, this hath touched thy lips; and thine iniquity is taken away, and thy sin purged.' 'Then', that is, not when this man was full of joy and rejoicing, but when he said, 'Woe is me!' – not when he was living in the sublimities of boastful self-consciousness, but when he was crying, 'I am undone'; 'Then flew one of the seraphims'. When he was consciously unfit, the Lord commissioned him; when he felt his uncleanness, when he owned the ruin of his nature, and the sad estate of his people, then it was that the seraphic messenger touched him with the living altar coal.

Brethren, do you so much feel your sinfulness that you are afraid that the Lord will never use you in the conversion of sinners? I am glad of it. Are you conscious that your lips are not worthy to speak for the holy God? Then I know you feel that, if ever God should save a soul by you, he must have all the glory of it. You feel that it is a wonder of grace that you are saved yourself, and if ever others are saved through your means, you confess that it will be a miracle of divine power. In all this I rejoice, for your hour of acceptable service has begun. I have noted, in my own experience, that whenever I have been most blessed in the winning of souls, it has generally been just after I have endured a thorough stripping in my own heart, or when by soul trouble I have been brayed as in a mortar among wheat with a pestle till I seemed ground into dust. Trial has preceded triumph. A wider field has been opened to me by the breaking down of my hedges. I have shrunk into self-oblivion, and then the Lord has moved me to speak in a burning manner to his glory.

I remember a foolish person coming to me once after I had been preaching, and he said to me, 'You said you were a sinner when you were preaching.' I replied, 'Yes, I did, and I meant it.' His answer was, 'What right had you to preach if you are a sinner?' 'Well,' I replied, 'my right to preach lies in the Lord's command, "Let him that heareth say, Come", but I think little of right, for I preach because I cannot help it, and I preach to sinners because I am a sinner myself, and feel a sympathy with them. If any man needs to be daily saved by Christ, I am that man, and therefore I delight to describe the salvation which is so dear to me. Sometimes, when I have been myself in bondage, I have preached in chains to men in chains, but made music with my fetters, by commending Christ when I could not have said a good word for myself.' Why, methinks that a man, who has taken medicine, and has recovered, is the very man to extol it to others; yea, and if he still feels that, in some measure, the disease is upon him though its deadly power is taken away, and if he feels that every day he must drink the healing draught, and wash in the healing bath, he is the very man continually to tell of the abiding power of that ever-precious heal-all which meets his case. Even when we walk in the light with God, still the precious blood of Jesus cleanses us from all sin, and still we declare from our own experience its gracious power.

My dear brethren and sisters, I want this to encourage you, if you feel unhappy in your work for the Lord. If you feel very much cast down, and are crying, 'Woe is me!' do not, therefore, cease from your service. If you did not get on last Sunday, when you tried to preach; if you blunder every day with those unclean lips of yours; if you have been unsuccessful in working among the people with whom you dwell; or if you have not succeeded with the children in your class, or with your own children at home, now is the time to seek the blessing, now is the time to pray for it in hope. 'Then flew one of the seraphims unto me, having a live coal in his hand, which he had taken with the tongs from off the altar'. The seraph does not come with live coals from off the altar to men of pure lips who never were undone, for such are exceedingly satisfied without altar coals; but when the chosen servant of the Lord is deeply conscious of his unworthiness, then shall the Lord inspire him from above. It is his delight to fill empty vessels, and to put his treasure into caskets which contain nothing of their own.

Very briefly, let us now speak of the third 'THEN'. 'Also I heard the voice of the Lord, saying, Whom shall I send, and who will go for us? Then said I, Here am I; send me.' Hear ye not, tonight, the voice which never ceases to cry in the church, 'Whom shall I send, and who will go for us?' Oh, that we may be ready to respond to it! Alas! We feel reluctant to answer, 'send me', because we feel that we are undone, and our lips are unclean; but, beloved, if while we are sitting here, the angel shall bring the live coal from off the altar – one of those coals wherewith our great Sacrifice was consumed – and touch each lip with it, and say, 'Lo, this hath touched thy lips; and thine iniquity is taken away, and thy sin purged', then we shall leap to our feet, and cry, 'Here am I; send me.' Knowing that we are now clean in the sight of God, through that altar which sanctifies all that it touches, we shall have all our fears removed, and then will grateful love burst out into the cry of full surrender and complete consecration, 'Here am I; send me.' Here is a man full of leprosy, and there is a healing bath. Jehovah Rophi cries, 'Who will go and publish the news of healing, sure and effectual?' He makes no answer because he is himself still full of disease; but the moment he has stepped in, and perceives that he is cleansed, he shouts, 'Eureka, I have found it', and begins at once to publish the joyful tidings. He longs for opportunities to tell his story. He rests not day nor night, but incessantly publishes the glad tidings of salvation.

> Then I will teach the world thy ways;
> Sinners shall learn thy sovereign grace;
> I'll lead them to my Saviour's blood,
> And they shall praise a pardoning God.

'Here am I; send me.' Who among you will say this in reference to missions abroad, or holy works at home? I expect to hear it come from those who love much because they have had much forgiven. The coal which purges will also fire your lip, and burn the bonds which restrain your tongue. 'The love of Christ constraineth us.' How can we be silent? The beam out of the roof and the timber from the wall would cry out against us if we did not witness for our Lord. Others may be able to be silent; as for us, we must cry out, 'Here am I; send me.' I could most heartily wish that more of you deeply felt your unworthiness till it filled you with an-guish, and that you felt anew the altar's purifying flame, for then would you be fired with fervour and enthusiasm, and a great work would be done for my Lord. Fresh from a sense of sin, you would pity careless sinners; newly blessed with a sense of sac-rificial cleansing, you would earnestly point men to the Saviour, and the fire which kindled your life would communicate itself to many other hearts.

These are the three 'thens': 'then', when I had seen God, I said, 'I am undone'; 'then', when I felt I was undone, the seraph brought the burning coal and touched my lip; and when that lip was touched and I was purged, 'then' I said, 'Here am I; send me.' May this be a word in season to many! Then will they be blessed, then will we rejoice together and then will God be glorified.

17

Pruning the Vines

*Every branch that beareth fruit, he purgeth [or, pruneth]
it, that it may bring forth more fruit* (John 15:2).

The prayer of one of our brethren, just now, made me think of
something upon which I will say a few words to you. I have
recently watched, more carefully than ever I did before, the
treatment of vines; and I have observed how true are the Saviour's
words: 'Every branch that beareth fruit, he purgeth [or, pruneth]
it, that it may bring forth more fruit.' All fruit-bearing trees, or
all that I am acquainted with, more or less need the knife to
cut away the superfluous shoots from the wood; but the vine is
probably selected by the Saviour, among other reasons, for this
fact, that it has to endure the pruning knife more than any other
tree. When I saw the vines, the gardeners had cut them back
dreadfully; there seemed to be nothing left but old, dried stems,
with a few knuckles, as it were, sticking up here and there, like
swans' necks, but to all appearance hard, and withered, and
dead.

As I looked at them, I thought they were just like myself,
I have been cut back terribly.* I hoped to have had many branches, from which there might have come large clusters of luscious
fruit for my blessed Master; but, instead of that, the knife has
been used upon me, and there has been the cutting away of
a shoot here, and a branch there, until I wondered what would
be left when the Vine-dresser had finished his pruning.

While a vine is being pruned, or after the pruning process
is over, there is a wonderful change in its appearance. You
would hardly know it to be the same as when it was covered

with leaves, and laden with fruit. On our journeys to Mentone, we pass through some of the principal vine-growing districts of France, and the view of the vines that we get in the winter is by no means charming.

As we look at them, we understand why the Saviour was likened to 'a root out of a dry ground', of whom many say, 'he hath no form nor comeliness ... no beauty that we should desire him'. I was told, when at Mentone, that the best vines were cut back the most. The vine-dressers pruned them until I thought they might as well root them up out of the ground, they seemed quite destroyed. But the men told me that they would not yield one-half such sweet and choice grapes if they were not thus cut. They said that there are coarser vines, which can grow upon trellis work, and climb over arches, but that the grapes they produce are very poor, compared with those that are brought forth upon the other vines. The scenery gains in beauty; but the fruit loses in sweetness and flavour. The best vines must be cut back most. I am sure this is a rule which applies both in nature and in grace. I do not say that it is a proof that we are the best Christians because we suffer most; but I do say that we ought to try to be the best branches of the true and living Vine if we have been the most cut back.

Notice the exact words of our Lord: 'Every branch that beareth fruit, he purgeth it, that it may bring forth more fruit.' This pruning must be personal: 'Every branch that beareth fruit, he purgeth it'. The pruning of any other branch will not avail; the knife must be used upon this particular branch. This pruning process must be applied to you, my brother, and you, my sister, who are in Christ, and who are bringing forth fruit because of your union to him. It is not sufficient to be a member of a fruitful church, or class, or family; each one must be fruitful if we are to accomplish the end for which we were elected by our Lord. He said, 'I have chosen you, and ordained you, that ye should go and bring forth fruit, and that your fruit should remain.'

And note, that it is the fruit-bearing branch that is to be pruned. Fruitless branches are cut off; but those that bear any fruit are cut, that they may bring forth 'more fruit' (v. 2), and 'much fruit' (vv. 5 and 8). The heavenly Husbandman takes away the fruitless branches, and he takes away from the fruit-bearing branches everything that would hinder them from being full of fruit. The clinging tendrils of self-conceit, the too-luxuriant foliage of outward profession or anything that would prevent the fullest possible production of fruit must be pruned with unsparing hand.

'He purgeth it.' However sharp the knife may be, it is held in the hand of unerring wisdom and infinite love. 'Shall not the Judge of all the earth do right?' Ay, that he will, even though the pruning makes the branch to bleed, as if its very life were being taken away. He will not prune either too much or too little. Be thankful if the Vine-dresser thinks you worth pruning, and does not cast you away with the fruitless branches that are thrown aside for burning.

'[H]e purgeth it.' The Revised Version has it, 'he cleanseth it'. In speaking to his disciples, our Lord explained how the purging or cleansing is effected. 'Now ye are clean through the word which I have spoken unto you.' Many godly people speak of affliction as the Lord's pruning knife; and, doubtless, the Vine-dresser often uses it for that purpose; and if he wills it to be so, it is a most efficient instrument for effecting his divine purposes. I bear my willing testimony to the blessing that affliction and trial have been to me. I owe more to the fire and the file than I can ever describe. Still, the teaching of this passage is that it is the Word of the Lord which is to purge and cleanse believers. Affliction may be the handle of the pruning knife, or the ladder by which the gracious Gardener reaches every branch of the vine; but it is the Word itself which is used to accomplish the needed purging or cleansing.

The great end that the Vine-dresser has in view, in pruning the fruit-bearing branch, is 'that it may bring forth more fruit'. Other trees may be useful for various purposes; but the vine exists that it may bear 'fruit'. Before we were converted, we brought forth evil fruit; but now, by the grace of God, we bear 'fruit unto holiness, and the end everlasting life'. Writing to the Galatians, the apostle Paul makes a catalogue of the fruit of the Spirit: 'love, joy, peace, long-suffering, gentleness, goodness, faith, meekness, temperance'. Men are not to be judged by their profession, or by their appearance; the Lord's test is, 'The tree is known by his fruit.' If we are bearing fruit, it is an evidence that we are abiding in the true Vine. Our Lord Jesus said to his disciples, 'As the branch cannot bear fruit of itself, except it abide in the vine; no more can ye, except ye abide in me.' The purging, pruning, cleansing is only to make us abide still more closely in the Vine that all the vital sap flowing into us may be used in the formation of fruit. 'He that abideth in me, and I in him, the same bringeth forth much fruit: for without me [margin, severed from me] ye can do nothing.' The more fruit we bear, the more will God be glorified, and the more shall we prove that we are Christ's followers, to whom he can say, 'I am the vine, ye are the branches'.

This is just what has happened to the vines that I have watched. If I had not seen it so often, I could not have believed that such a change could have been wrought. The vines that were cut back so terribly before my illness are now adorned with lovely leaves, and, better still, there are flowers from which the clusters will come, and the branches have grown marvellously during the time that I have been laid aside. It looked like a miracle to see the poor dried vine again springing up, and throwing out hopes of abundant fruitage by-and-by. This ought to encourage all of us who are being pruned. If we have been cut back by the Lord, it is only that we may gather strength that shall not be spent to waste in producing wood and leaf, but that shall be used in bringing forth fruit for our dear Lord and Master. That ought to be the case, and will be the case, with each branch of the living Vine.

Our friend prayed that, now that I am better, I may have strength I never dreamed of. I hope every one of you will have strength you never dreamed of. It would be a blessed thing if every branch in the true Vine should bear clusters as large as that which came from Eshcol. Oh, to bear for King Jesus such fruit, to abide in him so closely and to glorify him so completely that no more could have been done by us! I fear we do not, any of us, reach that standard; but let us all seek to get as near to it as we possibly can.

You must have noticed, in reading the lives of men who have been very fruitful unto God and his church, how much they have been cut back. You remember how it was with Martin Luther. At the very time that he seemed to be most wanted in the world, when he was returning from the Diet of Worms and hoping soon to be again preaching in his beloved Wittenberg, he was surrounded by a band of soldiers and carried off to the castle of the

Wartburg, and there he was shut up for awhile and unable to mix with men, as he longed to do. He was not confined as a pris-oner, for he went out hunting and riding; but he was always at-tended by guards, and the rest of his time he spent in reading and studying. He wanted to be preaching and thundering away against the evils of the papacy; and he said that he believed it was the devil who had come and shut him up just when he wanted to be in the thick of the fight. It was, however, the act, not of Satan, but of his faithful friend the Elector Frederic who knew that, at that time, his life would be in great danger if he were out abroad; so he kept him out of the way of harm, and in that castle of the Wartburg he was able to do more for the cause of God and truth than if he had been at liberty. It was there that he threw the ink-stand at the devil's head, and it was there that he began to throw the inkstand at the devil's head in another sense by his transla-tion of the Bible, and by his other writings. It was a good time for Luther, and it was a good time for the whole world. He was able to take active exercise, and also carefully and prayerfully to study the Scriptures, thus preparing himself for future service.

Luther was also cut back in another fashion. That faithful servant of God – the bravest of the brave, I think I might call him; one who seemed dauntless as a lion before the Lord's ene-mies – was throughout his whole life tormented by such doubt, unbelief and horrible attacks of Satan that I suppose there has scarcely existed a man who has gone through a more trying ex-perience. No barque that ever rode the waters endured fiercer tempests than Martin Luther when he was driven before the blast of Satanic assaults. He would get down his violin, and play, in the hope of driving away the foul fiend; he would talk with Catherine von Bora, his wife, his queen, his empress, as he called her, and she would reason with him and sometimes scold him. But it was no use: poor Martin went down, down, down, till he cursed the day of his birth, and wished himself in his grave. Imagine, if you can, what he would have been without all these trials. With such a spirit as he had, he would have been like a wild boar, rooting up everything that was growing in his pathway; and he would have acted towards a great many people in a way that would not have been for their comfort, or his own good name. So he was cut back and was not allowed to grow according to the vigour of the sap that was in him, and thus he was enabled to render such noble service to the great Protestant Reformation, with which his name will be eternally associated.

I have spoken thus in the hope of cheering any of you who are being tried, you that have been doubting, you that have been troubled in your minds. Cry to God that this pruning process may make you fruitful in every good work, and cheerfully submissive to the will of the Lord. Do not so much ask for deliverance from trouble as for the sanctified use of it; and may the Lord bless you all, and save any unsaved ones who may be present! Amen.

18

'Write the name of Jesus on all Your Crosses'

And Pilate wrote a title, and put it on the cross. And the writing was, JESUS OF NAZARETH THE KING OF THE JEWS (John 19:19).

Sweet is this hour of prayer, all the sweeter because outside in the world we meet with so much of trouble and disquietude. We have each a cross to carry, a burden which we may not and cannot refuse. What shall we do with our crosses? For once, we will go down to the Philistines, and learn from them.

I know of nothing in which I could hold up Pilate as an example to you, save in this one thing; he placed the name of Jesus on the cross. Writing these words with his own hand, he refused to alter them: 'Jesus of Nazareth the King of the Jews' must stand over the cross, whether the high priests rage or submit. The vacillating governor for once stuck to the truth, and would not be driven from it.

Now, whenever you have a cross, write the name of Jesus, the King, above it, and stand to what you have written.

Let us consider Pilate's inscription word by word. Over your cross take care that you set the name of JESUS. Bear your cross for Jesus, with Jesus and after Jesus: this is a grand recipe for making it as light as it can be. Remember it is only a wooden cross that we have to carry, though our fears often paint it with iron colours. Neither do we bear upon our shoulder a cross which will destroy us, but one upon which we shall triumph, after the manner of our Lord. We have not to bear it first in the procession of sorrow which is wending its way through this ribald world, but 'to bear it after Jesus', along a pathway which he has beaten for us. He has himself carried a cross far heavier than ours, and his hearty sympathy is with us. He is so united to us that all our crosses are his own. Bear your cross for the sake of Jesus. What could you not suffer for him? Bear it with Jesus. What can you not bear in his company? In this way you may joyfully carry your appointed load; the strengthening touch of Jesus will make the yoke easy and the burden light.

Oh, that name of Jesus! I could talk till midnight of its depth and meaning, its sweetness, its power; and when the twelfth hour struck, you would say to one another, 'Why, it is midnight, and the Pastor is only as yet upon the threshold of his theme!' There is so much to be said about the name of Jesus that all the tongues of men and of angels would fail to tell the half thereof. It is the joy of heaven above; and, meanwhile, it is the solace of sorrow below. Not only is it the most majestic name, the most instructive name, the most truthful name, the most powerful name, the most sanctifying name, but it is also the most comfortable name that was ever sounded in this valley of weeping. If you will keep your mouth flavoured and your heart perfumed with the dear name of Jesus, you will find that every bitter thing becomes sweet, and the most unpleasant becomes fragrant. Jesus, Emmanuel, God-with-us – why, this is as the opened windows of heaven, and as the inner melodies of the King's chamber! Our Saviour is the great Cross-bearer, Jesus is the Crucified; and, therefore, we gladly take up our cross, and follow him, finding, to our astonishment, that our cross has grown light in the presence of his cross.

The Roman governor did not fail to write, 'Jesus of Nazareth'. Those last words meant scorn of the bitterest kind, as if he had said, 'The wise man of Gotham', or Tom of Bedlam. To him, it meant that an ignorant country fellow had set up to be a king. Marvel not if, upon your crosses, there should fall a bitter rain of contempt. Accept shame and ridicule as a part of your life's burden. Be thou also called 'a Nazarene'; be not ashamed to own that 'thou also wast with Jesus of Nazareth'. Who are we, that we should receive praise where Jesus received spittle? Let us settle it in our hearts that, if there be an epithet of derision, it may as well honour us as anyone else. The world will not know us any more than it knew Jesus. If they have called the master of the house Beelzebub, the servants must not expect fair titles. Write Jesus of Nazareth on your crosses, and henceforth contumely and sarcasm will lose their edge.

Very significantly for us, the name of Jesus, in Pilate's super-scription, is followed by the words the King: Jesus, the King. These also are highly consolatory words, because our hearts prompt us to say, 'Did the King bear a cross infinitely heavier than mine?' Then I, a servant, may well take up my load, which is comparatively so light. Jesus, the King, does he condescend to this shame? Then, to follow him is the utmost height of honour. Jesus, the King, does he ordain a cross for me? Then why should I question his love, or doubt his wisdom? If he bids me take the cross, what remains to a loyal subject but to obey? If he be my King, I should be a rebel if I kicked against the burden which he lays upon me.

Jesus, the King: is it not sweet to think that, even on the cross, Jesus is the King? When he dies, for the first time in his mortal career his sovereignty is acknowledged by official authority among his countrymen, and the representative of Caesar sits down in Jerusalem, and writes, 'This is Jesus, the King of the Jews.' Hebrew and Greek and Roman had it, under Pilate's hand and seal, that the Crucified One was indeed a King. Then, my soul, if Jesus triumphed on the cross, canst thou not triumph under the cross if his grace be in thee? Art thou not still a priest and king unto the living God, despite thy griefs, and reproaches, and crosses? He that hath made us kings and priests unto God has not given us an empty title, neither does the fact of our cross-bearing in the slightest degree cast a doubt upon our royal dignity. We wear our coronets by patent of the King of kings, and our royalty none may question. Even when the cross weighs heaviest upon us, let us still rejoice that we are honoured to suffer with Christ, and are thus crowned as well as crossed. See the royal name set on our cross, and it will become at once lovely in our sight.

But Pilate wrote, 'This is Jesus, the King of the Jews.' 'Well,' says one, 'what has that to do with us?' I answer, write this also on that great cross which the whole church has to carry after Christ. He is a King whom his subjects refuse. The heaviest cross the church has to bear is that the world will not bow to Christ. Perhaps, in our younger days, we said, 'We have only to tell men the gospel, and they will obey it'; but we soon found out our mistake. We thought that there was very little for us to do except to push the world before us, and to drag the church behind us; but, today, we have a different opinion. We see the legions of darkness still in their entrenchments, and though we have won many a victory, yet how small our success compared with what still remains to be done! Africa, China, India, why, these are all parts of the great cross for the church to carry. Jesus is King of all these countries, for he is 'Head over all things'; but as yet we see not all things put under him, and this is our cross.

Write on the burden of your service these words, 'Jesus, the King of the Jews'; and be encouraged. Jesus possesses a throne which rules over Israel, even though Israel be not gathered. 'Oh!' says somebody, 'the Jews are the last people that will be converted.' Perhaps so, for judicial blindness has fallen upon them; but, still, Jesus is their King, and he will yet bring them to bow at his feet. He despairs not of them, he doubts not that Israel shall yet adore him; wherefore, be ye also of good courage. Do you wish it had been written, 'Jesus, the King of the Gentiles'? Ah! but this is better still; for when the Jews bow the knee to Jesus, then the fullness of the Gentiles shall be gathered in. Their conversion will be the capture of the innermost citadel of unbelief. I remember how Luther used to talk of the Jews in his wild, cruel way; he did not believe in their salvation at all; but we have made a great advance upon so unchristian a feeling. We hail with acclamation the title, 'King of the Jews'.

My point, however, here is this. The Jews rejected Jesus, and yet he reigned over them upon the tree; and we, too, shall triumph in that very point in which we are most tried, and perhaps most overcome. Tribulations crush us, but we 'glory in tribulations also'. The cross was Christ's throne over Israel, and our affliction is our conquest over sin through the work of the Holy Spirit, sanctifying it to our purification. Let us not hesitate, therefore, to bear the cross which bore our Lord, and to write over our cross the same claim of kingship which was written over him.

Very plainly let us label our crosses with the regal title in full. Hebrew, and Greek, and Latin were the three common languages of Jerusalem; all men in the Passover crowd would know one or other of these tongues, hence the superscription was repeated in three varying characters. Let it be plain to ourselves, and then to all others, that we have fellowship with Christ in his sufferings, and that our griefs are akin to his, and shared by him. Then our sorrows will build us pulpits from which to preach Jesus; or, at least, they will be pillars upon which we can uplift the adorable name of our Lord. Our afflictions will teach us many languages, we shall speak to the many sons and daughters of woe, and each one shall hear, in his own tongue wherein he was born, a brother voice proclaiming comfort to the mourners in Zion. It is well to carve the name of the Well-beloved everywhere; but the cross is a peculiarly suitable pillar for uplifting the dear memorial. This title will be read by many if we affix it to the cross. Some will scoff, but others will turn aside to indulge in thought awakened by our thoughtfulness, and to assuage their sorrows by learning how to make them golden links with the Man of sorrows. Sure I am that you will find it wisdom to –

WRITE THE NAME OF JESUS ON ALL YOUR CROSSES.

19

Pentecost and Whitsuntide

And when the day of Pentecost was fully come, they were all with one accord in one place. And suddenly there came a sound from heaven as of a rushing mighty wind, and it filled all the house where they were sitting. And there appeared unto them cloven tongues like as of fire, and it sat upon each of them. And they were all filled with the Holy Ghost, and began to speak with other tongues, as the Spirit gave them utterance. And there were dwelling at Jerusalem Jews, devout men, out of every nation under heaven. Now when this was noised abroad, the multitude came together, and were confounded, because that every man heard them speak in his own language (Acts 2:1-6).

'Therefore being by the right hand of God exalted, and having received of the Father the promise of the Holy Ghost, he hath shed forth this, which ye now see and hear. For David is not ascended into the heavens: but he saith himself, The LORD said unto my LORD, Sit thou on my right hand, Until I make thy foes thy footstool. Therefore let all the house of Israel know assuredly, that God hath made that same Jesus, whom ye have crucified, both Lord and Christ. Now when they heard this, they were pricked in their heart, and said unto Peter and to the rest of the apostles, Men and brethren, what shall we do? Then Peter said unto them, Repent, and be baptised every one of you in the name of Jesus Christ for the remission of sins, and ye shall receive the gift of the Holy Ghost. For the promise is unto you, and to your children, and to all that are afar of, even as many as the Lord our God shall call. And with many other words did he testify and exhort, saying, Save yourselves from this untoward generation. Then they that gladly received his word were baptised: and the same day there were added unto them about three thousand souls'. (Acts 2:33-41).

These two passages remind us of the great events which make the day of Pentecost still remain to us a standing encouragement and inspiration. It comes down to us, today, almost as a tradition, and the tradition has wrought such sad changes that the very glory of that memorable time is to a large extent hidden. People now talk of 'Whit-Sunday, Whit-Monday, Whitsuntide', these names are given to this period because of a custom that was prevalent in the early church. Now, I do not pay any attention to what the early church did, any more than to what the late church has done, unless there is reason to believe that it was the will of the Lord that they should act as they did. In many matters, that were not subjects of divine revelation, they were no more right than we are; in some things, far less so. 'Well,' they said, 'this is the day of Pentecost, and we must have a special observance of the day.' I do not know that they were right in what they did, nor can I see what particular use there was in their action; for, after the ceremonial law was abrogated, all its festivals were also abolished, and it would have been far better not to keep such days in any unusual manner, but to sanctify all days alike as holy unto the Lord. I always consider that the religious observance of 'Christmas-day' and 'Good Friday' is only a piece of modern Judaism, which tends to support the pretensions of the church of Rome. Still, rightly or wrongly, these early Christians said to one another, as the anniversary came round again, 'This is the day of Pentecost; three thousand believers were baptised on that day, and we should like to commemorate that great event by baptising our candidates every year on that day.' So it came to pass that, year by year, there were crowds of persons, believers in the Lord Jesus Christ, who had waited till the day of Pentecost that they might be baptised.

'But,' asks someone, 'why is it called Whitsuntide?' That is easily explained; for it was the custom to dress the candidates, the word 'candidates' conveys the idea of persons robed in white, it was the practice to dress them in white, and so the day was called White-Sunday. We have a similar custom now, when our sisters come to be baptised here, not because we have any superstitious belief concerning their being dressed in white, but because it appears to be appropriate to the service, and is the best and easiest to be washed; blue or green would do just as well, though it might not look so comely. To the Christians of the first century it seemed suitable that the men and women who came to confess their faith in Christ should be clad in white, that being in accordance with the taste of Orientals; so everyone who was accepted for baptism wore a new white garment. The great numbers who had waited until the Pentecostal day probably made it impossible for all to be baptised on the White-Sunday, so I dare say they continued the services on the next day, and therefore called it White-Monday, and possibly the day after as well, White-Tuesday. I only wish that we might have such a White-Sunday, and WhiteMonday, and White-Tuesday that the Lord would give us such a multitude of converts that we should be obliged to have baptisms day after day because there were so many to be baptised.

To the praise of God's grace, I must here say that this is very much what we have had these many years: long church meetings, church meeting after church meeting, held almost exclusively for the reception of candidates for baptism and fellowship, all being the result of one long-continued Pentecost which God has most graciously given us. I sometimes make our friends from the country open their eyes when I tell them that we have as many as half-a-dozen church meetings in a single month. They ask me, in the greatest astonishment, 'What can your members find to do so often?' Well, we do not find any quarrelling to do, and we do not call a meeting to decide whether they shall use mottled soap or yellow for cleaning the Tabernacle. That is the sort of subject that they have for discussion in some churches, or little insignificant matters of detail of no more importance than that; some of their church meetings are concerning nothing at all, and that is a grand subject to fight about. That is not our ideal of a church meeting; we meet very often for no other purpose than to take in the candidates, who wish to come forward, and in the waters of baptism confess their faith in Christ; and they keep on coming in great numbers, thanks be unto God! We can truly say, 'The Lord hath done great things for us', and he continues to do great things for us, blessed be his holy name!

But, my dear brethren and sisters, notwithstanding this glorious fact, does not your heart often grow heavy as you remember that, in this city of London, there are vast masses of people
who never go to hear the Word of God at all? In some parts of the
metropolis you might go through street after street and scarcely
find a Christian family, or you might find large families without
a single member attending the means of grace. The irreligion and
indifference of the people are perfectly appalling; the few who
are godly are like speckled birds in the midst of multitudes who
are altogether careless. I have lived in country villages where I do
not believe there was any habitual breaking of the Sabbath-day;
if you spent the Lord's day there, you would see the whole population going either to the Baptist Chapel or the Parish church, or
the Wesleyan or Primitive Methodist Mission-room. Everybody
went somewhere or other to the house of God; a man who never
entered a place of worship would have been looked upon as an
utter heathen; but here, in London, we have multitudes sunk in
this kind of heathenism; and do what we may, we do not seem to
have any power to influence these masses of irreligious people.

Then there is a growing infidelity: not an infidelity that talks
much, it is a great deal too respectable for that, but an infidelity
that refuses to think about the things of God. What is to be done?
What is to be done? There are a great many places of worship
that are not half full, and a great many more with a little handful
sprinkled about; the difficulty is to get the people in, to get the
kind of man that the people care to hear, and to give them the
kind of word that will attract and retain them.

Is not the case difficult? Is not the case hopeless? It is neither
hopeless nor difficult, because it is both hopeless and difficult. If
we had to do the work by ourselves, it would be both hopeless and
impossible; but since the Lord alone kills and makes alive, since
he wounds and he heals, since salvation is of the Lord alone from
first to last, we have passed out of the sphere of difficulty, and
consequently out of the region of hopelessness and impossibility.
He can send us men from quarters where we never expected them;
the boldest advocates of error may become the ablest defenders
of the faith. This has happened before, and the Lord can make it
occur again and again. He can take the most wicked and most
blasphemous of men and cleanse them and make them chosen
vessels to bear his name and his gospel to the people. He can

employ you, dear friends, in your homes, or in your workshops; he can make any one of you, nay, he can make all of you to be the dispensers of life, and grace amidst the masses of the people, as it was, when the newly-slaughtered Christ, by his almighty Spirit, inspired those who were but a handful, and a very feeble folk, and made them do exploits which, without the Holy Ghost, they would never have dared to attempt. Let the Lord but make bare his holy arm in our midst, let him but fill each of you and me, and every one of his servants, with his Holy Spirit, and who knoweth what may come of it? He has ways and means of working where we have none. He is the mighty God, our strong Rock, and our ever-present Helper.

I am sometimes greatly strengthened in my faith by the awful wickedness of men. I had today a letter; I often receive letters containing abuse and blasphemy, and become so used to seeing them that I take no notice of them; I had today a letter in which a man has written all the passages in the Old Testament in which God commanded the Israelites to slay their enemies. After citing these texts, the writer says to me, 'And this is your God, is it? I do not wonder that he wants a bloody sacrifice to appease his anger if these are his orders to his ancient people.' Yes, sir, if you are here; I say without hesitation that Jehovah is my God, and that I am not ashamed of anything that he ever said or did.

Why, friends, when we think of the judgments of God upon the wicked, in days gone by, we need never feel the slightest shudder at what some call God's cruelty. When I think of the abominable sinfulness of men, I wonder that the Lord, in punishing them, was not a thousand times more severe than he was; and when I have heard the way in which some men speak of him now, I ask myself, 'How is it possible for him to continue to bear with them as he does?' After he has formed them, and fed them, they neglect him, and despise him, and fight against him, and some of them even deny his very existence; why does he not destroy them? It is because he is God, and not man, that they are not all consumed; and if, sometimes, he does lay bare his mighty arm, and teach them terrible lessons with the edge of his sharp sword, still I adore and bless the angry God. Let him be what he may, he is to me altogether perfect; and though he slay me, yet will I trust in him Jehovah, the God of Abraham, and of Isaac, and of Jacob, the God of the whole earth shall he be called, that selfsame God is my God, and he will win the day despite all his adversaries.

But perhaps you ask me, 'How can you draw any comfort out of the blasphemy of men?' Why, in this way! It will stir up the Lord to jealousy, it will move him to say, 'Now will I do a great work in the midst of these rebellious and sinful people.' I used to wonder what John Bunyan meant when he said that he had great hope of the world because he saw so many young men who were terribly wicked. He felt that, if the Lord should save such big sinners as those, they would be great saints indeed. This is a prayer that the Lord will hear from his people: 'It is time for thee, LORD, to work: for men have made void thy law.' There is a good deal in that argument; we do have confidence in God, brethren, even amidst the prevailing wickedness of men. Oh, what a mercy, it is to have such a God to whom we can go in prayer! Let us turn again to the mercy-seat and plead for the masses of men who are still far from God by wicked works. It was while the apostles were all with one accord in one place, continuing in prayer and supplication, that the Holy Ghost came upon them, and they were endued with the power from on high which their Lord had promised. So may it be with us, for his dear Name's sake! Amen.

20

The Pastor's Need of the People's Prayers

Ye also helping together by prayer for us (2 Cor. 1:11).

Here is a short sentence, written by the apostle Paul, which I very earnestly commend to your serious attention, though I shall only speak upon it briefly. In the second Epistle to the Corinthians, the first chapter, and the eleventh verse, you will find these words;

'YE ALSO HELPING TOGETHER BY PRAYER FOR US'.

Dear friends, we are most of us members of one church, we are enlisted under one banner, and we are sworn to be faithful to one great purpose, namely, to live for Jesus, and to seek to glorify God. Now, we cannot all of us do the same thing for our Lord; we have each one some office, differing from all the rest of our brethren and sisters in Christ. Here let me pause, and say that everyone who has a work to do for Christ needs the prayers of his fellow Christians, therefore I urge you all to ask for them. You may be the teacher of the infant class in the Sunday school, or you may be only able to talk with one or two individuals now and then about your Saviour; but, whatever your service is, do not neglect to entreat the prayers of your brethren for a blessing upon your work; however limited may be your sphere, you will not get on without the supplications of others. 'Ye also helping together by prayer for us' may be the utterance of the weakest and feeblest brother; and he may, because of his weakness and feebleness, all the more powerfully appeal to his Christian brethren and sisters to help together by prayer for him.

But the most conspicuous person in the church is the one who has, from week to week, to preach the gospel to the great assembly; and he may, therefore, as the apostle does in this case, plead for himself, and say to the saints, 'Ye also helping together by prayer for us'. Oh, dear friends, do pray for all who preach the gospel, whether to many or to few! They all need your sympathy and help; but I make a specially earnest, personal appeal for my own self. I crave, beyond all things, your constant prayers; for I think a burden is laid upon me more than is borne by any other man, because of the vastness of this congregation, and because of the multitude of agencies connected with this great church. Many of the works are carried on by others, and I can take small personal part in them; and yet, somehow, I have to take the most difficult part, that of helping in every time of need, mending up any weak places when they are discovered and keeping all things in good order. A great care comes upon me, and not for this church only, but for many other churches, in various parts of the country, which have been formed by the brethren who have gone out from the College; and I have to deal with all sorts of difficult cases all over England, and I might almost say all over the world – things that try the mind, and exercise the judgement, and sometimes fret the heart; and therefore I must have your prayers.

Now, there are some of you who cannot do anything in the way of preaching; I do not want that you should try, and there are other agencies to which you could not put your hand; to you especially I may say, 'Ye also helping together by your prayers for us'. Here is a way in which you can really help, substantially help, wonderfully help; and this you can do even if you should become bedridden, you could even then lie still, and invoke a blessing from God upon our ministry. You can do this also if you are dumb so far as public speaking is concerned; you can, in the silence of your spirit, lay hold upon the Angel of the covenant, and wrestle and prevail. Amazing possibilities lie within the reach of the believing man. 'All things are possible to him that believeth.'

I have always, with my whole heart, and without any sort of untruthfulness, ascribed all the success I ever had to the prayers of God's people, and I unfeignedly do the same now. God the Holy Spirit has ever given the blessing in answer to your supplications. You have asked in faith for a blessing, and it has come, and it will come as long as such prayers are continued. If I should be called to lie down in the grave, if I should retire from the Lord's service through utter inability, it would be infinitely to be preferred to the sad end of the man who falls because those who used to hold him up are gone. It is hard to fight like Joshua when there is no Moses on the hilltop, nor any Aaron and Hur to hold up his hands in prayer. I appeal to those of you who have been with me from the beginning that you will never cease crying to God at the throne of grace. Never neglect that holy privilege and sacred duty, I implore you. I appeal to those who have been converted here, and they are not a few, that they will not forget to ask for a blessing upon others: 'Ye also helping together by prayer for us, that for the gift bestowed upon us by the means of many persons thanks may be given by many on our behalf.'

You want to praise God, you say. I was glad our brother, who prayed just now, began by praising the Lord for his goodness. Many pray for their minister, and they are the people who also praise God for their minister; how many there are who have praised God for us, we could not possibly tell. I have a family of spiritual children in heaven, and no small one; they will go on praising and magnifying the name of the Lord to all eternity; and among believing men and women on earth I speak not egotistically, but only utter the plain and simple truth; I think no one has more friends who are constantly praising God for the ministry in this house of prayer, and for the blessing they have received through reading the printed sermons. Therefore, while you are on your knees on earth, your prayers and praises are in harmony with the melody of the harps of heaven, and by your supplications you are calling down blessings which will make music for God in thousands of hearts of persons whom you never will know till you meet them in glory.

I wonder whether it strikes anybody that it is a very difficult task to keep on preaching when almost every word you say gets printed; I do not know whether anyone ever thinks of the sore travail of this brain in trying to find fresh subjects, and fresh matter upon those subjects. If I begin to repeat myself in the pulpit, we shall have a great sleeping society here instead of a living church, or the members will go their way to some other place. And what if the subject and material upon it are given, yet how is one always to keep up a lively spirit without the continual supplication of believers? Do you not feel, sometimes, my brother, or my sister, that you are very stupid when you are studying your subject? I know that I do; and then I say to myself,

'This will not do, sir, this will not do; you cannot go to the pulpit in this way, you must wake yourself up, you must get to your knees, you must draw nigh to God somehow, it will not do to go into the pulpit like a dead man, to talk of a dead gospel to dead hearers.' Mr William Olney seems to be always alive, and active, and earnest; but I have no doubt that he would ask your prayers that he may be kept so. At any rate, I do, with my whole soul, ask you to carry out these words on my behalf, 'Ye also helping together by prayer for us'.

It is not selfish to ask the prayers of so many for one man, since the reason is that, afterwards, the blessing may go out to the many through the preaching of the gospel. If we are filled, it is that we may be emptied; if we receive, it is that we may give; for the apostle says what I, in my humble measure, can also say, 'whether we be afflicted, it is for your consolation and salvation ... or whether we be comforted, it is for your consolation and salvation.' I do verily believe that, many a time, we have been chastened that we might be made a blessing to others; and we have had to carry the yoke of Christ more than we might have had to bear it on our own account, that so we might be better enabled to sympathise with the Lord's tried and afflicted people, 'whether we be afflicted ... or whether we be comforted', it is for the same reason, 'for your consolation and salvation'. And here, too, can I add with the apostle, 'we were pressed out of measure, above strength, insomuch that we despaired even of life: But we had the sentence of death in ourselves, that we should not trust in ourselves, but in God which raiseth the dead: Who delivered us from so great a death, and doth deliver: in whom we trust that he will yet deliver us; Ye also helping together by prayer for us'. Paul implicitly trusts in his God, yet he asks the people's prayers as much as if he rested entirely in them, and so must we do. Oh, give us continually more and more of your supplications!

I should like to ask a special favour of all who are present tonight that, some time this week, each believer here would not only pray for a blessing upon the work of God in this place, but that each one would pray with some other one, better still, with some other two, or three, or four, or five, or six, but at least with some other one, and ask for a blessing on this church. Could you not each one make a point of saying, 'I know whom I will get to join me'? You will do it, my sisters, I have no doubt; I am rather afraid of the brethren, yet I think all will join in this good work. Many of you will get together, I feel sure; and I cannot imagine a greater service that you can do to me, and to the church, than for two sisters, or two brethren, or more where it is possible, to meet together thus. Would you not also come together just a little before the Thursday-night service, say, at six o'clock, in the lecture hall? I will be there at six o'clock, to have a little prayer with you, so as to sharpen my sword before I come into the pulpit. And then one other thing I should like. Will everybody here try and bring some other person on Thursday night to hear the gospel preached in this place, and I will ask the Lord to give me a soul-winning sermon, and I shall be very glad if you will all try to bring some fresh hearer to listen to it? Well, now, that is a little task for some of you; it may take some thought, and time, and effort for you to accomplish it; but I really think it might be done. Let us see if every one of us can bring an unconverted person, I would aim at that; let each one say, 'I will try what I can do, I think I know somebody I can get.' Let us do so, then, and also pray much about it, and then we will watch and see whether it be not a good thing. I hope many will, somehow or other, find the necessary time for it; try for once, and see what you can do. It appears to me to be a good suggestion: what do you think of it, Mr William Olney?

Mr William Olney: 'It is a very excellent thing indeed, sir. I promise, by God's help, to bring my one, and more if I can. I will try to bring some of the men who work for me, and I will give them an hour less work on Thursday so that they may come.'

Others of you have workmen in your employ, some of you have servant girls, or else there is somebody in the house whom you could bring if you made an effort. Why might we not thus really bring some to the Saviour who, to all outward appearance, are at present beyond our reach? I shall be grateful to God and I shall also be thankful to you if it is so. What is more, God will bless this effort; I am sure he will, and you may live to thank God for what I have proposed to you this evening; and if not, many of those whom you bring will eternally have cause to bless the Lord for your loving service and your believing prayers.

If I could not preach, I do think that one of the things I would do would be to bring others to hear the preachers of the Word. I should like to have a large number of friends like my brother

Hobson, who used to sit up there in the gallery. Many persons joined the church through that dear old man, who is now in heaven: men who might not have come in here at all, but he used to be on the lookout for them, in Hyde Park and other places, and he would tell them that they must come and hear Mr Spurgeon; he would offer them a seat in his pew, and, through coming, God met with them, and blessed and saved them. Well, then, there is a task for you, but set about it with prayer. I come back to that point; my aim is to hit this nail on the head, and drive it home, and clinch it: 'Ye also helping together by prayer for us'. Oh, may God send this rich abounding spirit of prayer upon us all at this very hour, and to him shall be the praise!

I think I am right in begging this favour, for I remember that our dear brother George Muller, who is, as you know, a man mighty in prayer, yet found it needful, after he was seventy years of age, to make an appeal like this to the people, 'I beseech you deny me not your prayers', and he stated that he rested, under God, in the prayers of the saints. Now, he is a man who can have anything he likes in answer to prayer; yet he entreats the petitions of others. We are none of us worthy to be placed beside him; but, if he needs prayer, and he does, how much more do we, who are weaker, need it; therefore, deny us not your supplications, I earnestly beg you.

Now let us come back to prayer again, and ask the Lord's blessing upon this new work that we are hoping to do for him.

21

Why We Have Not

[Y]e have not, because ye ask not (James 4:2).

The Holy Ghost, by the mouth of his servant James, has said, '[Y]e have not, because ye ask not.' I would not willingly be censorious, but crying evils demand open rebuke. Do you not think that this text applies to the case of many of our churches? They have no prosperity, their numbers do not increase and the congregations are small; and, as the main cause of it all, they have scarcely a prayer meeting. I hear perpetually of prayer meetings abandoned, or, what is much the same thing, blended with the weekly lecture. From various sources I gather that, in many instances, the meeting for prayer is so small that it is difficult to spin out the hour; and as the same few persons come from time to time, variety is out of the question; indeed, in some places, the prayer meeting only exists to reveal the nakedness of the land. Now, if there be no conversions, and no additions to such churches, what is the reason? Is it not found here, '[Y]e have not, because ye ask not'?

A lack of interest exists in many places, so that the assembly for prayer is despised, and put down as a second-rate affair: 'only a prayer meeting'. Is this a right view of the throne of grace? Will this bring blessing? In certain churches, there is no union, and consequently no agreement in prayer: 'their heart is divided; now shall they be found wanting'; and wanting they are in their assemblies for prayer. In such a case, a feeble prayer meeting is an effect as well as a cause of disunion; and till this is altered, we may expect to see more and more of 'the divisions of Reuben'. Prayer is a grand cement; and lack of prayer is like withdrawing the force of gravitation from a mass of matter, and scattering it into so many separate atoms. Some churches are feeble all round; the members are a race of invalids, a body of infirm pensioners who can hardly hobble about in the ways of godliness. They have no life, no energy or enterprise for Christ; and do you wonder at it when their meetings for prayer are so scantily attended?

In some places where there are good, praying people, the prayer meetings are badly attended, because certain long-winded brethren spoil them. I know a church which is endowed with an excellent deacon, a real godly man, but he will pray without ceasing at every meeting, and I fear he will pray the prayer meeting down to nothing unless he is soon taken home. The other night, when he had talked for a full twenty minutes, he intimated, both to heaven and earth, that all he had said was merely a preface, a drawing near as he called it, and that he was then going to begin. None of his friends were pleased to receive that information, for they had begun to cherish the hope that he would soon have done. They were all too sadly aware that now he would pray for 'our own beloved country', 'from the Queen upon the throne to the peasant in the cottage', then for Australia and all the Colonies, and then for China and India, starting off afresh with kindly expressions for the young and for the old, for the sick, for sailors, and for the Jews. As a rule, nothing was really asked for by this most estimable brother, but he uttered several pious remarks on all these subjects, and many more.

It is a great pity when highly esteemed brethren fall into the notion that they must deliver themselves of long harangues; the better the men, the worse the evil, for then we are forced to tolerate them. I am sorry when a good man gets the idea that praying means telling out his experience, or giving his theological opinions. I am told that our Salvation Army friends strike up a tune whenever a friend becomes long and prosy, and I have great sympathy with the practice. It removes the responsibility of stopping the man from the minister to the people, and by dividing the action among many it operates like a round robin for the screening of anyone. When prayer is an earnest asking, it may occasionally be lengthened to advantage; but the less of mere holy gossip, the better. If prayer meetings degenerate into gospel gossip, we cannot wonder if no blessing comes. In such cases, the word is true, 'ye have not, because ye ask not.'

If any believer should chance to live where the prayer meeting is neglected, let him now resolve to revive it. Let us make a solemn league and covenant that the churches shall pray, or that it shall not be our fault if they do not. To strengthen a prayer meeting is as good a work as to preach a sermon. I would have you vow that the prayer meeting shall never be given up while you live. Be like the good woman who, when it was decided to close the prayer meeting in a certain village, declared that it should not be, for she would be there if no one else was. She was true to her word; and when, the next morning, someone said to her rather jestingly, 'Did you have a prayer meeting last night?' 'Ah, that we did!' she replied. 'How many were present?' 'Four,' she said. 'Why,' said he, 'I heard that you were there all alone.' 'No,' she said, 'I was the only one visible, but the Father was there, and the Son was there, and the Holy Spirit was there, and we were agreed in prayer.' Before long, others took shame to themselves at the earnest perseverance of a poor old woman, and soon there was a revived prayer meeting and a prospering church. I have heard of a Negro, who was found sitting out the time of service all alone when his coloured brethren had grown cold and prayerless; in his case also, the rest were shamed into fresh energy. I beg you, then, to maintain this holy ordinance even if the attendance should have dwindled down to two or three. Surely a church, if it be a church of Christ at all, must feel the rebuke which would be given by your perseverance. Oh, never let us leave off praying unitedly for a blessing! Solemnly settle it in your hearts that the fire upon the altar shall never go out. As for me and my church, we will serve the Lord by maintaining this sacred exercise in full vigour; and I beseech all other believers to come to the same resolve; or, if not, there will be dreary days for the church of Christ.

But now let us apply this passage to ourselves as individuals: 'ye have not, because ye ask not.' I wonder whether there is a brother here who has been tugging and toiling and struggling for years after a certain thing which seems farther off than ever; and does the reason of his failure lie in the fact that he has never prayed about it? Do you wonder, dear brother, that you have not when you do not ask? With one hundredth part of your present trouble, you may obtain the desired boon if you seek it at the

Lord's hands. I mean, even as to temporal things it is our duty to work for our daily bread, and to earn what is necessary for this life; but do recollect that everything about a Christian should be a matter of prayer, because everything about a child that ought to be the child's business is his Father's business. If a child should have a perfect father, that father would be interested to hear about the child's play as well as about the child's suffering. He would take an interest in his boy's lesson-books at school, and cheer him in reference to the little trials of his playhours, for that which may be very little to a stranger may be great to a father who measures things by his love to his child. Though a matter might be little to the father, considering him as a man alone, yet since it is great to the child, and the father puts himself into the child's place, his sympathy makes insignificance important. I have heard of a great king who was one day waited upon by an ambassador, who found him upon all-fours upon the floor, making himself into a horse for his little son. He said to the ambassador, 'Sir, are you a father?' 'Yes, your majesty, I am.' 'Then,' said he, 'I will finish my game with my boy, for you will understand me.' So he went on round and round the room till the little one had enjoyed his full share of romp, and then his majesty turned to the ambassador, and said, 'Now I am ready to attend to the affairs of state.' I honour the king for thus showing that he was a man who had a father's heart. So our heavenly Father takes an interest in the trifles which concern his children, if they are such as ought to concern them; and therefore you need never fear to tell everything to your God. Little things are often more troublesome than great things. If a tiny splinter of wood gets into your finger, it may be more serious than a heavy blow, and even so a minor sorrow may work us grievous ill.

Take your daily troubles, wants, longings, aspirations and endeavours to the Lord; for if they are such as are right and true, they should be laid at his feet. 'In everything by prayer and supplication with thanksgiving let your requests be made known unto God.' Do you not think that many desires of your heart and many domestic troubles may continue – the desires to be unfulfilled, and the troubles to be unremoved – because they have not been made the subject of prayer? '[Y]e have not, because ye ask not.' May not that be the case with many a merchant, student, mother or worker? Success in life, comfort, employment, health, friends may, in some cases, be found by asking, and missed by neglect of prayer.

Certainly, with regard to spiritual things, this must often be so. A brother has heard of the high joys of God's saints, and of the lofty places to which they have attained, so that they pass through life as if their feet trod lightly on the mountain-tops. He sighs, 'I wish I had their faith.' How many times has that brother said the same! Let me speak to him. Have you ever sought this faith of the Lord? If you had once prayed for it, it might have been better than wishing for it a thousand times; peradventure, strength of faith and elasticity of step have been denied you because you have not yet asked for them. May there not be a hundred other boons, which you have missed because you have never asked for them? You have envied others who had them, you have picked holes in their characters in consequence and you have complained of the Lord for withholding them; yet, all the while, the secret of your spiritual poverty has been this fact, 'ye have not, because ye ask not.'

Sometimes you will not ask because the thing is too little, sometimes because it is too great, and oftener still because it does not occur to you to ask for it. Is there anything about which a Christian ought not to pray? Then be sure of this, it is a matter with which he should have nothing to do. Mr Rowland Hill, in his Village Dialogues, proposes the composition of a form of prayer to be offered by a young lady before going to the theatre, and another to be said when she returns from a dance. 'There,' cries one, 'I call that mere hypocrisy. Who ever heard of praying in connection with such matters? It is preposterous.' Just so, and thus it is clear that these things are not for Christians, for they must do nothing which they cannot pray about, and it was to exhibit the incongruity of such actions that Mr Hill wrote as he did. A beloved brother said, the other night, and I heartily agree with him; that we ought not to pray anything that we could not suppose our Lord Jesus Christ praying. He allows us to ask in his name, and thus to use his authority in prayer. Now, what right has anybody to use my name in favour of that which he knows I should not approve of? This may test your prayers. If there is anything that Jesus would not pray for, do not dream of praying for it; but humble yourself for being guilty of a desire which would be contrary to his pure and holy mind.

This rule will be an excellent guide to you, for as you may only ask for that which Jesus would endorse, so you may only seek in your daily life that which Jesus would support you in seeking. Pray over everything; and that which you dare not pray over, do not touch. You are proposing a new course in business; well, go and pray over it. Are you going to issue bills announcing 'an alarming sacrifice' of your goods? Can you pray over them? You say that you will sell off 'under cost price'. Is it true that you hope to get a profit on all that you sell? Then how can you ask the God of truth to prosper your sales? This simple rule, if fully followed, would work a revolution in trade; and, truly it should be followed by all who call themselves Christians. Even in commerce, men have not, because they ask not; they think cheating to be a surer way of profit than praying. Hence evil practices arise, and at length become so usual that they lose their efficacy, and everybody allows discount for them. Should not godly men, in every case, set their faces against dishonest customs? 'Yes,' says one, 'but they would be great losers.' That might be, and yet the Lord is able to make it up to them in a thousand ways if they tried the power of prayer. In questions of business complication, where there is a will to do right, there is sure to be a way; and if you have not found out such a way, I must again quote the text, 'ye have not, because ye ask not.'

It may be that many a spiritual thing, for which you may pray without doubt, has never become yours simply because you have never asked for it. Is not that a pity? What! Nothing to pay; the priceless treasure a free grant, and yet I have it not because I do not ask for it! This is such a folly as we do not see in common life. Few people miss an alms for want of asking. Our poor neighbours are generally fast enough in begging. Poor frozen-out gardeners are out in the streets pouring out their complaint long before the ponds will bear a mouse. Few need to be encouraged to apply for charity; and yet, while spiritual gifts are to be had for the asking, many have not, because they ask not. Open your mouth wide, brother, and ask for a great deal. Begin asking in real earnest, and never let it be said that your spiritual poverty is your own fault.

If it is ever true of us, 'ye have not, because ye ask not', what does it mean? It means that there are needful spiritual blessings which you do not desire with all your heart. In what a wrong condition your heart must be! When a person has no appetite for wholesome food, it is a sign of disease; and if you have no appetite for divine grace, you must be sick in soul. Healthy children have large appetites; and God's children, when they are healthy, hunger and thirst after righteousness. Why is it we do not desire these precious things? Very often, it is because we do not feel our need of them; and what a proud ignorance that is which does not know its need! If you were to look at yourself, brother, though you think yourself rich, and increased with goods, and needing nothing, you would see that you are naked, and poor, and miserable. What a sad thing it is that you should miss priceless blessings because you fondly fancy that you already possess them!

Or, possibly, you know your need, and are anxious to be supplied, and yet you do not ask because you have no faith in God upon the matter. How long have you known the Lord? Have you known him a year? Is not this long enough to have gained confidence in him? There are many persons whom you would rely upon at once, and hundreds whom you could trust with untold gold after having known them for a few hours. Cannot you thus trust God? How is it that you dare to doubt him? What a sin it must be to distrust One so faithful and true!

Or else it may be that you do not doubt either God's ability or willingness to help you, but you have grown rusty in the knee: I mean, out of order as to prayer. It is a very great evil when this is the case. When I have pains in my wrist, or in my foot, I have some hope of speedy recovery, but I am always despondent when the weakness is in the knee; then it is a very serious business. O brethren, well doth the Scripture say, 'Confirm the feeble knees.' If we are not at home in prayer, everything is out of order. He who goes often to a room knows how to gain admittance, but a stranger loses himself in the passages. Familiarity with the mercy-seat is a great point in the education of a child of God; be sure that you gain it.

There are two or three matters for which I desire to ask your earnest prayers just now. Do pray for a very large blessing on the congregation here. In the early summer weeks, I thought that this house was not so full as usual, and I was greatly troubled about it; but the fact was that the major part of our friends had taken their holidays early. Of late, the crowds have exceeded those of past years, and we are all amazed at the attendance at the prayer meeting and the lecture. The sickness of the minister, no doubt, tended to make the public fearful of not hearing him, and his continued health reassured them, so that now our great building will not hold all who come. We have the people, to our heart's content; do you wonder that I tremble lest the opportunity should be lost in any measure? Do pray that I may preach with power. Plead with the Holy Ghost to convert these eager thousands. Persons of all nations, ranks, ages and religions come hither. I beseech you, agonise in prayer that they may be saved. Let it not be true, in their case, that we have not, because we ask not.

Greatly do I need your prayer for the work and ministry of this huge church. What a load rests upon me! Here are about 5,500 of you; and with all the help I have, I find I have enough upon me to crush me unless heaven sustains me. My brother and the elders do for me what the elders in the wilderness church did for Moses, else should I utterly faint; but the more difficult cases, and the general leadership, make up a burden which none can carry unless the Lord gives strength. I loathe to speak thus about myself; and yet I must, for there is need. Beside all this, there cometh upon me the care of many another church, and of all sorts of works for our Lord. There, you do not know all, but you may guess; if you love me, if you love my Master, I implore you, pray for me. A good old man prayed, before I came to London, that I might always be delivered from the bleating of the sheep. I did not understand what he meant; but I know now, when hour by hour all sorts of petitions, complaints, bemoanings and hard questions come to me. The bleating of the sheep is not the most helpful sound in the world, especially when I am trying to get the food ready for the thousands here, there and everywhere, who look for it to come to them regularly, week by week.

Sometimes, I become so perplexed that I sink in heart, and dream that it were better for me never to have been born than to have been called to bear all this multitude upon my heart. Especially do I feel this when I cannot help the people who come to me, and yet they expect that I should do impossibilities. Moreover, it is not easy to give wise advice in such complicated affairs as those which come before me, and I hope I shall never be content without using my best judgement at all times. Frequently, I can do nothing but bring the cases before God in prayer, and bear them as a burden on my heart. These burdens are apt to press very heavily on a sympathising heart, and cause a wear and tear which tell upon a man. I only say this because I want more and more the sympathy of God's people, and perhaps I may not have even this if I ask not for it.

If you put me in so difficult a position, you must uphold me by your prayers. If I have been useful to you in any measure, pray for me; it is the greatest kindness you can do me. If the word as spoken by these lips has been a means of grace to your children, plead for me that others of the young may be brought to Jesus by my teaching. If you would find my ministry more profitable to your souls, pray for me still more; and let it not be said of your minister that you do not profit by his preaching, and that you have not, because you ask not. Beloved, let us wrestle in prayer; for untold blessings are to be had for the asking. As a church, we have been specially favoured; but we have not exhausted the possibilities of prosperity, or the resources of heavenly power. There is a future for us, if we pray. Greater things than these lie behind that curtain; no hand can unveil them but the hand of prayer. The singular blessings which have rested upon us in the past call upon us to pray; the marked prosperity and unity of the present invite us to pray; and the hopes of the future encourage us to pray. Behold, the Lord says to you, 'Ask, and ye shall receive.' Brothers, sisters, slack not your asking; but, for the love of souls, multiply your petitions, and increase your importunity.

PART 3
Incidents
and
Illustrations

22

An Interruption Improved

(A few words spoken by Mr. Spurgeon, at a Tabernacle prayer-meeting, when a friend had been carried out in a fit.)

Possess your souls in quietness, beloved friends. When we are engaged in prayer, or in any other form of worship, interruptions may occur, especially in large assemblies. We cannot expect all nature to be hushed because we are bowing the knee. Permit not your minds to be easily distracted, or you will often have your devotion destroyed. Rather let us learn a lesson from a painful incident. I seemed to hear a voice in that sorrowful cry of our friend, and it bade me have pity upon the many whose life is one long agony. Let that doleful moan awaken sympathy for thousands in the hospital, and out of it, who are grievously tormented. We are in good health, and are sitting in the midst of a happy company of our fellow Christians; let us be grateful that we have not been struck down, to be carried out amid the distress of anxious friends. Sympathy and gratitude are two choice emotions; and if both of these are aroused by this interruption, we shall have gained more by it than we can possibly have lost.

Sympathy, or fellow feeling, may well be excited by the sight or hearing of pain in our fellow creatures. We may indulge it freely, for it is not only due to the sufferer, but exceedingly beneficial to the humane heart which feels it. Those who are never out of health themselves, and keep aloof from the poor and the sick, are apt to undergo a hardening process of the most injurious kind. It is a sad thing for the blind man, who has to read the raised type, when the tips of his fingers harden, for then he cannot read the thoughts of men which stand out upon the page; but it is far worse to lose sensibility of soul, for then you cannot peruse the book of human nature, but must remain untaught in the sacred literature of the heart. You have heard of 'the iron Duke', but an iron Christian would be a very terrible person. A heart of flesh is the gift of divine grace, and one of its sure results is the power to be very pitiful, tender and full of compassion.

You would feel all the greater sympathy with some afflicted ones if you knew how good they are, and how patient they are under their sufferings. I am delighted with the diligent way in which some of our tried sisters come out to religious services. When many in good health stay away from the meetings upon the most frivolous excuses, there are certain dear sick ones who are never absent. There is one among us who has many fits in a week, but how she loves to be here! I beg her to sit near the door, for her fits may come upon her at any moment, but she is an example to us all in the constancy of her attendance. Have sympathy with all the sick, but especially with those who might be spoken of in the words applied to Lazarus, 'Lord, he whom thou lovest is sick.'

I mentioned gratitude also, and I hope it will not be forgotten. Let the cry of pain remind us that we owe our Lord a song of thanksgiving for screening us from the greater ills of life – consumption sapping the constitution, asthma making it misery to breathe, epilepsy tearing us to pieces or palsy causing every limb to lose its power. Blessed be God for our limbs and senses, and for health which sweetens all. We shall never become too grateful; let us abound in thanksgiving.

This interruption speaks to us with a still deeper and more solemn tone. Our friend is not dead, but might readily enough have been so. That cry says to me, 'Prepare to meet thy God.' We are liable to death at any moment, and ought always to be ready for it; I mean, not only ready because we are washed in the blood of the Lamb, but because we have set our house in order, and are prepared to depart. I feel it right, when I lay my head upon my pillow, to ask myself, 'If I never wake on earth, is it well with my soul?' and then to reply

Sprinkled afresh with pardoning blood,
I lay me down to rest,
As in the embraces of my God,
Or on my Saviour's breast

Could we now, dear friends, at this moment, resign our breath, and without further preparation enter upon the eternal world? Breathing out the prayer, 'Father, into thy hands I commend my spirit', could we now ascend from earth, made meet for the inheritance above? It should be so. Everything about us should be in such order that, if our Lord should come while we are in the field, we should not wish to go into the house, but could depart at once. I agree with the great scholar Bengel that death should not become a spiritual parade, but should be regarded as the natural close of our ordinary life, the final note of the psalm of which each day has been a stanza. We ought so to live that to die would be no more remarkable than for a man in the middle of business to hear a knock at the street door, and quietly to step away from his engagements. There should be no hurrying for a clergyman to administer 'sacraments' as some call them, or for a lawyer to write a hasty will, or for an estranged relative to make peace; but all should be arranged and ordered as if we kept our accounts closely balanced, expecting an immediate audit. This would make noble living, and do more for God's glory than the most triumphant death scene.

A friend remarked to George Whitefield that, should he survive him, he would wish to witness the preacher's death, and hear his noble testimony for Christ. The good man replied, 'I do not think it at all likely that I shall bear any remarkable witness in death, for I have borne so many testimonies to my Lord and Master during my life.' This is far better than looking forward to the chilly evening or actual sunset of life as the time of bearing witness. Let us set about that holy work immediately, lest swift death arrest us on the spot, and seal our lips in silence. Be faithful every day that you may be faithful to the end. Let not your life be like a tangled mass of yarn, but keep it ever in due order on the distaff, so that, whenever the fatal knife shall cut the thread, it may end just where an enlightened judgement would have wished. Practise the excellent habit of Mr Whitefield, to whom I before referred, for he could not bear to go to bed and leave even a pair of gloves out of place. He felt that his Master might come at any moment, and he wished to be ready even to the minutest details.

Now that disturbing incident is over, we shall settle down again, all the more ready to unite in prayer and praise.

23

Fishing

I fear I have gathered but few illustrations during my holiday in the North, though I am almost always upon the lookout for them. I have spent nearly all my time on board a friend's yacht cruising by day in sunny seas, and usually anchoring at night in lonely bays, far off from the busy haunts of men, where you hear neither rumble of traffic nor hum of city life, but are startled by the scream of seabirds, the cry of the seal and the splash of leaping fish. The profound quiet of those solitary regions is a bath of rest for a wearied brain: lone mountain, and sparkling wave, and circling gull, and flitting sea swallow, all seem to call the mind away from care and toil to rest and play. I am grateful, to the last degree, for the brief furlough which is permitted me, and for the intense enjoyment and repose which I find in the works of God. No exhibitions, or picture galleries, or artificial recreations, or medical preparations can afford a tithe of the restoring influence which pure nature exercises.

I have been resting, but not idling, relieving the mind, but not smothering it. Very frequently, I have seen others fishing; and as I have looked on with interest and excitement, I have been sorry to have been able to take so small a share in it. Perhaps, however, I have gained as much from lines and nets as those who personally used them; they took the fish, but I preserved the silver truths which the creatures brought in their mouths. These pieces of money I have taken, like Peter, not for myself only, but 'for me and thee', and so let us share them. We have a good company of spiritual fishermen in our midst tonight, for here are the young members of 'the College of Fishermen', who are making and mending their nets; here, too, are eager members of a church in which, when the minister says, 'I go a-fishing', all the members say, 'We will go with thee.' Here are the fishers of the Sabbath schools and of the Bible classes, fishers of the Tract Society and of the Evangelists' Associations; all these have heard our Lord say, 'Follow me, and I will make you fishers of men.' Not for the hurting of our fellows, but for their good, we seek to 'take up all of them with the angle, to catch them in our net, and gather them in our drag'; and therefore we are willing to learn from others who are fishers, too.

Fishermen speak of what they call gathering bait, and they say, such a fish is 'a gathering bait', and another is 'a killing bait'. We need both. The gathering bait brings the fishes together, and thus becomes very useful. You cannot catch the fish if they are not there, and it is therefore wise to throw in your groundbait pretty freely to attract the finny multitude. I wish some of my fellow fishermen were a little more liberal with gathering bait, for one would like to see the creeks and bays of their pews and galleries swarming with life. Some of them appear rather to frighten the fish away than to attract them around their hooks; they are so dull, so monotonous, so long and so sour. All spiritual fishermen should learn the art of attraction; Jesus drew men to himself, and we must draw men in like manner. Not only in the pulpit, but in the Sunday school class, you need gathering bait, to draw the little ones together, and maintain and increase their numbers. In every other sphere of Christian service, the same is true. If faith cometh by hearing, we should first endeavour to gain interested listeners, for how shall they believe if they will not hear? Common sense teaches us that the people must be drawn together first, and must be induced to attend to what we have to put before them; and, therefore, we must lay ourselves out to this end, because it is essential to our highest aim. A pleasant manner, an interesting style and even a touch of wit may be useful. I have sometimes been blamed for making use of pleasantries, but I have done so partly because I could not help it, and chiefly because I have perceived that the interest is sustained and the attention excited by a dash of the familiar and the striking. A sufficient quantity of that which will draw men to listen to our message we not only may use but must use, unless we mean to be content with empty nets and useless hooks.

A good temper is a fine gathering bait in a Sabbath school. There are some of our brethren and sisters whose very faces are enough to gather the children round them. If I were a little girl, I could not help being drawn to some of the sisters who teach in our schools; and if I were a boy, the kindly manners of many of our brethren would bind me to them at once. Kindly teachers need not bribe children with gifts, their looks and words are irresistible bonds. Cheerfulness and good humour should be conspicuous in all our attempts to catch men for Jesus; we cannot drive them to the Saviour, but they may be drawn. There is a way of offering a tract in the street which will ensure its acceptance, and another way which will prejudice the receiver against it: you can shove it into a person's hand so roughly that it is almost an insult, or you can hold it out so deftly that the passer-by accepts it with pleasure. Do not thrust it upon him as if it were a writ, but invite him to accept it as if it were a ten-pound note. Our fish need delicate handling. A certain painter, when asked how he mixed his colours, replied, 'With brains, sir', and we must fish for the souls of men in like fashion. If you are to win souls, you must not be fools. Men will no more succeed in the Lord's business than they will in their own unless they have their wits about them. If Christ's work be done in a slovenly or churlish manner, it will answer no man's purpose, but prove labour in vain. We cannot make the fish bite, but we can do our best to draw them near the killing bait of the Word of God; and when once they are there, we will watch and pray till they are fairly taken.

The fisherman, however, thinks far less of his gathering bait than he does of his catching bait, in which he hides his hook. Very numerous are his inventions for winning his prey, and it is by practice that he learns how to adapt his bait to his fish. Scores of things serve as bait; and when he is not actually at work, the wise fisherman takes care to seize anything which comes in his way which may be useful when the time comes to cast his lines. We usually carried mussels, whelks and some of the coarser sorts of fish, which could be used when they were wanted. When the anchor was down, the hooks were baited, and let down for the benefit of the inhabitants of the deep; and great would have been the disappointment if they had merely swarmed around the delicious morsel, but had refused to partake thereof.

A good fisherman actually catches fish. He is not always alike successful; but, as a rule, he has something to show for his trouble. I do not call that man a fisherman whose basket seldom holds a fish; he is sure to tell you of the many bites he had, and of that very big fish which he almost captured; but that is neither here nor there. There are some whose knowledge of terms and phrases, and whose extensive preparations lead you to fear that they will exterminate the fishy race; but as their basket returns empty, they can hardly be so proficient as they seem. The parable hardly needs expounding: great talkers and theorisers are common enough, and there are not a few whose cultured boastfulness is only exceeded by their lifelong failure. We cannot take these for our example, nor fall at their feet with reverence for their pretensions. We must have sinners saved. Nothing else will content us: the fisherman must take fish, or lose his toil; and we must bring souls to Jesus, or we shall break our hearts with disappointment.

Walking to the head of the boat, one evening, I saw a line over the side, and must needs hold it. You can generally feel, with your finger, whether you have a bite or no; but I was in considerable doubt whether anything was at the other end or not. I thought they were biting, but I was not certain, so I pulled up the long line, and found that the baits were all gone; the fish had sucked them all off, and that was what they were doing when I was in doubt. If you have nothing but a sort of gathering bait, and the fish merely come and suck, but do not take the hook, you will catch no fish; you need killing bait. This often happens in the Sunday school: a pleasing speaker tells a story, and the children are all listening, he has gathered them; now comes the spiritual lesson, but hardly any of them take notice of it, they have sucked the bait from the hook, and are up and away. A minister, in preaching, delivers a telling illustration, all the ears in the place are open; but when he comes to the application of it, the people have become listless; they like the bait very well, but not the hook; they like the adornment of the tale, but not the point of the moral. This is poor work. The plan is, if you possibly can manage it, so to get the bait on the hook that they cannot suck it off, but must take the hook and all. Do take care, dear friends, when you teach children or grown-up people, that you do not arrange the anecdotes in such a way that they can sort them out, as boys pick the plums from their cakes, or else you will amuse, but not benefit.

Then your tackle is in good trim, it is very pleasant to feel the fish biting, but it is quite the reverse to watch by the hour, and to have no sign. Then patience has her perfect work. It is very encouraging to feel that a large creature of some sort is tugging away at the other end of your line. Up with him at once! It is better still to have two hooks, and to pull up two fish at a time, as one of our friends did. To do this twice every minute, or as fast as ever you can throw the line, is best of all. What an excitement! Nobody grows tired, and the day is hardly long enough. Up with them! In with the lines! What, another bite? Quick! Quick! We seem to be all among a shoal. The basket is soon filled. This is good fishing. Our great Lord sometimes guides his ministers to the right kind of bait, and to the right spot for the fish, and they take so many that they have hardly time to attend to each case, but in joyful haste receive the converts by the score, and fill the boat. It is grand fishing when the fish flock around you, but it does not happen all the day long, nor yet all the days of the week, nor yet all the weeks of the year, else would there be a great rush for the fishers' trade.

When amateurs are at sea, and the fish do not bite, they have nothing to do but to give over, and amuse themselves in some other way; but it must not be so with us, to whom fishing for souls is a lifework and a vocation; we must persevere, whether we have present success or not. At times, we have to spend many a weary hour with our line, and never feel a bite; but we must not, therefore, go to sleep, for it would be a pity for the angler to lose a fish by negligence. Draw the line in every now and then, look to the hooks, try a new bait, or go to the other side of the vessel, and cast your tackle into another place. Do not be disappointed because you do not always fish as you did once; have patience, and your hour will come.

Our captain, one evening, when we were in a very lovely bay, came up to me, and said, 'Look at this; I only just threw the line over the side, and this fine cod has taken the bait in a minute.' A cod is noted for the thorough manner in which it swallows the bait. Being of a hungry nature, it is not in a picking humour, but feeds heartily. I remarked, at the time, that the cod was like earnest hearers who are hungering for divine grace, and so greedily snatch at the Sacred Word. Hungering and thirsting, their souls faint within them; and when the promise of the gospel is placed before them, they seize it directly. Tell them of Jesus and full deliverance through his precious blood, they do not make two bites of the gracious message – they dash at it, and they are not content till they have it, and it holds them fast. Oh, for more of such hearers!

All fish are not of this kind, for some of them are cautious to the last degree. The author of 'The Sea Fisherman' introduces us to an old salt, who says of the Conger eel, 'he don't bite home, sir', that is to say, he does not take the hook if he can help it. In the instance referred to, it had stolen the bait six times, and yet was not captured. Alas! we have an abundance of hearers of this kind, who are interested but not impressed, or impressed but not converted; 'they don't bite home', and we fear they never will.

This fishing with a line is a suggestive subject, but I must leave it to say a word about fishing with the net, a mode of fishing to which our Saviour makes more numerous allusions than to angling with a hook.

When we came home, on the Monday, after visiting Rothesay we cast anchor in the Holy Loch. My friend said to me, 'Look at the fish. Just look at them out there, they are leaping up on all sides; and there are the men, let us go and see what they are getting.' We were soon in a boat pulling towards them, while all around us were the fish leaping in the air and splashing back into the water. We reached the fishers, who were just getting out the net. I suppose you all know how this is done. A certain number of men remained near the shore with one end of the net, while others in a boat encompassed a great circle of water, letting out the net as they went along. Thus they enclosed a large space, and the salmon within that area were fairly imprisoned. When all was ready, the fishers began to pull at both ends, so as to make the circle smaller and smaller. We followed the decreasing ring, and kept just outside the edge of the net. The fish, which had still been leaping all around us, now began to do so in great earnest, for those within the range of the net seemed to know that they were in an undesirable position, and strove to leap out of it. Some escaped, but many more failed in the attempt. The men kept pulling in, and then it became very exciting, for it was evident that the net was full of life.

Here is a very good picture of what we should do as a church. I am to go out on the Sabbath with the net, the grand old gospel net, and it is my business to let it out, and encompass the thousands who fill the Tabernacle; then, on Monday night, at the prayer meeting, we must all join in pulling in the big net, and looking after the fish. So we bring to land all that have been caught. Many, who were surrounded by the net during the sermon, will jump out before we secure them; but, still, it is a comfort that it is not every fish that knows how to get out of the gospel net. Some of them will be in a rage, and bite at the nets; but they will only be the more surely held prisoners. To me, it was a very pleasant sight to see within the net a mass of living, twisting and struggling salmon-trout, most of them fine fish. There were thirty-seven large fish taken at one haul. Oh, that we may often succeed in taking men in larger numbers still! Let us drag in the net tonight. Let us pray the Lord to bless the services of last Lord's day, and recompense the fisher's toil.

We must never be satisfied till we lift sinners out of their native element. That destroys fish, but it saves souls. We long to be the means of lifting sinners out of the water of sin to lay them in the boat at the feet of Jesus. To this end, we must enclose them as in a net; we must shut them up under the law, and surround them with the gospel, so that there is no getting out, but they must be captives unto Christ. We must net them with entreaties, encircle them with invitations and entangle them with prayers. We cannot let them go away to perish in their sin, we must land them at the Saviour's feet. This is our design, but we need help from above to accomplish it; we require our Lord's direction to know where to cast the net, and the Spirit's helping of our infirmity that we may know how to do it. May the Lord teach us to profit, and may we return from our fishing, bringing our fish with us! Amen.

24

'Trespassers Beware!'

In proclaiming the gospel, we endeavour to set forth both its fullness and its freeness. We put up no hedge, fence or barrier; we raise no question, and utter no prohibition; for the invitation runs thus, 'Whosoever will, let him take the water of life freely.' We sometimes meet with the opposite of this in the world without, and the contrast serves to enhance our idea of divine liberality. This afternoon, I saw a large board, conspicuously lettered and elaborately printed, which bore the following inscription: 'Trespassers Will Be Prosecuted. No Dogs Allowed in These Waters.'

The 'waters' were a little, miserable, stagnant pond, green with duckweed, and the estate into which no trespassers were allowed to enter was about half an acre of what would have been a meadow if the grass had not been too much trodden down. I was cheered by the reflection that the dogs of the neighbourhood must have been highly intelligent, and that there was no need for the School Board in that region; for, of course, it would have been no use to put up the notice, 'No dogs allowed in these waters', unless the dogs could read. I have before heard of learned pigs, but reading dogs are even more an evidence of the culture of the district. The exclusiveness of the notice is not altogether new; but being placed so prominently, it struck my attention.

Frequently, we are warned that 'trespassers will be prosecuted'; but there is no sentence of the gospel which breathes such a spirit. You cannot trespass there, for the rule is, 'Whosoever will, let him come.' You may come to the richest banquets of the gospel; you may walk up and down through all the length and breadth of the land of promise, but you shall never be questioned as to your right to be there, for the Lord says, 'him that cometh to me I will in no wise cast out'. An open door is set before us which no man can shut, and we may enter freely. I know an hotel, in a Continental town, in front of which there is a fine garden, and at the gate you may read this notice, 'Strangers not residing at this hotel are invited to enter and enjoy the garden at all times.' Now that is generous, and deserves all praise; it is indeed after the manner of the gospel; enter and enjoy yourselves. 'Hearken diligently unto me, and eat ye that which is good, and let your soul delight itself in fatness.' 'Come in, thou blessed of the LORD, wherefore standest thou without?'

The Lord draws men to him with the cords of a man, and with the bands of love; but he never did drive a soul from him yet, and he never will. So long as this dispensation of grace shall last, no trespassers can ever be found on the domain of grace, for all who come are invited guests. The Queen permits certain favoured persons to drive through her private park, but the Lord sets the gate of mercy open to all comers, and gives all believers a golden key which will admit them at all hours to his own palace. Who then will refuse to come?

The board also said, 'No dogs allowed in these waters.' But no such intimation is given concerning the living waters of divine grace, for the poorest dog of a sinner that ever lived may come to drink, and swim, and wash here. No doubt it is advisable to keep dogs out of little shallow pools, for the water would soon become defiled, and the cattle would refuse it; but we do not need to preserve a great river, and no one cares to put up a notice informing the dogs that they may not wash in the sea, because there is no fear whatever that, however many dogs may come, they will ever pollute old Father Thames or defile the boundless sea. Where there is infinite abundance, there may well be unlimited freeness. The vilest dog of a sinner that ever ate the crumbs which fell from the Master's table is invited to plunge into the river of the water of life, which is clear as crystal still, though thousands of uncircumcised and defiled lips have drunk of it, and myriads of foul souls have been washed whiter than snow in its streams.

'Come and welcome, come and welcome' is the note which sounds from Calvary, from the wounds of the expiring Saviour, yea, it sweetly comes upon mine ear from the lips of the glorified

Christ, who sits at the right hand of the Father. 'Let him that is athirst come. And whosoever will, let him take the water of life freely.' No one can be an intruder when the call is so unconditional; and whoever tries to keep any sinner back is doing the devil's work. They are trespassers who keep away from Jesus, and not those who come to him. Some are afraid that they would be presumptuous should they believe on the Lord Jesus, but presumption lies in the opposite direction: it is the worst of presumption to dare to question the love of God, the efficacy of the blood of atonement and the saving power of the Redeemer. Cease from such proud questionings, and trust in Jesus.

> Come, hither bring thy boding fears,
> thy aching heart, thy bursting tears;
> 'Tis mercy's voice salutes thine ears;
> O trembling sinner, come!

25

The Silent Steamroller

Did you observe, last Sunday, a notice at the bottom of a street, at the back of this Tabernacle, warning us in large letters against a terrible monster? Thus ran the oracle: 'Beware of The Steam-Roller.'

I always feel inclined to turn down a side street when I see the red flag and that admonitory sentence; for useful as the steamroller certainly is, I cannot persuade horses to believe that it is their true friend. On this particular occasion, there was no cause to fear the steam-breathing, coal-consuming leviathan, for its fire was out, its steam was a thing of yesterday, and the creature rested in perfect quiet, under cover of a tarpaulin. It is quite right that even engines should have their Sabbath.

I thought, as I passed it, a steamroller at work is the pattern of what a church ought to be; but this particular steamroller is a type of what many churches are. A church should be 'terrible as an army with banners'; but, oftentimes, it is not. 'Beware of The Steam-Roller!' seemed rather a humorous notice, under the circumstances. Why, a kitten need not be afraid of the huge machine, or its big wheels, when the fire is out. Satan, who is said to tremble at the sight of a single praying man, might laugh in the presence of some of our churches, for there is no fear of their doing any harm to his kingdom. We must have the steam up if we are to crush the granite, and prepare a highway for our God. The weight of our numbers, and the excellence of our machinery, will go for nothing unless the inward fires are glowing, turning lukewarmness into heat, and impelling every wheel to strong, all-subduing motion.

The steamroller could do nothing without the stoker, and his coals and fire; and a church can do nothing if love, and fervour,

and enthusiasm are not produced in it. It is my longing desire
that we may ever be filled with the divine energy. I see in our
congregations, and in our societies, the altar and the wood; but
what sacrifice can we offer to the Lord if we lack fire? One of the
great uses of a prayer meeting is to keep the fires burning. By
earnest pleadings, we heap on the fuel; and the Holy Spirit comes
to us as a heavenly wind, and makes the fire burn vehemently.
There may be wildfire about, and, if so, I deplore it; but as far
as my observation and experience have gone, I am more afraid
of the want of fire than of the excess of it. The majority of our
brethren are in no danger of becoming fanatical; the danger
lies in the opposite direction: they are more likely to have their
boilers cold, and their wheels rusted, than to burst with excess
of force, or fly to pieces with perilous velocity. At any rate, let us
cry for the fire tonight.

At the same time, we must not be satisfied with heat; for
a steamroller needs weight, or it will accomplish no useful end.
As a church, we need sound doctrine; or else our ministries
will be mere sound and nothing more. We need to be taught by
God ourselves that we may be able to teach others. Go ahead,
my young and fervent brethren; but, as you run, mind that you
have a message to carry, or to what end will you run? You must
have something to tell the people, and real instruction to impart
to them, or your zeal will be 'much ado about nothing'. If you
gather the people together, or call at their houses, or talk to them
individually, you must have precious truth to impart. Clouds are
well enough; but clouds without rain are disappointing.

Any mother will tell you that it is a very bad thing for a baby
to suck an empty bottle; if it gets no food from the bottle, it
sucks down a deal of wind, and does itself hurt. Beware of giving
an empty bottle to those whom you desire to benefit. I am afraid
that, in many exciting meetings, there is more clatter of plates,
and rattling of knives and forks, than anything else. Men may
bawl and stamp, but if they do not teach the gospel, they are
doing no more good than acrobats in a circus. The babes of
Christ need the unadulterated milk of the Word, that they may
grow thereby; and if they do not get it, they will starve, even
though you try to amuse them with rattles and corals. I will
accord you great liberty as to how you shall say it, but there
must be something in what you say. Why, in certain Evangelical

meetings, if you listen to one address, you have heard all that you are likely to hear if you wait for half a century. Under a prosy minister, a little boy once turned to his father, and said, 'Father, what are we all sitting here for?' And a similar question might be asked when earnest ignorance repeats its commonplaces till they are as well known as the street cry of 'scissors to grind'.

We must have something to communicate, or we shall be like a gun which has plenty of powder in it, but no shot; we shall make a great noise, but produce no result. Better to teach the simplest truth with great quietness than to make a great fuss and teach nothing. The steamroller needs the fire; but if it were itself light as a feather, however fast it moved, it would never crush down the stones, and prepare the highway. Be solid as well as earnest, instructive as well as impassioned.

I am thankful to say that among us, as a church, this state of things is largely realised; our most zealous brethren are the most attached to the old, old gospel; they are as enthusiastic as the Salvation Army, and as true to the old faith as the staunchest of Calvinists.

Often, when I get letters concerning our evangelists, Fullerton and Smith, I meet with the remark, 'Your brethren preach the truth as fully as if they were pastors, and yet they exhort the people with all the freeness of evangelists.' This is what I desire: I would see the doctrine of the Calvinist associated with the fire of the Methodist and the holiness of the Puritan. I thank God that you, my brethren, know the difference between thunder and lightning, between beating a drum and breaking a heart. Make all the stir you please, but do not forget that claptrap has nothing in it, and that shouting is not grace. The gospel truth which is communicated is the true means of blessing, and not the excitement which may go with it. Dust will rise as an express train rushes along the metals, but the dust is not what the traveller admires, or the engineer depends upon. By all means give us truth red-hot, but mind that it is truth, or you cannot expect the Lord to bless it. Let us all be anxious to know more and more of Christ personally, and to be filled more and more with the divine Spirit, without whose aid all our teaching will be in vain. Unless we are made partakers of the fiery energy of the Holy Ghost, the best instruction we can give will be cold, and lifeless, and powerless to affect the hearts of men.

As for me, I beg a special interest in your prayers that I may be sustained in the tremendous work to which I am called. A minister must be upheld by his people's prayers, or what can he do? When a diver is on the sea bottom, he depends upon the pumps above, which send him down the air. Pump away, brethren, while I am seeking for my Lord's lost money among the timbers of this old wreck. I feel the fresh air coming in at every stroke of your prayer-pump; but if you stop your supplications, I shall perish. When a fireman climbs upon the roof with the hose, he can do nothing if the water is not driven up into it. Here I stand, pointing my hose at the burning mass. Send up the water, brethren! Send up a continual supply! What will be the use of my standing here with an empty hose? Every man to the pump! Let each one do better still, let him turn on the main. The reservoir is in heaven; every saint is a turncock; use your keys, and give me a plentiful supply. What I ask for myself, I seek for every true minister of Christ. Let not one be left to himself. We all cry with one voice, 'Brethren, pray for us.'

Thus, with a church with its steam up, sowers with their baskets filled with precious seed, and officers of the Lord's army supported by a valiant soldiery, all things will be ordered as they should be, and we shall see greater things than these. Only let our dependence be wholly fixed upon the Lord our God; and because it is so at this moment, let us pray.

26

The Steamroller
and the
Stone-Roller

Dear friends, each saved one must try to serve his God according to his calling, position and ability. Our powers vary greatly, and our modes of action must vary also; but each one ought to do his very best, and he should try to raise that best to something better. The largest capacities are none too large for our holy service. If we could each gain ten talents, our Lord would deserve ten times as many. The Lord Jesus is such a good Master that he deserves to have good servants, and to receive perfect service. Oh, that I could honour him with a thousand voices, and continue to extol him through a thousand lives! It may be that some of us will never be able to gain any remarkable degree of mind or influence; well, then, we must use what capacity we have. Whatever our work may be, we must throw our whole energy into it, and let it stand as a pattern of how work can be thoroughly done; and then, whether large or small, it will be acceptable. It is astonishing how much zeal and perseverance can accomplish with very little ability; and even if there be not much in quantity, the little may be so fine in quality as to be very precious. He who carves ivory does not expect to fill so large a space as if his tools were used upon wood.

As I came to this service, I met an old acquaintance, for whom I have a respect almost amounting to dread; for my horse is too much impressed by him; I mean the steamroller. He is the friend of all who travel upon wheels, and deserves first place among public benefactors. Rough roads, which make your ride like a voyage upon a stormy sea, are transformed into smoothness by this giant's power. When a long stretch of road has been broken up with picks, it is then covered with bits of granite which are all sharp edge and pointed corner, and every step becomes painful both to horse and rider. With the help of the water-cart, our weighty friend comes in, and makes the rough places smooth. It is wonderful how every unruly stone subsides into order as soon as the roller appears. It does its work grandly, with a steady, immovable determination which mortal men might envy.

If ever I were, or could be, a steamroller upon the road to heaven, crushing down those stones, which now hinder travellers, I am afraid I might become proud of my own prowess, and therefore I will not covet so hazardous an office; but yet I would earnestly desire and eagerly seek after all the force and ability that may be within my reach, that I may employ them for my Lord and his people. We may all ask that the power of Christ may rest upon us, that out of weakness we may be made strong: strong in the Lord, and in the power of his might. Of such power, the steamroller may be a type; for all the impediments which lie in its way are most effectually overcome, and used to make its road better. The very things which look like difficulties are treated as instruments for the accomplishment of its design: granite stones are the material which the steamroller subdues to its purpose. If a man receives great grace from on high, and the Lord endues him with much of his Holy Spirit, what work he can do for Christ!

But there may be much mental and moral force, and it may remain unused. If God has made you capable of being a steamroller, I hope you will set the fire alight, and keep the steam up, and be ready for constant work. But it is not so in every case; those who could do much, and should even do most, often do the least. Many men have ability, but there is no 'go' in them; there is plenty of roller, but no steam; plenty of weight, but no driving power. Many a preacher is heavy; oh, that we could put force into him, and set him to work! What is learning if a man will not teach? What is the profoundest knowledge of theology if there be no love to souls? What is the use of that young man's biblical information if he merely reads and studies for himself? Grace to make us zealous in the Lord's cause must abound in us, or else our weight will create responsibility for ourselves, but it will have no salutary influence upon other minds and hearts. It is a small matter for a pitcher to be full, if nothing can be poured from it to slake the thirst of the fainting. It is well to have the talents, but it is better to trade with them for the Master.

To my big brothers, comparable to the steamroller, I offer earnest entreaties that they will consecrate every ounce of their power, and use it diligently. Oh, how much we need the help of all men of light and leading! Forcible characters are not so plentiful among us that we can afford to let one of them waste his energies. Indeed, my brothers, we are surrounded by so many feeble folk who need assistance but can render little efficient aid in return, that our work is rendered hard from the want of capable and sagacious workers. May God send us a legion of strong men; but may he fill them to the full with his grace! My district would be all the better for a few more steamrollers: I find plenty of stones in my road, and I have need of all the force I can enlist in preparing a highway for our God.

We cannot expect all of you to be steamrollers; perhaps it is not needful that you should be. If all ships were ironclads, or huge frigates, how would shallow rivers be navigated? If all were learned and cultured, simple folk might never hear a plain sermon.

At Mentone, I have seen another kind of roller used on the road. The remembrance of it amuses me much. Often as I have seen it, it has never failed to make me smile. In the mending of roads in the South of France, things are done in a special manner; it wears the appearance of an endeavour to employ the largest number of men, and to give each one as little fatigue as possible. It is a fine country for going about work in a deliberate fashion. There is a bit of road to be mended, and it is done in detail, patch by patch; those who undertake too much at once may fail in their endeavours. A man picks the road over just a little, but he does not wear himself out with rash haste; he thinks between each stroke, and thus he performs his important office with wisdom and judgement. Having disturbed that little bit of road, of about the size of a doormat, or possibly of a small Turkey carpet, another man comes along with a little water-cart, which he draws himself by the help of a hard-working comrade who pushes behind. Inasmuch as it would be a pity for one man to do the work that might be done by two, or which might do itself, the water is not allowed to flow out from the cart, through an arrangement of a pipe with holes in it; but a tap is turned, and a watering-pot is filled, and a rose is put upon it, and the section of road is thus moistened with tender discretion, as if it were a bed of tulips. Another hard-working person now appears on the scene with a barrow-load of stones, a discreet load, such as may be pushed along without breaking one's back. You imagine that these stones will be shot down; but you are in too much of a hurry; they do things so much better in France. A small basket is provided, and a large shovel; the stones are shovelled into the basket, and then carefully deposited upon the prepared ground. A barrow of earth is also fetched, measured into the basket, and daintily used to mix with and cover the stones, even as a cook puts a crust over her gooseberries and makes a pie.

It is quite beautiful to observe these children of toil when occupied with their sore travail; they may well be a terror to British workmen, and make them dread competition with them! We should all mend our ways; but should we not do it with care, and thought, and deliberation? So our French brethren rightly judge. Now comes in our roller, after a little discreet touching-up of the stones and earth with a rake.

The beauty of the whole concern to me lies in this stone-roller. It is a roller similar to that which any one gardener would cheerfully drag over our gravel paths; but this roller has a horse to move it to and fro. I confess it is a very old horse, and that you may tell all his bones; but still it is a horse, and a big horse for so little a roller. An excellent man led the horse with care over the difficulties of the selected portion of road. He fastened the traces to the roller and gently led the horse to the end of the little bit of road; then he took off the ropes, and hooked them on to the other side of the roller, and walked the steed back again, and so on, with persevering continuance. It is a beautiful instance of how the thing should be done in order to utilise a large quantity of unexhausting labour for which the payers of taxes may give a bountiful reward.

Here, however, is the point of the whole affair; when I rode over roads which had been dealt with in this fashion, I invariably found that they were effectually mended. The old-fashioned method produced first-rate results. It took a good while to do; but when the work was done, it was well done; and complaint turned into good-humoured criticism.

It struck me that I knew certain friends who do their work for God very calmly and deliberately, and with as little of push as the old man and the old horse and the stone-roller at Mentone get through their labours, and yet what they perform will bear inspection, is of a lasting character, and wears well. It is therefore no business of mine to find fault, but, on the contrary, to commend; and if I smile, it shall be in all good fellowship. So far from disturbing our quiet, steady workers, I wish we had thousands more of them. Brother, let not the rush and worry of this boastful age disturb you. Move more quickly, if you can; but if not, be not distressed by the criticisms of the flippant. If you cannot be a steamroller, and should happen to be more like a common stone-roller, keep on steadily at your work, and roll well the little bit of road that you travel.

It may be, you could do nothing if you quitted your own ways and methods; don't quit them, but stick to ways by which you have done good work. Don't try to wear Saul's armour, nor even Solomon's robes. Only do your work conscientiously, prayerfully and with faith in God, and somebody will yet say, 'Well, it was a slow business; but it was a sure one.' Have we not often seen workers do a great deal which has all ended in nothing? What a noise and fuss they have made! The papers have been ablaze with their mighty deeds; and yet we have passed that way, and the spreading bay-tree has vanished, not a leaf has remained. The bulk of us may never be more than humble plodders; but let it be our resolve that we will do good sound work by the help of God's Holy Spirit.

Better that one soul should be savingly converted than that hundreds should crowd the enquiry-rooms, and turn out to be only excitable persons, temporarily wrought upon, but not brought to Jesus in spirit and in truth. Better one yard of wall built with gold, silver and precious stones than a mile of wood, hay and stubble.

While speaking to those who are saved, I remember sadly that some of my hearers cannot do anything for the Saviour. Who are they? Those who are bedridden? Ah! they can speak of Christ upon their beds. Those that have but one talent? They can use that one talent for the Lord. A little candle may give great light. But who are the useless ones? They are such as are not yet alive from the dead, those who have not yet come to Jesus. How can they do anything for Jesus, or even attempt it? Your first business, my friend, is to find the Lord yourself, and yield yourself to him, that he may give you a new heart and a right spirit. Then may you go forth, and serve him. In one of the letters brought to me this evening, asking for our prayers, the writer says, 'If God will but hear me, I will tell everybody of his goodness.' Is not that the resolve of each one who has tasted that the Lord is gracious? Do not all believers cry, 'Taste and see that the Lord is good'?

27

Two Common Dangers

Two great dangers are common in the streets of the City of Vanity in which we are called upon to sojourn for a season. If we were to shut ourselves up within doors, and never go abroad, we might possibly avoid one of these dangers; but we should certainly fall into the other. The two perils are those of getting harm from others, and doing mischief to others; the latter we can fall into by doing nothing at all; possibly, we may, in this way, occasion more mischief than by mistaken activity. These dangers are equally great, and equally imminent, unless we are strictly upon our guard. Happy is that man who shall reach heaven unharmed and harmless, having neither gotten nor given a wound.

Illustrations sometimes come in our way, and demand a hearing. I have lately been instructed by two parables which have met me on the road and compelled me to learn from them whether I would or not. I cannot refrain from telling them to you.

As I rode home, the other evening, I had like to have fallen a victim to the Drink Traffic in a very literal sense. A loaded dray came thundering along the road with its freight of barrels. It was hard to tell which side of the way it would take, and certainly there was nothing to be done but to yield it the road without dispute. As it was very much upon the wrong side, there was nothing better for my driver to do than to get on the path, and shout, in the hope of arousing the attention of the Jehu in command. No such person was visible; there was no Jehu to say, 'Gee-woah!' Nevertheless, the sensible horses steered more nearly to the centre of the road; and as they went by at a great rate, we saw that they were their own masters. We escaped that peril, and were thankful. Their driver was refreshing himself at the next public house; and his poor steeds, having waited patiently till they felt the cold night air, were making the best of their way home, to the serious peril of her Majesty's subjects.

There are a great many runaway teams upon the road of life in these evil days; indeed, it was always so in the best of times. If we would not be run down by transgressors of one sort or another, we shall have need to be always on the watch. One cannot go into the street, the shop or the workroom, without being exposed to more or less of risk. Immense damage may befall us through the evil deeds or wicked words of unregenerate men and women. Satan assails us through our fellows. He has his apostles, evangelists and ministers everywhere; nor is he without his house-to-house visitors and tract distributors. With great noise or with none, the drays and chariots of the evil one rush along the road, and will soon run us down unless we get out of their way. This is so difficult a task that when we have prayed, 'Lead us not into temptation', we are bidden to add, 'but deliver us from evil'; for the most careful avoidance of evil will not suffice to prevent our being in peril.

The devil does not keep to his own side of the road, but drives in where we least expect him. When the sons of God came together, did not Satan come also among them? Yes, he is not omnipresent – that none can be but the Lord himself – but it is very hard to tell where he is not. 'Watch and pray, that ye enter not into temptation.' We are careful not to go into harm's way. In places where sin is open and rife, we are never found; but we must watch even in the safest places lest, in an hour when we are not aware, we should be battered and bruised by some mighty evil.

The second peril is that of doing harm to others. This would be sadness indeed. If we are run into by others, we must bear the damage, and in due time we shall get over it; but if we were to cause grievous harm to another, how could we bear the painful reflection? A sensitive mind would be driven into the depths of misery by considering the injury which it had unwittingly inflicted. Now it happened to me that almost my next journey to London was on the Bank Holiday; and, alas! there were on that day sadly abundant signs of the dominion of John Barleycorn in the open streets. An intoxicated man fell from the pavement full upon his back. It was an ugly fall for the back of his head; but, by the good providence of God, a worse evil was averted. We were passing at that instant; and, as I looked out of the carriage window, I saw that a few inches further would have laid that drunken cranium, or the neck of the beery one, right under our wheel. Had we passed over his prostrate body, we could not have helped it, for his fall was altogether unexpected; but what a horrible event for us as well as for the poor tippler! I would very much have preferred an accident to myself.

It is not easy to avoid injuring others, and you may do it when you are where you have a right to be, and when you would gladly empty your purse to avoid it. I rejoiced exceedingly to have escaped this second peril. I think I was more glad on this occasion than on the former one. To injure another is worse by far than being injured ourselves. It is always painful for me to cause the least pain to those around me, or indeed to anyone.

On the highway of life, such minor accidents as treading upon people's corns are very common to me; I have been doing it rather much of late, without the slightest intention of so doing. I shall have to buy a pair of list slippers, and muffle my oratorical feet in them; for I fear my boots must have rather heavy soles, since people complain of their weight even when I think I am tripping very lightly. I hope the crushed corns will soon forgive me.

It is worse when there is somewhat in our example which becomes an unavoidable but real injury to others. Though we may not be aware of it at the time, we make a sad discovery when we find out, in after days, that what we did without a thought was turned to sad account by some young observer, and made the occasion of evil. We did not, at the time, look around for all the consequences of our act, neither did we foresee what would be sure to be made of it; and so the deed was done, and a wound inflicted which we would give our eyes to cure, but cannot. We may yet have to make very humiliating discoveries of the evils wrought inadvertently by us. Who among us can hope to be quite clear? A look of vexation, or a word coldly spoken, or a little help thoughtlessly withheld, may produce long issues of regret. This should warn us to walk circumspectly both in the present and in the future, and go carefully in and out among men. He who has to deal with young lambs, or little children, has great need to guard his movements.

I see that great objection has been taken to my warning you not to be partakers of other men's sins by setting an example in the matter of drink, which it would be unsafe for others to follow. I thought that I put the case very temperately. I neither said nor implied that it was sinful to drink wine; nay, I said that, in and by itself, this might be done without blame. But I remarked that if I knew that another would be led to take it by my example, and this would lead him on to further drinking, and even to intoxication, then I would not touch it. I did not urge abstinence as a duty to one's self, as I might have done; but I gently placed it on the footing of concern for the welfare of others. I thought every Christian man would agree to this. I did not make it a matter of law, but of love. I set forth no doctrine of salvation by meats and drinks, and I laid no ban upon the exercise of your liberty. I did, however, entreat you not to endanger others by an inexpedient use of things lawful. It was saying no more than Paul meant when he said, 'If meat make my brother to offend, I will eat no meat while the world standeth.' This has made some brethren very angry; but, in truth, I see no cause. May I not express my opinion? Are they so insecure in their own position that they are afraid to have it challenged, even in the gentlest manner? I sincerely hope that this is the case.

One friend asks, 'Are we to give up shaving because people may cut their throats with razors?' To which I answer that, if I had an insane friend in my house, who was likely to commit suicide, I would far rather leave my beard alone than put a razor in his way. If I knew of even one poor friend who had cut his throat with my razor, I should hate the sight of it, and I would make sure that no second person should be tempted to destruction by any razor of mine. It would be an awful memory to have carelessly contributed to a suicide, and it would be still worse to have aided in ruining a soul by strong drink.

The same friend enquires, 'If I am a skater myself, must I keep off the ice because my skating would induce another to come upon the ice, who might fall down?' This also is not a difficult question. If my skating caused no further mischief than a tumble or two to those inexpert in the exercise, I should not feel called upon to abstain; for the only result would be an increase of merriment, with a possible bruise or two which would soon be gone. But if I saw legs broken, spines injured and lives lost,

I should never forgive myself if I enticed a single person into such peril. But the subject under consideration is no child's play. The falls in this case are not such as boys may get upon a slide. Oh, that they were such harmless casualties! The skating which is now under consideration is performed on a more dangerous element than frozen water; it causes jeopardy to character, to position, to eternal well-being, and it is not for Christians to speak lightly of it. When I think of the poverty, misery and crime which are caused by drunkenness, I can see no parallel between these things and healthy sport upon the ice. It may seem trivial to some; but to those who come in daily contact with the evil, it is a solemn business.

Brethren, let us have all our eyes open, that in the highway of life we neither suffer injury from others nor inflict injury upon them unawares.

28

A Little Sermon from the Painter's Brazier

I saw a painter doing up the posts of a gate which led into a gen-tleman's grounds. The paint was very foul, so the workman had a brazier, filled with glowing coals, which he held close to the paint, to burn it off. His aim was to paint the posts, and he be-gan his work by scorching them with hot coals. He was no sim-pleton, but knew his business well; and he knew that before he could put on fresh paint he must first burn off the old paint, or else the work would be badly done.

Seeing that painter at work, I said to myself, 'That man is doing what the Lord has often done to me'; and it is what he may be doing to some of you who are now suffering greatly in the process. You have been seeking the Lord, and you had hoped that you would be con-verted, and enter into peace at once; instead of which, the sermons you have heard have made you feel worse and worse. You are more troubled now than when you began in earnest to seek salvation. It is all right; the old paint is being burned off. Your self-righteousness and self-sufficiency are being destroyed, and you are keenly feeling the fire of the Lord's wrath against sin burning into your very soul.

If the old self had been left, the colour of grace could never have soaked into your mind: the old stuff would have kept it out; you would have taken a mere film of grace, and soon the old rubbish of nature would have appeared through the new colour of grace. The more completely the old paint is burned off, the better will the new work stand; and it is for this reason that the Holy Spirit is to you a Spirit of judgement, and a Spirit of burning, before he works for your renewal. See this, and understand the wisdom and loving-kindness of the Lord.

A similar process goes on with godly people, as well as with the unconverted. Your spiritual beauty gets old with the wear and tear of life; you lose your freshness, you get into a mouldy and defiled condition; for this is a damp and smoky atmosphere in which you stand, even the best of you. Then the Lord comes to you, to restore your soul, and give you the renewing of the Holy Ghost. In order to do this, he removes the old comeliness, and turns your beauty into corruption. There is nothing like the burning process for really, effectually preparing the way for a fair and abiding renewal.

No mill has yet been invented for grinding old people young again; but if ever it should be invented, the old man will have to be crushed very small, and broken into the finest powder. I am afraid that most of us would steal away rather than endure the grinding. But yet the crushing is the only sure way to the restoring; we must die daily that we may fully enter into life. By the gate of death, multitudes of saints find their way into heaven; and by a deeper death to sin and self, we rise more fully into an experimental enjoyment of newness of life.

Some of us owe a great deal to the brazier of glowing coals, for this is a chief instrument in the process by which we renew our freshness. Our youth is renewed like the eagle's, and the eagle renews its youth by moulting; it loses its glorious feathers, and seems worn and haggard, and then newer, fresher and brighter plumage covers it. The ways of the Lord are only strange to inexperience; faith sees how perfectly natural they are.

Learn, also, another lesson from the brazier. I said to a friend, as we looked at the painter burning off the old paint, 'That is what the devil tries to do with me; he endeavours to burn the doctrines of grace and the old Evangelic faith out of me.' Ah, friends! the hot brazier of ridicule and unkindness has been laid very close to my soul! But the attempt is not successful; for those truths, in my case, are not paint, and so they cannot be burnt off. The Gospel is in the very grain of my soul. Even the devil himself cannot burn off that which is part and parcel of myself, my life, my all. When the doctrines of the Word are taught us by God the Holy Ghost, and made to tincture and season our inmost life-blood, no burning process can take them from us, or cause us to give them up. That which is in the grain of the wood becomes more apparent the more deeply the plane cuts its way. My belief in the Gospel of the grace of God, and especially in the doctrine of our Lord's substitution, is no veneer; but is in me and of me. I live upon this truth, and by God's help I could die sooner than renounce it. The true child of God does not hold truth so much as truth holds him; it cannot be taken away from him, for he cannot be taken away from it. All the power of fire or water, time or eternity, life or death can never separate us from the love of God which is in Christ Jesus our Lord, nor take away from us the blessed truth which he has engraved upon our hearts. This, then, is our little sermon from the painter's brazier.

29

A Life-Belt for Daily Use

Somebody wrote in the newspaper, immediately after one of our great passenger steamers had gone down, that it was a very advisable thing that everybody who went on board a ship should wear a life-belt. He suggested that we should have the apparatus affixed to us, so that, just as we felt the ship sinking, all we should have to do would be to float away from the vessel until we were picked up. It did seem to me to be about the last thing that mortal man would ever attempt to do; but the proposal was a very natural one, and in a spiritual sense, and for the highest purposes, it may suggest an equipment which would be exceedingly wise.

If we always went about with life-belts around us, we should look very awkward, and they would be often in our way in following the ordinary business of life if we walked or rode on dry land prepared for swimming or floating; but suppose there could be a life-belt invented which would make our ordinary garments more comfortable, which would be of use to us while on the land as well as in the water, which would give ease to us while we were sitting in the pew, and which would positively put strength into us while walking, as well as help us to float instead of sinking, which would be useful to the housewife in the kitchen, to the merchant at his desk, to the ploughman in the field and to the workman in the shop; suppose there were such a life-belt as that, every one of us would want to have it on, and would never want to put it off.

Now it so happens that, if we would be prepared to die, that preparation will not in the least degree interfere with the duties of this life; but our best preparation for the life that now is will be that which prepares us for the life that is to come. If we were to be immortal on earth, and never see death, the very best thing that we could do in order to live a happy, useful, successful life would be, first of all, to be reconciled to God, and to receive from him a new heart, and a right spirit, by which we should be enabled to live in a way which would be acceptable with him. Now, dear friends, you know how needful it is to be prepared to die; but ought it not to commend that solemn consideration to your soul that the very thing which fits us to die is that without which we are not fit to live?

'Are you prepared to die?' is thought to be a very solemn enquiry, and so it is; but, 'Are you prepared to live?' is quite as solemn a question, if a man would weigh it by the light of eternity. If my believing in Jesus unto eternal salvation would make me miserable in this life, it would be worthwhile believing and being miserable through this little mortal span in order to inherit eternal life, would it not? When we once pass into the eternal state, how the ages of time will dwindle into nothing! But, beloved, believing in Jesus will not make you miserable, it is the path of happiness and bliss. To believe in Christ is to be unloaded of a terrible burden, and to have your heart filled with a sweet serenity. So there is a double advantage in believing; the result would be worth the having if it brought us a lifetime of misery; but it will not have that effect, for it will bring us present as well as perpetual joy. As we often sing:

> Tis religion that can give
> Sweetest pleasures while we live;
> 'Tis religion must supply
> Solid comfort when we die.
>
> After death its joys will be
> Lasting as eternity:
> Be the living God my Friend,
> Then my bliss shall never end.

Suppose that, from this time forth, if you became a Christian, you had to be always poor, always sick, always baffled, always afflicted, it would be worth all that, it would be worthwhile suffering anything of which a human being is capable, to be eternally saved, and to have the joy of dwelling at the right hand of God for ever; but if you believe in Jesus Christ, it will not necessarily deprive you of anything that is really worth having; indeed, there are many who have proved that, although the great gain of godliness is in the world to come, yet even here it has brought them untold blessedness. I remember the story of an old man and his wife who were once called upon for a subscription to the Bible Society, or some other good work. The old lady said they had lost so much by their religion that they had no money to spare. The old gentleman said, 'Yes, we have lost a great deal. I used to have a suit of clothes all ragged and greasy and filthy, and I never could get another suit because I was a drunkard; and you know, Mary, that by my religion I lost my old ragged clothes. I used to be out till late at night, and then came home drunk, and very often through fighting I brought with me a pair of black eyes; I lost all that by my religion. I also had a nose that began to show the effect of drinking; and I lost that fine rosy tint, you know, Mary. That is only a small part of what we have lost by religion; and I think we can well afford to give a good subscription.'

Lost by religion! Why, where would some of you have been but for the grace of God? Where does a course of drunkenness and vice lead men? Where does even morality lead many? They have the chilly moonlight of self-satisfaction; but, in the hour of trouble, they have not the warm sunshine of the Lord's love and grace to cheer them. Yes, although our brightest joys are yet to be revealed, God has been pleased to attach many temporal blessings to the yielding up of ourselves by faith in his dear Son. Who, then, would not be a Christian?

'There are drawbacks,' says one. 'If we are Christians, we shall get ridiculed and laughed at.' I think I have had a tolerable share of that sort of thing; but it has not hurt me, I have not had a bone in my body broken through it, and I have not been robbed of an hour's sleep by it. Dr Watts said:

Let dogs delight to bark and bite,

and I think we have come to that pass, and can say the same with regard to ridicule for Christ's sake; that is a very small matter.

'Oh! but it is at home that we are so cruelly persecuted,' says somebody. Yes, I know that is a very severe trial, and yet it produces most blessed results. If your persecution were to cease, it might be the worst thing that could happen to you. I knew right well a young man, in a good station in life, a believer, apparently a very earnest believer, and the most indefatigable worker I ever met. He was constantly opposed at home on account of his religion, yet he never yielded an inch, but kept on earnestly working for Christ. The opposition is all gone, and he has a house of his own; but I do not see any earnestness in him now, it disappeared as soon as the persecution ceased.

Some of us are very much like those gas bags that we have when we are exhibiting dissolving views; we put heavy weights on them to press out the gas so that we may have a more brilliant light. I do believe that most of our troubles at home and abroad are just like the weights on the oxygen bags. I am not disposed to wish that every young Christian should have a smooth path, for I notice that the bravest believers are often those who have had the severest struggles to maintain their integrity. 'It is good for a man that he bear the yoke in his youth.' If you have too much fine weather, you will be like some gardeners' plants that grow too fast; they never get much heart, they had too much sun at the first, they would have been all the better for a little early nipping. You know that celery is not really good till it has had a sharp frost on it, and there are some Christians who seem all the better for a little persecution or trial; it seems to pinch them back; and, at the same time, it sends a sweetness into the very heart of their religion. If you ask me, 'Do you like to hear of our being opposed?' I answer, 'No, I do not; but I would not take this burden off you if I could, for it is best that you should have at least a little of it to bear.'

To be truly saved, to be a Christian, to be on Christ's side, to know that you have an everlasting Saviour is worth a great many fools' laughs, is it not? You can bear to let all the asses bray at once and yet not be troubled if you know that you have Christ, and eternal life in him. My dear young friends, I do pray that you may be led to weigh and estimate these things, and that you may be drawn by the divine Spirit to say, 'Jesus shall be mine, I will trust myself to him whatever the consequences may be.' You will never come to Christ unless you feel your need of him, unless you are convinced that you are really sinners, and confess it in penitence before God; but if the Lord has made you realise your true condition, come and welcome the Saviour who died for the guilty; stand not back through shame or fear; the great gates of divine mercy are set wide open that all sinners who believe in Jesus may come through them, and enter the Kingdom of heaven, 'For God so loved the world, that he gave his only begotten Son, that whosoever believeth in him should not perish, but have everlasting life.'

Then, dear friends, having trusted Christ for yourselves, remember that all whom you meet with need to hear about the Saviour who has delivered you. I have known some good earnest Christian people who have hardly known when to stop talking about religion, and some of them have at times spoken very indiscreetly. Well, well, I had rather hear of a hundred such indiscretions than that you should be indifferent to the welfare of the souls around you. Never you mind about being called 'imprudent' now and then; there is nobody worth a button with the shank off who has not been imprudent sometimes; there is no one who has ever done anything for Christ who has not been lacking in discretion in the judgements of other people. They have been so prudent that they never spoke to anybody about Christ; they have been so prudent that they never lived as Christians should live; they have been so prudent with their saving faith that they have saved all their money, and not given any to the cause of Christ; they have been so prudent that, when they came to die, they had seriously to raise the question whether they were Christians at all; and they have been so prudent that, when they were dead, their friends did not know what to say of them, but they hoped that the Lord would see some sign of grace in them, although nobody had ever seen it while they were alive.

For my own part, I do not wish to be the chip in the porridge; and I hope you will be something that has a flavour in it, and show it by speaking to others of what you yourselves have experienced. There are some things that have flavour in them, but it is never known until they are boiled or bruised; and there are some Christians whose excellence is not revealed till they are persecuted. Therefore, do not shrink from the fiery trial that may await you; but look up to your Lord for grace sufficient in the trying hour, and go joyfully forward singing:

If on my face for thy dear name,
Shame and reproaches be,
All hail reproach, and welcome shame,
If thou remember me.

30

The Eye, an Emblem of Faith

Dear friends, before we return to the holy exercise of prayer, in which we will spend most of our time this evening, I want to say just a few words to you so as to put the Gospel before you all once more, very simply and plainly. My subject will be:

THE EYE, AN EMBLEM OF FAITH;

and, singularly enough, I have an illustration of my theme, and a very painful one, too, in my own eye. I mean that expression quite literally; I do not know what it is, but a little something or other has found a lodging in my eye, and it causes me much pain. I shall not mind the suffering if some of you learn the lesson that it has already taught to me.

I was thinking that the eye is the type and symbol and emblem of faith. Nobody in his right senses wishes to have anything in his eye; he wants his eye to be, just as an eye should be, without anything at all in it, but bright, and strong, and clear: and that is precisely what we want our faith to be; bright, and strong, and clear; with nothing in it, so that we may just simply look away to Christ, and be saved.

My eye does not see itself; I cannot see my own eye unless I stand before a looking-glass. There are some people who are always wanting to see their own faith, but that is not the right thing to look at or to look for; you might as well desire to take out your eyes to examine their structure and uses. No, no, the object on which your faith rests and relies, that upon which your salvation depends, is not your faith, but what your faith sees. Do not try to see your own eye; look through your eye, as the window of your body, and gaze at the object you desire to see;

and just in that fashion use your faith in a spiritual sense. Jesus Christ is the sinner's Saviour, and faith is simply the eye that looks to him. Oh, that you would, dear hearer, look unto him now at this moment, for:

> There is life for a look at the Crucified One;
> There is life at this moment for thee;
> Then look, sinner; look unto him, and be saved;
> Unto him who was nail'd to the tree.

Do not think so much about your faith as about the Christ at whom you are by faith looking. Do not wish to have anything in your eye; if you do get anything in, it will have to come out, for it cannot help you to see, and will probably cause you much pain and suffering. 'Oh!' says one, 'I wish I had a tear in my eye; I do want to feel repentance.' Yes, my dear friend, but tears do not help a person to see; on the contrary, they hinder a clear sight of the object before him. Your business is not to look at your own repentance, but at Christ. Looking at Christ alone, you will repent aright; but looking at your repentance, you will not.

I recollect a striking expression in that precious book by Thomas Wilcocks which I have often mentioned to you, *A Choice Drop of Honey from the Rock Christ Jesus*. There is some such expression as this in it: 'When thou art seeking Christ, if thou dost look to thy repentance, away with thy repentance; for if thy repentance come into the place of Christ, it is a repentance that will need to be repented of.' So I say to you, dear friends, do not even wish to have a tear in your eye as a part of the means by which you hope to be able to see Jesus as your Saviour. Remember what we so often sing:

> Could my tears for ever flow,
> All for sin could not atone:
> Thou must save, and thou alone.

'Oh, but!' says another, 'I wish I had more feelings.' It is a curious thing that, very often, those persons who feel the most are the very ones who think that they do not feel at all. One says, 'I am in an agony because I cannot feel.' Surely, that 'agony' is a plain proof of very acute feeling. Another says, 'I am quite brokenhearted because I have got a heart of stone.' No heart of stone ever feels itself to be broken; yet it is true that they who feel most, feel that they do not feel at all; their cry is:

> If aught is felt, 'tis only pain
> To find I cannot feel ...

Yet that is feeling, and no mistake. You need not wish to have feelings, dear friends; they are like this bit of dust, or whatever it is that I have in my eye; far better out than in.

You have nothing to do with anything else but Christ as the ground and object of your faith. Remember the epitome of the Gospel which Paul wrote to the Corinthians: 'I delivered unto you first of all that which I also received, how that Christ died for our sins according to the Scriptures.' The apostle Peter put it with equal clearness: 'Who his own self bare our sins in his own body on the tree.' If you mix up anything of your own, your feelings, or your tears, with Christ, you do dishonour to him. Will you stitch your filthy rags on to the glistening robe of his stainless righteousness? Far be it from any one of us to attempt such a thing. Go and yoke a gnat with one of the cherubim, and see how they will work together; but never seek to join Christ and yourself in trying to do the work that he has completely and for ever finished. Why, it would be an impertinence akin to profanity! Shake thyself clear of everything like trust in what thou art or canst be.

You may have seen a balloon ready to ascend into cloudland; and, perhaps, as you gazed upon it, you have asked yourself, 'Why does it not go up? The supply of gas is furnished, the voyagers are in the car, everything appears ready; why does it not go up?' The attendants have cut most of the ropes; but there the balloon hangs because there is one rope that still holds it to the earth, and it is not until they cut the last one that away it bounds off towards heaven. That is what you need to do. Perhaps you have a little goodness of your own, a little something to which you think you can trust. Well, if so, you must cut that rope, and all others; for you must get rid of anything and everything upon which you can rely for salvation except Jesus Christ, the only Saviour. 'He hath made him to be sin for us, who knew no sin; that we might be made the righteousness of God in him.' 'Christ is all.' 'Ye are complete in him.' 'Perfect in Christ Jesus.' 'Who of God is made unto us wisdom, and righteousness, and sanctification, and redemption.' This is the teaching of the Scriptures. You cannot have Christ, and mix him up with something else; you must have 'JESUS only'.

I wonder whether this little thing in my eye will be remembered by some of you, whether you will say, 'I must have my eye single, and clear; I must look right out of it to Christ.' You know, if a person is in good health, he does not think about his eyes. You may ride a thousand miles in a train, and as long as your eye is all right, you do not think anything about it; and the less you think about your faith, the better; and the more you think about Christ, the better; for, after all, what is your faith by itself? Apart from Christ, there would be nothing to believe in, and therefore there would be no faith; and really to believe in Christ Jesus, to trust in him, if we ever weigh it in comparison with Christ himself, what is it? Then, away, away, away from all thou hast, and all thou art, and look alone to Jesus Christ, thy Lord and Saviour, for again I remind you that

It is not thy tears of repentance or prayers,
But the blood that atones for the soul:
On him, then, who shed it, believing at once
thy weight of iniquities roll.

31

'Nothing to Say'

Dear friends, when I stood up, a few minutes ago, and tried to think what I should say to you, I discovered that I had –

NOTHING TO SAY.

I have often found the theme for a brief address while meeting with you here on these happy Monday evenings, and my experience tonight has suggested a subject on which I think we may profitably meditate for a few moments, and then return to the holy exercise of prayer, in which we always like to spend most of the time. Perhaps some of you are wondering whether I ever before felt that I had 'nothing to say'.

Yes, more than once in my life has this been true; and, first, it was very specially the case with me when I was under conviction of sin. Through the Lord's restraining grace, and the holy influence of my early home-life, both at my father's and my grandfather's, I was kept from certain outward forms of sin in which others indulged; and, sometimes, when I began to take stock of myself, I really thought I was quite a respectable lad, and might have been half inclined to boast that I was not like other boys: untruthful, dishonest, disobedient, swearing, Sabbath-breaking and so on. But, all of a sudden, I met Moses, carrying in his hand the law of God; and as he looked at me, he seemed to search me through and through with his eyes of fire. He bade me read 'God's Ten Words' – the Ten Commandments – and as I read them, and remembered what I had been taught about their spiritual meaning as interpreted by the Lord Jesus Christ, they all seemed to join in accusing and condemning me in the sight of the thrice-holy Jehovah. Then, like Daniel, 'my comeliness was turned in me into corruption, and I retained no strength'; and I understood what Paul meant when he wrote, 'Now we know that what things soever the law saith, it saith to them who are under the law: that every mouth may be stopped, and all the world may become guilty before God.'

When I saw myself as guilty before God, I could say nothing in self-defence, or by way of excuse or extenuation. I confessed my transgression in solemn silence unto the Lord; but I could speak no word of self-justification, or apology, for I felt that I was verily guilty of grievous sins against the Holy One of Israel. I remember that it was a dreadful silence that reigned within my spirit at that time; even if I had tried to say a word in my own favour, I should have been self-condemned as a liar. I felt that Job's words might be applied to me, 'If I wash myself in snow-water, and make my hands never so clean; yet shalt thou plunge me in the ditch, and mine own clothes shall abhor me. For he is not a man, as I am, that I should answer him.' So I said nothing, when I was under conviction of sin, because I had 'nothing to say'.

I will tell you another time when I had 'nothing to say', and that was when I first saw the Lord Jesus Christ as my Saviour and realised the meaning of John Newton's hymn:

> I saw One hanging on a tree,
> In agonies and blood,
> Who fix'd his languid eyes on me,
> As near his cross I stood.
> Sure never till my latest breath
> Can I forget that look;
> It seem'd to charge me with his death,
> Though not a word he spoke.
> My conscience felt and owned the guilt,
> And plunged me in despair;
> I saw my sins his blood had spilt,
> And help'd to nail him there.

> * * *

> A second look he gave, which said,
> 'I freely all forgive;
> This blood is for thy ransom paid,
> I die that thou mayest live.

I remember well how he told me that he had loved me with an everlasting love, and that he had given himself up to die for me. I can never forget his wondrous words, nor the effect they produced upon me; I wanted to shout, 'Hallelujah!' I wanted to borrow all the angels' harps, and to set all heaven ringing with my Saviour's praise; I wanted all the stars to speak in his honour, and every voice in heaven and earth to be jubilant with thanksgiving unto him who had done such great things for me; and failing all that, I could only sit down, and weep to the praise of the mercy I had found.

It was not long, however, before I began to tell others of my Lord's great love to me; and now I can truly say to him:

> E'er since by faith I saw the stream
> thy flowing wounds supply,
> Redeeming love has been my theme,
> And shall be till I die.

Ay, that it shall as long as I have a tongue to speak; but tell it all out, I never shall; and, sometimes, under a sense of his great goodness to me, I can sing, with good John Berridge:

> Then my tongue would fain express
> All his love and loveliness;
> But I lisp, and falter forth
> Broken words, not half his worth.
> Vex'd, I try and try again,
> Still my efforts all are vain:
> Living tongues are dumb at best,
> We must die to speak of Christ.

It must be so, my brethren; to speak of Christ as he deserves is quite impossible while we are in this imperfect state.

I hope that none of you will ever be in the condition of having 'nothing to say' in the presence of God the Judge of all. Recollect the man who came in to the marriage of the King's Son without putting on a wedding garment; and when the King came in to see the guests, he said to him, 'Friend, how camest thou in hither not having a wedding garment? And he was speechless.' O you who hear the gospel but do not receive it; you who join us in the outward act of devotion, yet do not yield yourselves to the Lord Jesus Christ; especially you who prefer the rags of your own righteousness to the perfect robe of the righteousness of Christ, you will not be able to say a word in self-defence! Shame will tie your tongues, conscience will prevent your utterance of a single syllable; and the King will say unto his servants, 'Bind him hand and foot, and take him away, and cast him into outer darkness; there shall be weeping and gnashing of teeth'; and you will be driven from his presence for ever. O my hearers, do not let it be so with any of you! May the Holy Spirit work in you, even now, repentance towards God and faith in our Lord Jesus Christ! God grant it, for Christ's sake! Amen.

32

Fasting and Backsliding

Dear friends, I asked you specially to pray, just now, for those who are backsliding, for those who are declining by little and little from the ways of God, that eternal mercy may stop them, and bring them to a better and happier condition.

You have noticed in the papers, lately, an account of a fasting man; and I am afraid there are some people who are doing spiritually what that foolish fellow is trying to do physically; he is seeking to find out how long he can fast; I think he is going to see whether he can live for forty days without eating. I do not recommend any of you to follow his example; and it strikes me that, if I did, you would not be likely to try it; there are not sufficient fools in the world to make such an experiment as that practicable on a very large scale. God has made it a law of our being that we should eat in order to live; but this stupid man means to ascertain how long he can violate that law, and still live.

I have known some professing Christians who seemed to be trying to see how long they could live without eating spiritually. Prayer is neglected, the reading of the Scriptures is forgotten, attendance upon the means of grace is very much slackened; and as for coming out to a weeknight service, that is given up altogether. If they are not quite going without all spiritual food, yet they are trying to find out on how little they can exist. If they try the experiment long enough, they will be like a valuable horse that a Frenchman had, which managed to live on next to nothing. He had at last brought the poor creature's allowance down to one straw a day, and then the experiment failed, for the animal died. Some professors have got down to one service on the Sunday as their spiritual food for the whole week, and we have not been greatly surprised when their poor form of religion has died altogether. They tried how little their souls could live upon, and there is an awful risk in such an experiment as that.

Now, first of all, the man who tries to live without food denies himself a natural pleasure. Whatever may be said about eating for the nourishment of the body, this is certainly true concerning spiritual food; for, to feed upon the Word is a great delight to the heart, to feed upon Christ is a heavenly banquet. You felt it to be so once, did you not? Then, you must be out of health if you do not enjoy your spiritual food now. If you cannot eat, you take it as a sure token that there is something wrong with you. The psalmist speaks of 'fools' whose 'soul abhorreth all manner of meat'; and he significantly adds, 'and they draw near unto the gates of death'. God grant that we may not be such fools in a spiritual sense!

We are not surprised to learn that the fasting man is gradually losing weight. That might not be so great a calamity to anyone who is overburdened with flesh as I am, but it is a serious thing for most people to be losing weight; and if you do not have spiritual food, you will certainly lose weight in many ways. You will lose weight of moral character; you will lose weight of influence; you will lose the weight of solidity and restfulness of mind; you will lose power in prayer; you will lose force in every direction; and, if you do not actually die, you will get to be a living skeleton.

I know some professors who, if they are Christians at all, are nothing but skeletons; they are a bony kind of people, very bad to run against, for they bore holes in you. The moment you come into contact with them, they begin to bore you about modes of worship, or about the Second Advent, or about high Calvinism, or about low Arminianism, or anything else which is their special craze. They have lost weight, they have lost enjoyment, they have lost all pleasure in religion and they become uncomfortable people to associate with, for they are very apt to make others as miserable as they are themselves.

That fasting man is also losing strength. He has no vigour, he could not run up a hill, he can do very little now; and, soon, he will not be able to do anything at all if his foolish experiment be continued. As for the man who does not feed spiritually, what can he do? What can be done by those professors who do not take spiritual food? Go and get a number of consumptives from Brompton Hospital, and say to them, 'Come along, you poor weak-kneed creatures, we are going to make a railway cutting. Here are the planks, and the picks, and the shovels; so set to work, and get the cutting made as fast as you can.' They stand still, or lie about on the ground, and you say to them, 'Why do you not get to work?' They cannot do it, poor things! One of them tries to lift his pick, but it is as much as he can do simply to lift it; he could never use such a tool as that. Another takes hold of his spade, and puts his foot on it, but there is no force in him; so we say to the whole lot of them, 'You had better go back to the hospital.' Now bring us a dozen stalwart navvies, tell them what you want done, give them the picks, and the shovels, and the planks; see there, they seem to walk through the hill, they have tunnelled it as if they had simply threaded a needle! So, let a man have spiritual force through feeding on the wondrous bread that Jesus Christ gives to our souls, and all things are possible to him; but let him go without his spiritual meat, and then what is there that he can accomplish?

PART 4

Miscellaneous Addresses

33

Preaching to Sinners

We shall always, I trust, as a church, cultivate an anxious desire for the conversion of all who come within our gates: yea, and of all who dwell around us. Never, I hope, will you wish the Pastor to preach so that you shall be fed, careless as to whether sinners are saved or not; nor will you make yourselves into a snug corporation for purposes of profit and mutual admiration. We long to see the wedding furnished with guests, and our Redeemer seeing of the travail of his soul. The public ministry must not be confined to a part of the truth, for it should reflect the whole counsel of God as far as mortal mind can do so. It is my delight to preach the doctrine of election, and all the other grand teachings which declare Jehovah's special love to his chosen; but, at the same time, I have felt it to be my duty to preach the gospel to every creature. We know no other limit to our invitation than this, 'Whosoever will, let him take the water of life freely.' 'Ho, every one that thirsteth, come ye to the waters, and he that hath no money; come ye, buy, and eat; yea, come, buy wine and milk without money and without price.'

I have been amused, lately, with a story told me by a dear fellow labourer in the gospel. One of his church-members came to him, and said that she was going to unite herself with another church, a church higher in doctrine, and less given to evangelistic efforts. She said, 'When you preach the doctrines of grace, I am very happy; but when I hear you inviting sinners to Christ, my heart goes down into my shoes.' 'That is a very sad thing,' said the minister, 'but I cannot alter my preaching on that account, for I think you are wrong.' When our brother met his people at the prayer meeting in the evening, he told them what had occurred,

and said, 'I cannot help preaching to sinners as I do; and even if
more of you go, it will be the same. I shall preach to sinners as
long as there are any sinners left.' Our friend then went on to
say that the mode of preaching among certain friends reminded
him of his schoolboy days. A boy had a nice, rosy-cheeked apple,
which he tossed up in the air before our friend's eyes, and then he
shouted to him, 'Do you see this apple?' ' Yes.' ' Well; now, take
a good look at it,' replied the boy, 'for that is your share of it'; and
he put it back into his pocket. Another playmate pretended to be
more generous, and said, 'Oh, give the poor fellow a smell!' Even
his liberality went no further. Have you never heard preaching
of that sort? 'Here is a precious salvation! I hope you sinners see
how precious it is, for that is your share of it.' The minister puts
the heavenly fruit back again into his pocket, and the sermon is
over; and this is called free grace! The most liberal of those who
dare not invite the sinner try to give him a smell of the gospel by
telling him of the peace and joy which it brings.

Now, when I am preaching to sinners, I feel inclined always
to beg every one of them to put the golden apple in his pocket,
for this choice fruit of the tree of life may belong to millions, and
yet the whole of it will remain for millions more. There is not
a sinner in the world who is to be told that he may not come to
Jesus, and receive the whole of the blessings of the gospel. What
a blessing to have a free salvation to preach as well as a full salvation! At least, I feel it to be so. Everyone must speak according to
his light; but while I see clearly the doctrines of distinguishing
grace, I see also the universality of the gospel command.

Many years ago, I had a good old friend, who, like myself,
had a very sweet tooth for Calvinistic doctrine; and I cannot do
with any other doctrine any more than he could. He said to me,
one day, 'I love to hear you preach the doctrines of grace, but
I feel very uncomfortable when you are giving free invitations
to sinners; I feel as if I could not sit in the place.' I said to him,
'Well, shall I give up inviting sinners in order to please you?'
'No,' he replied 'by no manner of means; for, a month or two ago,
my son-in-law, about whom I was very anxious, went to hear
your sermon, and you were very persuasive with sinners, and set
Christ before them most freely. I did not enjoy it at all; but when
I got home, I found my son-in-law in tears, and that sermon, by
the blessing of the eternal Spirit, brought him to the Saviour.

Therefore, I think you had better go on in your own style, and not alter your preaching to please a poor old man like me.'

I answered, 'That is just how I feel; I would gladly agree with you in everything, but I dare not try to appear consistent by leaving out one side of the truth.' He said to me afterwards, 'If I do not quite agree with your invitations to sinners, it is clear that God blesses them; and therefore I must look into the matter, and see whether I am right or not. You have declared the doctrines of grace, yet you have freely given the invitations of the gospel; and I hope, my dear sir, you will long continue to preach what you feel you have learned in your own soul.' I have followed his advice, and I hope to do the same as long as the Lord spares me. We shall proclaim the doctrine of God's sovereignty without toning it down, and electing love without any stuttering over it; but we shall proclaim the other truth also.

Those who differ from us, in one direction, ought also to remember that there are others who differ from us on the other side. A sister has written to me saying that, even if I do believe in election, she would not have me preach it, but keep it in my own mind, and get comfort from it for myself. I do not know who the friend is, for she forgot to put her name to her letter; but I would like her to know that I cannot accept her idea for a moment. I feel sure she does not expect me to do as she says; for, if I did, I should act like a Jesuit; I should say one thing and believe another, and that be far from me! I hope that no earthly power could bring me to do that: no, not even an anonymous letter from a good lady!

Everything that I believe to be in God's Word, I shall preach, whether my hearers accept it or not. It is to me a great comfort that such numbers do receive my teaching; and I never feel surprised when I meet with those who do not. I do not expect everybody to eat everything that I put on the table. I may flavour a dish with too much salt or too much pepper at times, but your own prayerful judgements will guide your tastes. We must preach all the truth; and this one thing is certain, we shall never give up loving the souls of men, or cease from trying to bring in the lost from the highways and hedges. We shall, throughout life, echo that blessed call of our Lord Jesus, 'Come unto me, all ye that labour and are heavy laden, and I will give you rest.' Labourers and burden-bearers shall hear continually that gracious

Word; and if they do not come to Jesus, their blood shall be upon their own heads, for the invitation is as free as the blessing is full. The gospel trumpet rings out clearly over hill and dale. 'The Spirit and the bride say, Come. And let him that heareth say, Come. And let him that is athirst come. And whosoever will, let him take the water of life freely.' We cannot make men come; that is the work of the Holy Spirit; but we can persuade them, by the love of Jesus, and by the terrors of the Lord. We can preach Christ to sinners if we cannot preach sinners to Christ; and we know that the Lord's Word shall not return unto him void.

34

A Full Christ for
Empty Sinners and Saints

That was a very neat way of putting the matter when someone spoke of 'a rich Christ for poor sinners and saints'. I think I might put another expression side by side with it, which would be equally good as descriptive of our experience of Christ's preciousness. It is this:

A FULL CHRIST FOR EMPTY SINNERS AND SAINTS.

There is emptiness in the sinner's heart, apart from the guilt which makes his heart worse than empty; and the believer, day by day, as much depends upon the continued grace of God as at the first, when, full of guilt, and covered with shame, he came to Christ for pardon.

So, first, let me speak a word or two about a full Christ for empty sinners. Are you empty, brothers, tonight? Then Christ's fullness is precisely what you want, and your emptiness is precisely what Christ is looking for; and when the two meet, then, as our brother just now said in his prayer, the right things are in the right place. Where could your emptiness be in a more suitable place than where Christ fills it? Where could Christ's fullness be more useful than in filling up the emptiness of a poor guilty sinner?

'Alas!' says one, 'I do not feel my emptiness.' Then, my friend, you are one of the very empty ones, because you have not even a sense of emptiness to fill you. I generally find that those who think they do not feel their sinfulness are those who feel it most; and if anybody were to say, 'I do sufficiently feel the burden of sin', I think I should tell him that he did not know anything at all about it. Fully to feel the burden of sin is utterly overwhelming;

and no man ever thinks he repents enough, or, if he does so think, it is evidence that he has not really repented at all of his sins.

> Could my zeal no respite know,
> Could my tears for ever flow

none of these would be as fitting or as full an expression as we need to denote all the repentance that we ought to feel because of sin.

'I am afraid,' says one, 'I have no good thing in me at all.' Then, my brother, you are another of the empty ones. 'But, oh, I am afraid to hope that I am such an one!' Then you seem to be even empty of hope and of courage. Well, well, you are empty indeed. 'I have sometimes thought that, if I could feel despair, then, strange to say, I could have some hope; but I have not even that feeling.' Well, friend, I see that you are empty. If I search you through and through, even with a candle, there is not a good thing, nor a rag of a good thing, to be found in you.

But what then? This only proves what an empty sinner you are; and there is a full Christ for all empty sinners. Only let them be but empty, and the Master is ready enough to fill them. Confess your emptiness, acknowledge that in you dwelleth no good thing; and ask him, according to the infinitude of his mercy, the multitude of his tender mercies, to fill you, even you. I am sure that the moment when we are accepted in Christ is the moment when we realise our need of Christ, and yield up our emptiness to be filled from his fullness. We generally get Christ, I think, when we acknowledge ourselves to be the very lowest and most unworthy of men. He that is bankrupt and beggared of all consciousness of creature merit, and of all human hope, is the man to whom the riches of the covenant of grace most surely belong.

> Tis perfect poverty alone,
> That sets the soul at large;
> While we can call one mite our own,
> We have no full discharge.

The Lord bring us down to realise what we are in his sight, to be in our apprehension what we are in fact, 'less than nothing, and vanity'!

But, dear hearers, whilst I have spoken these few words about your emptiness, I beg you to think much of the fullness of Christ. You are full of sin; well, but he is full of mercy. You are full of guilt; he is full of atoning merit. You are full of hardness of heart; he is full of long-suffering and tenderness towards you. You are full of mistakes; he is full of wisdom. You are empty of all power; he is full of might. Though you have nothing, he has everything. The mercy is that, just in those very points where you fail, Christ excels; and his merits just fit your demerits as the key fits the wards of the lock. Christ was prepared on purpose for such an one as you are! His character and his work precisely meet the needs of your sad and fallen condition.

Now, if you want Christ because you are empty, and Christ wants you because he is full, who forbids the banns when it is proposed that you two should be united? There is a tree laden with beautiful fruit; it is late in the autumn, and the apples are all of a red and yellow colour. They are all ready to be gathered; what, then, is wanted? Why, they want baskets. And what kind of baskets? 'See,' says one, 'there is a basketful here.' That is no use at all. Another says, 'Here is another full basket.' But that is of no use. What that tree wants, with its mellow fruit, is that somebody should bring empty baskets. Now there is Jesus Christ, the Tree of life, laden with the ripe fruits of his abundant grace. What does he want? Why, not you who are already full; no, but you who are like empty baskets, you who have need of Christ's glorious fruit of life. He wants you, and you want him. Now, who is here, I say again, to forbid the banns, when Christ loves sinners, and sinners want him?

But where is the ring? How shall we effect the marriage? The ring is faith. If thou wilt simply trust Christ Jesus, thou art saved. Persons sometimes say, 'What! am I to believe such-and-such a thing in order to be saved?' No, that is not the point; you are not saved by believing in things; it is not believing even doctrine that saves you; it is trusting a Person, relying upon Christ Jesus; and if you trust in him, your faith is the wedding ring which espouses you unto the Lord Jesus for ever. The marriage may be now performed in this very place, by the power of the Holy Ghost.

Now, secondly, I want to say a word or two about a full Christ for empty saints. I do not think we know much about Christ yet – at any rate, we who are but beginners in the things of God.

Some of our elder brethren may know more; but I think I know enough to say that, probably, he knows most of Christ who has discovered most of his own emptiness: that, in proportion as we go down, Christ goes up; and as we see more and more of the deep depravity of our own hearts, we shall see more and more of the amazing excellence of the person and work of our Lord Jesus Christ.

Now, how is a Christian made to feel himself an empty saint? Well, there are many ways. Some of us, at certain times, have been made to be empty of our own wills. Now, you who have had an invalid child, or a sick husband, or an ailing wife, or beloved sister, you have prayed and wrestled with strong crying and tears to God; and night and day you have carried your burden, and of course it has been very heavy. At last, you have been brought to this point: 'Lord, I see there is self here; I have wanted to have my own way'; and the Holy Ghost has brought you to say, 'Not my will, but thine be done.' It has taken a long time, perhaps, to bring you to that point; but, at last, you have laid self-will right down at the Lord's feet, and you would have nothing more to do with it. You have said, 'Nay, Lord, I will not complain; I will scarcely express a desire; there is the whole case, do as thou wilt. I have told thee what nature suggests, and thou hast helped me now to play the man of grace rather than of nature. The decision rests with thee; do as thou wilt.'

Well, now, it is at such a time, when you are emptied of your own will, that you begin to see the fullness of Christ; for I am persuaded that our self-will is the cataract on the eye, which prevents the soul from having a clear view of Jesus; but if self-will is brought into subjection to Christ, and if it can be kept under his dominion, what a sweet and comforting sense of the love of Jesus we may always enjoy! We should have a fullness of joy in the will of God, if we were emptied of our own will. It would be sweet to us to be in pain, and we should rejoice even to be in sorrow, if our will were quite subdued to the will of God; and we could even kiss the rod with which he corrects us.

Another kind of emptiness is emptiness of all power. We, who are constantly engaged in the Lord's work, have to feel that emptiness pretty often. You feel as if you were quite unequal to that next sermon, or to meet that class, or to talk with those who are in affliction. You often feel, like Jonah, as if you would like to take ship, and be off to Tarshish. The work is sweet; but you do not seem to feel any capacity for the task. You go to it, and are very graciously helped; but you go home complaining, 'Who hath believed our report?' and are as disheartened as ever. Some of those whom you thought were converted have gone back; others, whom you fancied able to meet sorrow with unshaken faith, have not been able to stand firm in the time of trial; and you go home greatly discouraged and bowed down. Oh, it is then that Christ rises! There is nothing that forms such a suitable frame to set the picture of Christ in as a thoroughly broken-down spirit. Then we come to him, and feel that he is the great All-in-all, and we are poor nothings; then we run to him, and ask him to make our work acceptable through his own merits, to plead before his Father for us that our infirmities may be removed, or else that even these may make room for the greater display of the grace of God, and that we may bring even more glory to God because through such weak instruments he can do such great exploits. You never see the fullness of Jesus Christ as the omnipotent Saviour so well as when you are emptied of all power.

And let me also tell you that there are times, with believers, when they seem to be emptied even of all spiritual life. Of course, they never are so emptied, because, while Christ lives, they must live also; yet it appears to them sometimes as if they had quite lost their religion, and there was not a spark of vital godliness left in them. You may rake and stir the embers, and go down on your knees and blow; but you cannot find even a spark. You ought to be grateful to God for all his goodness; but you feel as if a great stone had been rolled over the door of your heart, and that it had been turned into a sepulchre. You have no light. You want to pray, you feel that you must pray; you cannot do without prayer; yet your prayers are 'groanings which cannot be uttered'. You feel as if they would burst the bonds of your soul; and yet you feel as if you did not feel at all. You say with Cowper:

> If aught is felt, 'tis only pain
> To find I cannot feel.

There are promises, but you cannot grip them; there are threatenings, but you do not feel their power. At such times, it is a blessed thing to remember that Christ 'is able also to save them to the uttermost that come unto God by him, seeing he ever liveth to make intercession for them'. Empty saints rejoice that Christ is the sinner's Saviour still. Often and often are we driven to Christ alone, as at the first. We are obliged to look up, for we feel that if we could not look up, it would be death to look within, for within there can be nought to comfort. It is in looking up to Jesus, looking away from self, and looking into the wounds of Christ, and reading his heart's love that we get comfort. To believe that I am saved when the graces of the Holy Spirit abound in my soul is no faith; that is only sight. But to believe in Christ when you cannot see any evidence, when sin abounds, and doubts and fears roll over you, to come even in the dark, and in your consciousness of natural depravity to say, 'Lord Jesus, I believe; over all this mountain of sin, from the dark pit of this iniquity, right here out of the depth of my soul's abasement, I cling to thy cross. Though I feel myself to be by nature as a very devil, only fit to be an outcast from thy mercy, and to be driven into the lowest hell, yet I do believe thou canst save me, and I cast myself on thee, and thee alone.' Then it is that the empty saint, like the empty sinner, finds a full Christ exactly suited to him.

As I was singing those verses, just now, my mind seemed to picture our Lord Jesus Christ, and I stood before him in medita-tion, and did sing, I hope, from my heart:

If ever I loved thee, my Jesus, 'tis now.

There I see him stand, clothed with a linen garment down to his feet, and girt about the paps with a golden girdle; and as I look at him, how he remains ever the same, and yet how he changes! One moment, there is a mitre on his head, and he is my Priest; and I see that breastplate hung with golden chains, and set with precious stones, and I rejoice that he is my blessed priestly Intercessor!

And then I look again, and behold there is a crown instead of a mitre. He is a King, and how truly royal does he appear: King over heaven and earth and hell, King of my soul, my bosom's Lord! Look at the silver sceptre, how he wields it! If he should smite with it, he could break the nations as the potter's vessel is broken with a rod of iron; but he stretches it out, and bids me touch it; 'Thou,' saith he to each believer, 'thou hast obtained favour of the Lord.'

Now I look again, and the crown is gone for a moment; and I see him with the Prophet's mantle about him. How wise he is!

What wisdom drops from those blessed lips! How I wish to sit down at his feet, and to be taught of him! He is the infallible and the good Teacher, who teaches the heart, while others teach but the head or the hand.

Now look at him, and, as you gaze, one moment you catch a glimpse of the nail-prints, and you worship him as the Lamb that was slain. And the next moment the nail-prints are gone, and you see him as Solomon saw him, 'his hands are as gold rings set with the beryl: his belly is as bright ivory overlaid with sapphires'. His glory shines forth now resplendent with heavenly brightness.

> No more the bloody spear,
> The cross and nails no more,
> For hell itself shakes at his name,
> And all the Heavens adore.

See him again, and for the moment, as you gaze upon him, your eyes are dazzled, the Godhead is so grand and so glorious; but you turn again, and the manhood is so soft, so sweet! If that Deity were alone, you might flee from it; but when you see it shining through the transparent glass of Christ's manhood, you are comforted, and you say, in the language of the Song of Solomon, 'Let him kiss me with the kisses of his mouth: for thy love is better than wine.'

Can you not see him now? Do you not behold him? The angels bow before him around the glassy sea; and the elders, with their vials full of odours, and their harps of gold, cast their crowns before the throne. Can ye not see him, as, at the right hand of the Father, 'God blessed for ever', Jesus, the Son of the Virgin, sits supreme, Son of God, and Son of man?

Our hearts exclaim, 'Blessed be thy name for ever; be thou exalted in the highest Heavens; worthy art thou, O dying Lamb; worthy, O risen Lord! Let all the angels of God worship thee, thou Well-beloved, the Only-begotten of the Father!'

And what shall we say next to him? Just this, 'Lord, reveal thyself to us. Come, now, and if our hearts be shut up, put in thine hand by the hole of the door, and our bowels shall be moved towards thee. If thou standest at the door, and knockest, Lord, by the sweet influence of thy grace, let the door be opened, and come in, and sup with us, and we with thee. We will find the empty house in our poor hearts, and thou shalt find the feast, and we will sup with thee, and thou shalt sup with us.'

Do you not long for his presence, my fellow believer? I know you do, if you are empty; for there is no such fullness or such satisfaction in all heaven beside as can be found in him, under whose shadow we sit with great delight when he brings us into his banqueting-house, and his banner over us is love.

Two things I want you to recollect, and I have done. One is, believer, that you are altogether Christ's: body, soul and spirit. Do not pilfer anything that belongs to your Lord; do not be a traitor to him, and do not dispute your Master's right to all that he has so dearly bought.

The next truth is that Christ is all yours, every part of him, his Godhead, and his manhood; his time-life, and his eternal existence; all his promises, all his offices, all his graces; all he bought on Calvary; all he scattered among his followers when he ascended to his Father; all he has laid by in the covenant stipulation; and all he is to be when he cometh in the glory of his Father, and all his holy angels with him. Till he comes, glory in the truth that he is wholly yours, and you are wholly his; and live 'to the praise of the glory of his grace, wherein he hath made us accepted in the Beloved'. God bless you all! Amen.

35

'Steal Away to Jesus'

Return! O wanderer, to thy home,
thy Father calls for thee;
No longer now an exile roam,
In guilt and misery.

Steal away, steal away, steal away to Jesus,
Steal away, steal away home; for Jesus waits to
save you.

Return! O wanderer, to thy home,
'Tis Jesus calls for thee;
The Spirit and the Bride say, Come;
Oh, now for refuge flee!

Return! O wanderer, to thy home,
'Tis madness to delay;
There are no pardons in the tomb,
And brief is mercy's day.

May those sweet words of invitation be very graciously blessed!
I was smiling, while you were singing that refrain, 'Steal away
to Jesus', at the recollection of something that happened a long
time since. A brother minister was, years ago, almost as eccentric
as I am said to be, though the peculiarity after all is not in us,
but in other people who are not so concentric as we are. After
an evangelistic service, we were holding a prayer meeting, or
a meeting for enquirers. Among the rest of the anxious ones,

there was a young man in whom we were both interested. I was kneeling on one side of him, and my friend knelt down on the other side of him, and prayed a prayer which made me laugh; I could not help it. He said, 'Lord, here is a poor sinner, who has been a servant of the devil, and he has run away from his master, and never given him any notice.'

I was amused by the expression at the time; but there is a great truth in it, and I want, just for a few moments, to call your attention to that truth, for it may be of lasting service to any of you who long to escape from the slavery of sin and Satan. First, let me remark that, if you give the devil notice, you will never get away from him. If that prodigal son had gone to the citizen in the far country, and said to him, 'I am engaged to you for another week to feed the swine, but I give you notice that, at the end of the week, I shall quit your service', he would never have gone back to his father. The only way of escape for him was to steal away home; so he not only said, 'I will arise and go to my father', but at once 'he arose, and came to his father'. Imitate his example. Do not give the devil any notice. This is the very meaning of the refrain, with which we have been familiar ever since we first heard it so pathetically sung by the Jubilee Singers:

Steal away to Jesus.

That simple sentence may be a very delightful voice to someone here who has been living a life of sin. Do not go back into the midst of your old companions; but steal away to Jesus; steal away home. Perhaps your life has been a very evil one, altogether contrary to the law of God; yet here you are tonight, in the house of prayer, and among a company of praying people. Now, I beseech you, do not say what you will do tomorrow, or in a month's time, or when you have set some matters right; but steal away to Jesus at once, just as the poor slave in the Southern States did when he found a chance of gaining his freedom. I warrant you that he did not go to his master, and say, 'I's goin' to run away from you tomorrow, massa.' Oh, dear, no! But on some moonshiny night, when his master least expected it, he was away in the woods, and was being guided by the blessed Pole Star to the land of liberty. I say to you again, imitate his example, steal away, steal away to Jesus, if you are held in bondage by sin and Satan; I cannot give you any better advice than that. Procrastination is not only the thief of time, but the murderer of many souls. Remember those verses we sometimes sing;

> Today, a pardoning God
> Will hear the suppliant pray;
> Today, a Saviour's cleansing blood
> Will wash thy guilt away.

> But grace, so dearly bought
> If yet thou wilt despise,
> thy fearful doom with vengeance fraught
> Will fill thee with surprise.

Then again, as to the idea of giving the devil notice, you cannot give it. Some try to give this notice by attempting to escape from the power of some one sin, when all the while they are in captivity to other sins as securely as ever. There is many a man who has meant to break off wrongdoing by degrees, and to loose himself from his fetters one by one; but he has not been able to do it; it can only be done all at once, straightaway, there and then. Sin is like Joseph's mistress; you must not parley with it, you must leave your garment, and run away; your only safety is in immediate flight. We say to you, as Mentor did to Telemaque, 'Fly, Telemaque, fly! Your only hope of conquering is by flight.' Oh! get away at once, poor sinner. Steal away, steal away to Jesus. Let us sing that second verse and the chorus again very softly:

> Return! O wanderer to thy home,
> 'Tis Jesus calls for thee;
> The Spirit and the Bride say, Come;
> Oh, now for refuge flee !
> Steal away, steal away, steal away to Jesus,
> Steal away, steal away home; for Jesus waits to save you.

Just this word in closing. You know that, in the old slave days, when one Negro wanted to run away from his master, there was often someone who told him the way. There were some good people who worked what they called 'The Underground Railway', by which they passed the slaves on from one place to another till they reached the land of liberty; so, tonight, there are many friends all about this Tabernacle who would be only too glad to speak to any of you who want to steal away to Jesus; and especially if you will come to the platform when the meeting is over, you will find some of my brethren who will be delighted to tell you how to get out of the great dismal swamp of sin. They know the road; some of them have hardly brushed the mud off their own garments yet, and they will be most pleased of all if they can guide you into freedom. The all-important thing is to get to Jesus. He is the great Liberator, and 'if the Son shall make you free, ye shall be free indeed'.

If any of you have found your way to Jesus, let me say to you that it is all very well to steal away from the old master, but do not steal up to the new one. Come right up to him, and say, 'thine I am, Lord Jesus, and I am not ashamed to own thee as my Lord and Master'. Come out boldly on the Lord's side, be baptised according to his command, and his example, too, and unite with his people in fellowship and holy service. If you are truly the Lord's, you will never want to steal away from him, and he will never give you up to your old master again, for so hath he declared:

> The soul that on Jesus hath lean'd for repose,
> I will not, I will not desert to his foes;
> That soul, though all hell should endeavour to shake,
> I'll never no never, no never forsake.

36

An Address to
Sunday School Teachers

Dear friends, the Sunday-school teachers, I hardly think that I need to tell you tonight how greatly we value your work, and how thankful we are to God for your holy zeal and Christian love. There are some of you who are our most continual helpers in the work of the Lord; the very sight of your faces always gives me pleasure, because I remember how many of the dear children and young people you have brought to the Saviour's feet. Go on, brothers and sisters, with your sacred service, and the Lord be with you!

I should like you to think, however, not only of the benefit that you bestow on others by this holy work, but also of the great good you yourselves receive by teaching. Will you try, just for a moment, in order that you may be humbled by gratitude, to think how much you have gained by teaching others? Speaking for myself, I can testify that I owe very much to the Sunday school. I never was in a Sunday school as a child; but that was because my mother thought she could be a better teacher than anybody else, and so she taught me at home, and I think she did right. But after I knew the Lord, I soon became a great debtor to the Sunday school, because it gave me an immediate and important field of labour, and it also helped very materially to prepare me for future service.

I could not do much for my Lord at first; but I thought that I could go and teach a class in the Sunday school, and I did so. Then, through teaching a class, I was asked to give addresses to the scholars. I do not think I had any idea that I could speak in public until I began to address the children; but God gave them such attention that I was asked to speak to them every Sunday.

Some of the teachers, some of the young men, thought it was
a pity that any one of their number should always be the speaker,
and therefore it was agreed that they should take the address
alternately with me. Then the superintendent divided the girls
from the boys, and I had to speak to the girls once a fortnight, and
to the boys on the intervening Sabbath, and thus I was kept at the
happy employment every Lord's day. To my surprise, before long
I found the end of the schoolroom filled with grown-up people;
and soon I had more to hear me in the afternoon than my pastor
had to preach to on a Sunday morning. I could not make it out;
but I did know that the opportunity of speaking was blessed.

One of my friends was telling me, the other day, that he
recollected an address of mine to the boys in the schoolroom at
Cambridge. He said that I told them a story about a fly on the
window. I told them that I was standing in a farmhouse, and
there saw a fly on the window, and I tried to catch him; but as
soon as I put out my finger, he went a little lower down the pane;
and as I moved, he moved. I soon saw that the fly was on the
other side of the glass, so that I was not likely to catch him; and
my friend reminded me that I said to the boys, 'Now, there are
many people who are trying to be happy, and they are aiming
at happiness in this way and that way, and they think they will
get it here or get it there; but all their efforts are in vain, for it
is on the other side of the glass. It is only when they have been
renewed in the spirit of their minds that they will catch that
fly, and secure that happiness which they so much desire.' It
was a striking simile for boys, and I was glad my friend had not
forgotten it. I recollect a boy who was struck with that simile; he
was the worst lad in the school until the day when God blessed
that message to him.

Now, I feel so glad that I had an opportunity of opening my
mouth for God in a Sunday school, because it helped me to begin
preaching; and I have no doubt that many of our pulpits have
been filled by those whose first training in speaking for Christ
was received in a Sunday school, where they were asked to
address the children. I do not say this that all of you may become
preachers; you are not all wanted in that particular service; our
good sisters, for instance, are not required as preachers. Yet,
what a blessing it is for you to have an opportunity of doing good
to others, and, at the same time, of getting good yourself!

Nothing, I think, tends to keep piety so much alive as trying to bring others to Christ. If a man does not feel his own weakness, and his entire dependence upon the Holy Spirit as he once did, when he begins to teach others, he soon finds that old Adam, even in young children, is far too strong for him. Thus, trying to teach others teaches us humility. It also teaches us earnestness, for children, as a rule, will not listen to us if we are not in solemn earnest. I remember seeing the boys spinning round over a form, and twisting over and under the seats in a school while the teacher was addressing them, and I really wished I could do the same, for there was nothing to interest anyone in what he was saying. If all our people could amuse themselves in that fashion whenever we preached dull sermons, it would tend to wake us up.

They have done away with the good old custom of clapping or hissing the preacher, because, while the people applauded the minister, all was right, but when they hissed him, it was another matter; so they said that it was improper to have any manifestation of approval or disapproval, and they put it down. I am inclined to think that something or other of the kind would be good for some of us when we are dull, just to let us know that it will not do to waste our people's time, and our own, too, in that fashion. It is only natural that, when you are talking as if your hearts were miles away, that your hearers' hearts go gadding away, too. If you are not yourself interested in your theme, you cannot expect them to be much concerned about it. But when you do labour for your Lord with real earnestness, and especially when you do bring souls to Christ, what a blessing it is to yourself as well as to them! 'It is more blessed to give than to receive.' To be feasting in the house of God is good; but oh, to go out and speak for Jesus, and to bring others to him, is one of the highest felicities on earth! Go on, brothers and sisters, work away for your Lord, and God send you abundant success!

I do not think it is necessary to say to you, but I will say it in case it should be necessary, that the same gospel that saves grown-up people saves children. You must not give to the children a different gospel from that which we have to preach to their parents. Do not give your scholars a diluted gospel, the gospel and water. I have noticed that children are often told, 'You must love Jesus, and then you will be saved.' Yes, but that is not the Bible plan of salvation; it is, 'Believe on the Lord Jesus Christ, and thou shalt be saved'; and though, undoubtedly where love exists in the heart, it is an abundant proof of the exercise of faith, yet you were never sent into the world to tell people, either old or young, that they would be saved by loving Christ; you have altered your Master's commission, which you have no right to do. Those children need to know what they have to believe in order that they may be saved; and you must tell them that it is in Christ and him crucified that they have to trust, and that it is by faith that even little children are brought to Jesus, and saved.

I know you, my dear brethren and sisters, will do that; I have no fear that you will do otherwise; but I do know some Sunday schools where it is not so, and where the children are taught anything but the truth as it is in Jesus. There are other schools where there is nothing for the scholars but the reading and explaining of those regular orderly lessons that are issued by the Sunday-school Union. I suppose they are very capital things for those who can use them; but I know that my experience was that they were of no use to me. They were so often about David and Goliath, or about Ezra and Sanballat, or about Daniel and Nebuchadnezzar; but I wanted to get away to Jesus Christ at once. Now, whether you use the regular lessons or not, do seek to bring your scholars to Christ, and do the best you can to win every one of them for the Saviour, and remember that persuasion is a mighty force with the children.

All of you teachers, I am sure, will get a blessing if you pray for your children one by one, and speak with them one by one. Much more is usually done by a special, particular, personal word than by a general message delivered to a large number. If you were all bottles, and I wanted to fill you, I should not try to do it by squirting over you all at once; but I should come to you one by one, and pour the liquor into you one by one, slowly and gently. I think that, in your Sunday-school teaching, you can try to do too much, and accomplish nothing. You cannot get a quartern loaf into a child all at once; but it goes to be done by breaking it up, and putting some nice warm milk with it. So, when you have a great mass of truth, and you say to yourself, 'How am I to get this loaf into that child's mind and heart?' break it up small, and give it to them with some nice warm milk of affection; and thus, by God's grace, you will get it into the children, and they will be built up thereby. That is the way, I have no doubt, you are doing it. Go on doing it in that way; and may God bless you, dear friends, more and more! Amen.

37

Fellowship with God's Greatness

When I think of the great work of foreign missions, and of all that may result, with the Lord's blessing, from our obedience to his command 'Go ye into all the world, and preach the gospel to every creature', the chief emotion that thrills my heart is that of gratitude to God for enabling me to have some sort of –

FELLOWSHIP WITH HIS INFINITY,

with his greatness. It was enough for me, at the beginning of my Christian life, to have fellowship with God's mercy, to rejoice in his compassion as a pardoning God, 'merciful and gracious, long-suffering, and abundant in goodness and truth, keeping mercy for thousands, forgiving iniquity and transgression and sin'. I rejoiced to know, not only that God is merciful and gracious, but that his mercy and his grace had been displayed in pardoning my sins and iniquities. I praised the Lord because I could say with David, 'Great is thy mercy toward me: and thou hast delivered my soul from the lowest hell.' Ever since that glad hour when I first saw Jesus as my Saviour, I have delighted to sing to him, whose mercy endureth for ever. I have no sympathy with those who would set down as a vain repetition that oft-repeated refrain recorded in the hundred and thirty-sixth Psalm, 'For his mercy endureth for ever.' Long as we live, and till we die, this should be the grateful song of all who have tasted that the Lord is gracious:

> For his mercies shall endure,
> Ever faithful, ever sure.

This, then, was my first Christian experience: a sense of overflowing gratitude for the Lord's forgiving mercy.

When I had advanced a little further along the heavenward way, I came to have sympathy with God's justice: I began to see something of the horrible character of sin, both in myself and in other people; and, sometimes, I felt a burning passion of righteous indignation within my heart as I heard, or read, of vice and crime in some of their grosser forms, or as I became acquainted with sinful men's intense hatred of Christ, the altogether lovely One. Our modern doubters talk with contempt of 'the cursing Psalms' of David; but we have often needed just such language as he used – not for the purpose of vindictively calling for judgements upon our fellow creatures, but as a prophecy of the doom that certainly awaits evildoers.

Even under the milder radiance of the gospel, we have the awful apostolic anathema, 'If any man love not the Lord Jesus Christ, let him be Anathema Maran-atha' (let him be accursed, the Lord cometh). Preachers of 'another gospel, which is not another' (gospel), ought to take warning from Paul's solemn imprecation, 'If any man preach any other gospel unto you than that ye have received let him be accursed.' God's danger-signals have flamed forth from the time of our first parents' entrance into the Garden of Eden, and the red lamp of his inflexible justice is still undimmed. By its crimson light we can clearly read that 'the soul that sinneth, it shall die'. The righteous God 'will by no means clear the guilty'. 'God is angry with the wicked every day.' ' The Lord is a God of judgement.' As I thought of God's justice, and then saw how he had vindicated it by the great sacrifice on Calvary's cross, 'that he might be just, and the Justifier of him which believeth in Jesus', I think I rejoiced as much in his justice as I had formerly done in his mercy.

Since then, on many occasions, I have seemed to have fellowship with God's power. During the terrific thunderstorms that we have had lately, I have thought of Job's words, 'The pillars of heaven tremble and are astonished at his reproof. He divideth the sea with his power, and by his understanding he smiteth through the proud. By his Spirit he hath garnished the Heavens; his hand hath formed the crooked serpent. Lo, these are parts of his ways: but how little a portion is heard of him? But the thunder of his power who can understand?' I have had to get Dr Watts to help me to understand 'the thunder of his power', and I have joined him in singing:

> The God that rules on high,
> And thunders when he please,
> That rides upon the stormy sky,
> And manages the seas:
> This awful God is ours,
> Our Father and our love;
> he shall send down his heavenly powers
> To carry us above.

It is not easy for poor creatures, such as we are, to have sympathy with God's great power as manifested in the thunderstorm; some of us can scarcely do more than lie down, cowed by its majestic grandeur. What would become of us if the Lord were to let loose all his wonderful power? Our comfort is that all the might of omnipotence is pledged to defend us who belong to Christ, and that greater is he that is for us than all that can be against us.

Thus, you see, I have had fellowship with God's mercy, God's justice and God's power; but when I come to the mission field, and begin to think of the work of foreign missions, I get more communion with God's infinity there than I do in almost anything else. You look at the mass of mankind, and talk of the population of the globe as being nearly fifteen hundred millions! What do we know about fifteen hundred millions? We cannot comprehend what one million means; indeed, we do not know much about fifteen hundred: what can we know about fifteen hundred millions? When we get into these long figures, we may as well talk about a million millions at once, or any larger number that you please, for we are quite out of our depth even with the smaller numbers. It is like a man who cannot swim, and who is cast overboard where the sea is five thousand fathoms deep; he would have been drowned if it had been only five fathoms deep; and he would not have been any more drowned if it had been five million fathoms deep. The term 'millions' is one, after all, of which we have a very faint idea; and how can we think of the multitudes of men and women and children who swarm upon this globe, and not be overwhelmed with the magnitude of their numbers? Are these millions to be converted to God? That is our great aim and object, to seek to bring back this world to its rightful Lord and Master: that, filled with redeemed souls, it may shine among its sister stars with a fair, clear light to the praise and glory of God's grace.

We look back upon the ages past, and we mourn that so few have been brought to the Saviour. The years keep rolling on, and but slender progress is made, after all; and centuries, in which we hoped that so much would have been accomplished, pass away with comparatively little done for Christ and his cause and Kingdom. It is an awful struggle, this fight with sin; the cross against the tenfold midnight of human depravity; 'the foolishness of preaching' against the wisdom of this world; nothing against everything, so far as appearances go! Yet God, who is All-in-all, is able to effect his eternal purposes concerning the salvation of men by the feeble means that I have ventured to describe as 'nothing'.

When you come to the missionary meeting, you have gone beyond those trifling troubles with which some are so grievously perplexed. They are wasting their time in a fruitless discussion about the shape of a communion cup, or the colour of a vestment, or the position of a 'celebrant' at what he calls 'an altar'. You have left the puddles of the street, and are soaring upwards toward your God; you have forsaken the little molehills where the worldlings burrow, and you are high up among the Alps when you get to the work of foreign missions. Here is a field wherein the tallest of us may stretch his legs, and not be afraid of intruding into the domain of his fellow labourer. There are some men, and some women, too, who would be all the better if they would stretch their minds, and not always confine their thoughts to one narrow circle.

Look at our small country villages, how rife they are with slander and scandal! Very often, it is because the people have nothing better to think about. I believe that the daily newspaper, with all its faults, has rendered some service to the cottagers of our hamlets, for it has enlarged their ideas, and shown them that there are other people in the world beside those who live at Little Pedlington or Slocum-in-the-Marsh. You hear them talk about the President of the French Republic, or the President of the

United States, or the Emperor of Germany, or the Czar of Russia; and even if they talk nonsense, it is better than slandering their neighbours.

When you transfer this idea to a higher sphere, when you begin to read God's Word, when the Lord has brought you into fellowship with himself through the death of his dear Son, when he has made you a new creature in Christ Jesus, and put his Holy Spirit within you, and given you something of his own compassion for souls, then all things else shrink into nothingness compared with the great redemptive work of Christ, and your obligation to make that work known among the millions of men upon the earth. Compared with the tremendous conflict between God incarnate and the evil that still remains in the hearts and lives of millions of our fellow creatures, all the battles that ever were fought on the earth seem only to be like the fights of ants in their nests. There is no chivalry like that which is possible to a good soldier of Jesus Christ.

I seem to live in poetry when I get to the work of foreign missions. Some of our young brethren in the College, when they begin to make poetry (which is sometimes very poor-try, and at other times very cracked pottery), really imagine that one day they will become Miltons. Ah! well, there will be plenty of prose, and perhaps prosiness, too, in their ministry before it is finished; let us not take their poetry from them; but, brethren, if you want to be poets, think of missions to the heathen; there is a theme worthy of your muse. One feels as if his wings were beginning to grow as he contemplates the triumphs of the cross in foreign lands as well as in our own dear country. Are there not nations that are to be born to God, and are there not whole lands that are to be sown with the seeds of light for the reaping by-and-by?

Foreign missions supply a theme for the prophet as well as the poet. I like, as a rule, to prophesy after the event, or else when I am perfectly sure it is going to happen; and even then, I hold my tongue longer than most people would. But when a man begins to be a foreign missionary, he really does seem to grow into a prophet; there is something in his occupation congenial to the prophetic spirit, and he is linked on to the glorious company that in all ages has prophesied in the name of the Lord. He has higher objects and aims than he used to have, and nobler ambitions than many of his fellows have; his object, and aim, and ambition are to carry out God's purposes of mercy toward the sinful sons of men.

So, if nothing came of our mission work except the education of the workers, the lifting up of men until they are able to have some sort of sympathy with God, it were worthwhile to have our foreign missions; but, thank God, there is much more than that as the result of our efforts! Let India, China, Japan, Africa and the islands of the sea testify what triumphs have been won for King Jesus by the heralds who have gone forth in his name to all quarters of the earth. There remaineth yet very much land to be possessed, both at home and abroad.

Enlarge your sympathies, dear friends, increase your contributions; give yourselves to this glorious work, if you can; and if that is absolutely impossible, help to support those who are both able and willing to go. Do not imagine that the decrees of God can be shut up in a small box, and put away in a cupboard in one of your rooms. They are too great to be confined to any box, or any cupboard, or any room, or any house, or any street, or any town, or any country; nay, they are not confined to the world in which we live; for all worlds are comprehended within the influence of the everlasting purposes of God. His decrees concern the smallest grain of dust that can only be discovered by the aid of the microscope; but they equally have to do with the orbs of heaven: those starry hosts that he calleth by their names, and numbereth, as the Eastern shepherd does with his sheep. In this foreign mission work, I seem to get into the sweep of the spheres of God's eternal purposes; and there I hear again that note that first brought peace and pardon to my burdened heart, 'Look unto me, and be ye saved, all the ends of the earth: for I am God, and there is none else.'

38

Timely Cautions

We have great reason to bless God for the rich mercies we have enjoyed as a church and people for many years, in the unity of the brotherhood, the zeal of the workers, the number of conversions, the success of all our enterprises and the growth of the whole body. It is on my heart to say a word upon another subject: a subject which presses heavily upon my heart. I beseech you, by the mercies of God, and by the love of Christ Jesus, your Lord, that, as members of this church, you do nothing which would grieve the Spirit of God, and cause him to depart from among us. Remember how Israel suffered defeat because of Achan. One man only, and one family only, had broken the divine rule, but that sufficed to trouble the whole camp. Achan had taken of the accursed thing, and hid it in his tent, and all Israel had to suffer defeat because thereof; how much more may a people suffer if sin become general among them, and is allowed to walk abroad unrebuked! At this time, I am greatly mistaken if the church of God is not suffering grievously from the sin of its own members, sin in its own midst.

As I look abroad, I am grieved and have great heaviness of spirit at what I see among professing Christians, not here and there, but almost everywhere. Many Christians, nowadays, do not order their families with godly discipline as becometh saints. I am thunderstruck to hear of Christian men who allow their sons to drink, to keep late hours and even to swear, while their daughters are dressed as gaudily as the gayest of the gay. It grieves me that some professors have no family prayer, and have no command over their children whatever, but seem as if they thought that the duty of a father was to let his children have their own way in all things, and make him their slave. We have too many of the race of Eli, who perhaps say, 'Do not so', but exercise no authority, and put no real check upon the sins of their sons. This is a great source of evil.

The Lord said, 'I know Abraham that he will command his children and his household after him'; and where households are not ordered aright, we cannot expect that the Lord will show special favour to the parents. A husband is the king of his household; and if he allows everything to be in a state of anarchy, he must blame himself in some measure. A husband cannot always govern his wife, for here and there a Jezebel is to be met with; but there are certain things which he should never permit in her if he be a Christian man; and if he fails in his duty of preventing and forbidding sin, God will certainly visit him for it. In ourselves, and in our partners, children or servants, evils are not to be winked at, but put down with a strong hand. May God grant us wisdom and strength of mind to discharge our duty at home! To show piety at home is to show real piety. Time was when there was not a professing family without family prayer, but now there are scores in which it is never offered. You can some of you remember that, if your father was absent on business, your mother carried on the daily sacrifice; and when mother was sick, there was found a boy or girl who would read the Scriptures and pray, so that the holy fire was not allowed to go out. If there be no gathering together for prayer in the morning, how can we expect to be prospered in the duties of the day? If there be no meeting for prayer at night, how can we expect the Lord to guard the tents of Jacob through the night watches? If prayer be neglected in our families, how can we hope to see its spirit pervading our churches?

Another very serious matter concerns the amusements of professing Christians. I see it publicly stated, by men who call themselves Christians, that it would be advisable for Christians to frequent the theatre, that the character of the drama might be raised. The suggestion is about as sensible as if we were bidden to pour a bottle of lavender water into the great sewer to improve its aroma. If the church is to imitate the world, in order to raise its tone, things have strangely altered since the day when our Lord said, 'Come ye out from among them, and touch not the unclean thing.' Is heaven to descend to the infernal lake to raise its tone? Such has been the moral condition of the theatre, for many a year, that it has become too bad for mending; and even if it were mended, it would corrupt again. Pass by it with averted gaze, the house of the strange woman is there.

It has not been my lot ever to enter a theatre during the performance of a play; but I have seen enough, when I have come home from distant journeys at night, while riding past the playhouses, to make me pray that our sons and daughters may never go within the doors. It must be a strange school for virtue which attracts the harlot and the debauchee. It is no place for a Christian, for it is best appreciated by the irreligious and worldly. If our church-members fall into the habit of frequenting the theatre, we shall soon have them going much further in the direction of vice, and they will lose all relish for the ways of God. Theatre-going, if it becomes general among professing Christians, will soon prove the death of piety. One finds the taste for such things increasing on all hands, insomuch that we cannot enter places of entertainment once dedicated to science and art without finding ourselves before long in the presence of something like a theatrical performance.

I do not doubt that these things, which may be in themselves harmless enough, have tended to create and foster the taste which leads ultimately to the theatre and its surroundings. Who can suppose amusements surrounded with the seductions of vice to be fit recreation for a pure mind? Who could draw near to God after sitting to admire the performances of a wanton woman, and I am told that some who have dazzled London society are such. When manners are growing every day more lax and licentious, shall the Nonconformists of England cease from their godly protests, and lower the standard of their lives? If they do so, their spiritual power is departed, and their reason for existence is gone.

If there ever could be a time when Christians might relax their rigidity, it surely is not now when the very air is tainted with pollution, and our streets ring with the newsboys' cries vending filthy papers and abominable prints. It is sad to hear how people talk about acts of sin nowadays; how young men and women, without blushing, talk of deeds which deprave and destroy, as though they were trifles, or themes for jests. It is a thousand pities that the ends of justice should require the publishing of unsavoury details. I suppose there are grave objections to certain cases being heard more privately; otherwise, it would assuredly be better for public morals. As for those who not only commit lewdness, but take pleasure in those who do it, 'Oh, my soul, come not thou into their secret.' My heart often cries, 'Oh, that I had the wings of a dove, that I might fly away and be at rest.' It will, indeed, be ill for the church of God if her members should become impure. In these days, we must be doubly strict, lest any looseness of conduct should come in among us. Actual sin must be repressed with a strong hand, but even the appearance of evil must be avoided.

My dear brethren and sisters, be ye pure; whatever you are not, be pure in heart, and lip, and life. Never indulge an evil imagination, much less speak that which is unclean; let it not once be named among you, as becometh saints. A lascivious glance, a doubtful word, a questionable act must be earnestly avoided; anything and everything that verges upon the unchaste must be eschewed. Only the pure in heart shall see God. We are all subject to human passions, and this wretched flesh of ours is all too easily fascinated by those who would minister to its indulgences; and before we know where we are, the soul is led into captivity. Watch unto prayer; watch especially in these evil days. Cry, 'Lead us not into temptation'; and if the prayer be sincere, you will keep far from doubtful haunts. Make a covenant with your eyes that you will not look upon that which pollutes, and stop your ears from hearing of licentiousness. Pray God to keep your heart pure and holy. Watch your lips lest they spread corruption when speaking of sin. I do not fear so much your going into gross open sin as your doing that which will take you a little way upon the road to it.

I think it is Augustine who tells a story of a young friend of his, who had the greatest horror of everything connected with the Roman amphitheatre. A heathen friend tried to persuade him to enter the Colosseum; and as he was very hard pressed, and was under some obligation to that friend, he determined to go just once, but to keep his eyes and ears closed all the time. It would seem to be a very small risk to sit there as one who was blind and deaf; but, in the middle of the sports, the people so loudly applauded a certain gladiator, who had pleased them, that the young man opened his eyes to discover what it was about. From that moment, he was spellbound; he looked on, and enjoyed the sight; and though, before, he could not bear the very mention of it, he came at last to be a regular frequenter of the cruel sports, and a defender of them, and after a short time he abandoned his profession of Christianity. Beware of the leaven of worldly pleasure, for its working is silent but sure, and a little of it will leaven the whole lump.

Keep up the distinction between a Christian and an unbeliever, and make it clearer every day. Have you never heard of the minister who complained of the devil for running off with one of his church-members? The fiend replied, 'I found him on my premises, and therefore I claimed him.' I, also, may say, 'Stop!' to the arch-deceiver, but it will be of no use if he finds you in his domains. Every fowler claims the bird which he finds in his own net. This is the argument, 'I caught him in my net, and therefore he is mine.' We shall in vain try to dispute this right of property with the arch-enemy, for possession is nine points of the law.

Avoid the appearance of evil. 'But we must not be too rigid,' says one. There is no fear of that in these days. You will never go too far in holiness, nor become too like your Lord Jesus. If anybody accuses you of being too strict and precise, do not grieve; but try to deserve the charge. I cannot suppose that, at the last great day, our Lord Jesus Christ will say to anyone, 'You were not worldly enough. You were too jealous over your conduct, and did not sufficiently conform to the world.' No, my brethren, such a thing is impossible. He who said, 'Be ye perfect, even as your Father which is in heaven is perfect', has set before you a standard beyond which you can never go.

'Well, but,' says one, 'are we to have no enjoyments?' My dear friend, the enjoyments which are prepared for Christians are many and great, but they are not such as savour of sin and folly. Do you call vice and folly, amusements? Then I do not grudge you your mirth. When I go down into the country, I see the farmer's men carrying out great pails of hog's-wash for the swine, and I never grudge them their dainty meal. I never protest against their having a full trough twice over. But do I partake with them? Not I. Not I! I have no taste that way. Do I therefore deny myself? Certainly not! It never struck me that there was anything desirable in their rich mixture. I have no doubt that it has a fine flavour to the creatures for whom it is prepared; at least, it is very strong, and seems to be highly appreciated. So, when persons can enjoy the pleasures of the world and sin, let them have them; poor souls, they have nothing else to enjoy, they have no Paradise for their hereafter, they have no Jesus' bosom to lean their heads upon for the present; let them have that which makes them happy while they can be so. But when I am talking to the children of God, I adopt another tone, since for you these things have no charms if you have, indeed, tasted the high delights of fellowship with God.

'But,' say you, 'I should greatly enjoy a little of the pleasures of sin.' Judge yourselves, then, to be falsely called children of God. 'He that is born of God doth not commit sin': by which is not meant that he does not fall into sins of infirmity, but that it is not his delight to commit sin, it is not the way of him; he is a new creature, and he finds his joy and pleasure in living as near to God as possible.

'How far may we go in conformity to the world?' is a question that is frequently asked in some men's hearts, if not in so many words. Have you never heard the story of the lady who wanted a coachman? Two or three called to see her about the situation, and, in answer to her enquiries, the first applicant said, 'Yes, madam, you could not have a better coachman than myself.' She replied, 'How near do you think you could drive to danger without an accident?' 'Madam, I could go within a yard of it, and yet you would be perfectly safe.' 'Very well,' she said, 'you will not suit me.' The second one had heard the question upon which the other had been rejected, and therefore he was ready with his answer, 'Danger! Madam, why I could drive within a hair's breadth, and yet be perfectly safe.' 'Then you will not suit me at all.' When number three came in, he was asked, 'Are you a good driver?' 'Well,' he replied, 'I am careful, and have never met with an accident.' 'But how near do you think you could drive to danger?' 'Madam,' he said, 'that is a thing I never tried. I always drive as far away from danger as ever I can.' The lady at once replied, 'You are the kind of coachman I want, and I will engage you at once.'

Get such a coachman as that yourself to guide your own heart, and lead your own character. Do not see how near you can go to sin, but see how far you can keep away from it. If you do not take that advice, and if the Spirit of God does not work in you purity of life, by-and-by the church will have to hold up its hands, and say, 'Who would have thought it? These were the nice young people of whom so much was expected; these were the good people who used to say, "You must not be too strict", and where are they now?' To avoid the worst, keep clear of the bad.

As for your Lord's work, be bound to the altar of Christ, and be united for ever to him; and I am sure, if such be the case, you will not find that you are losers by giving up worldly pleasures. The Lord's ways are ways of pleasantness, and all his paths are peace. There is a safe and sweet pleasantness in holy living, and the pleasantness lies very much in the fact that an abounding peace springs from it. God grant us grace to keep in these peaceful paths, even though others should call us Puritans, and ridicule our holy fear of sin! Amen.

39

'Tempted of the Devil'

The letter, which I am about to read, comes from a certain county in Scotland. Each line begins in the original with a capital letter, so that it wears the appearance of poetry. I believe the idea is current in remote country places that this is the correct way of writing, and the writer is too earnest to do anything carelessly or contrary to rule. Here is the letter:

> To the Very Rev. C. H. Spurgeon; Believing that you are one of the faithful servants of God, and also that you have a large congregation, and that there is many a true believer among them; therefore I proposed to write to you in the hope that you and your congregation will remember me in your daily prayers, and also that it will be made public that I am requesting the prayers of the Lord's people for my soul and everlasting salvation, knowing that the effectual fervent prayer of a righteous man availeth much. Dear sir, I may tell you that I am suffering much from the adversary. It is true that I cannot compare myself to that holy man, John Bunyan; but in the book that he wrote under this title, 'Grace Abounding,' he tells us how he was tempted; and I feel that the old serpent, which is the devil, and Satan, who deceived Eve in the Garden, and who was tempting that saint, John Bunyan, with many of the same temptations, tempteth me on this day; and if you would know all that I am suffering from his fiery darts, you would have commiseration with me. I believe it will be twenty-five years now, if not more, since I began to pray to God, and yet my temptations are terrible. Yet I cannot say that I am in despair, for I know that my Redeemer liveth, and I will see him. My trials from the adversary are awful. It may be when I am on my knees praying to God that he will come to me as sudden as a gunshot, and I believe doing all he

can to steal my heart and affections away from God and heaven, and trying to make me say some wrong word; and many a time he will make my heart and flesh tremble while I am at my meat or talking, or in the house of worship, or travelling. In whatever condition I am, I feel that he is doing all he can to ruin my poor soul; therefore, I request the earnest prayer of all Christians for my poor soul, and I know for one, and for the first one, that you will not refuse this supplication to me. I believe that we never saw one another in the flesh, and God only knows if we will see each other on the face of the earth; but I hope we will see one another in heaven where the adversaries can never come near us. I hope this will be told before your congregation on Sabbath first – I am, dear sir, your obedient servant, who resides in the county of — – 'The Lord knoweth all them that are his.

P.S: I will be happy to see your kind advice either in a tract or in a newspaper. I am a reader of the Herald.

I very much demur to the commencement, 'To the Very Reverend C. H. Spurgeon', for no reverence is due to me. Romaine used to say that it was very astonishing to observe how many reverend, right reverend and very reverend sinners there were upon the face of the earth. Assuredly, reverend and sinner make a curious combination; and as I know that I am the second, I repudiate the first. To me, it is surprising that such a flattering title should have been invented, and more amazing still that good men should be found who are angry if this title be not duly given to them. However, the superscription is a small matter. I would make a few remarks upon the letter itself, in order that we may the more intelligently and fervently present our supplications on the writer's behalf.

And, first, we notice with pleasure that the writer is not altogether in despair, for he expressly says, 'I know that my Redeemer liveth.' If he would dwell more on his living Redeemer, and look less at the changeful current of his own thoughts, the snare would be broken, and he would escape. It is very charming to see how poor souls, when tossed to and fro by the devil, will yet hold on to their hope; half afraid to think that Jesus is theirs, they nevertheless feel that they could not give up what little hope they have. By a blessed inconsistency, they doubt and yet cling, dread and yet trust, condemn themselves and yet hope. Such souls are a riddle, puzzling their friends, and most of all confusing themselves. Could we but persuade them to give their thoughts to that blessed 'I know', they would soon chase away the enemy, for Satan abhors a believing 'I know'. He is more content with 'I hope', and best pleased with 'I am afraid'; but 'I know' stings him dreadfully; and if he, who can truly say it, will arm himself with that mind, he will ere long overcome the enemy. Satan dreads the Redeemer's name, and he falls like lightning from heaven before those who know how to plead it with confidence.

Having noticed the pleasing point in the letter, we are now forced to remark that it is a very dreadful thing to be tempted twenty-five years in this way, and yet this is not the only case we have heard of, in which temptation has been both long and strong. I have, in my library, a book by Timothy Rogers upon 'Trouble of Mind', in which he tells us of Mr Rosewell and Mr Porter, both ministers, the latter of whom was six years oppressed by Satan, and yet afterwards rejoiced in the light of God's countenance. Mr Robert Bruce, many years ago minister in Edinburgh, was twenty years under terrors of conscience, and yet found deliverance. Rogers says: 'You have, in *The Book of Martyrs*, written by Mr. Fox, an instance of Mr. Glover, who was so worn and consumed with inward trouble for the space of five years, that he neither had any comfort in his meat nor any quietness of sleep, nor any pleasure of life; he was as perplexed as if he had been in the deepest pit of hell, yet at last this good servant of God, after such sharp temptations, and strong buffetings of Satan, was freed from all his trouble, and was thereby led to great mortification, and was like one already placed in heaven, leading a life altogether celestial, abhorring in his mind all profane things.'

None of these cases extend to quite the length of time mentioned in the letter; but I remember to have heard of one who lay in the prison house some twenty-seven years, and yet came forth to perfect liberty: but even this is less remarkable than the case mentioned by Turner in his *Remarkable Providences* of Mr Charles Langford, the author of a book called *God's Wonderful Mercy in the Mount of Woeful Extremity*. He therein says that, for nearly forty years, he had been severely buffeted by Satan, who left no stone unturned to do him all the mischief he could. For forty years was he led through the uncomfortable wilderness of temptation; and his clearest day, all that time, was but dark: Satan filling his soul with cursed injections, blasphemous thoughts and dreadful temptations. The Lord was pleased to make use of his godly wife for his deliverance. He overheard her pleading at the throne of grace, as was her wont, after this fashion, 'My Father! My Father! What wilt thou do with my husband? He hath been speaking and acting still in thy cause. Oh, destroy him not, for thine own glory! What dishonour will come to thy great name if thou do it! Oh, rather do with me as thou wilt; but spare my husband ...' 'God, who delights to advance his own power by using small and unlikely means, came,' said he, 'and owned his own ordinance, and crowned the cries, and faith, and patience of a poor woman with such success that my praise shall be continually of him. Mine adversary, the devil, was sent to his own place by my dear Lord Christ, who brake the door of brass, and rescued me from his fury.' So, you see, that long temptation by Satan is not so rare a trial as some would suppose.

But these temptations of the devil, do they come to really gracious men? Certainly. The instances I have given prove it; and, besides, our reason would lead us to expect it. If a footpad were on the road, and knew something about the travellers, he would not stop beggars, for he would know that they have nothing to lose. Would he try to rob the rich or the poor? Those that have money, of course, would be his game; and, just so, Satan assaults those who have grace, and leaves those who have none.

When a sportsman is engaged in duck-shooting, he does not hurry himself to pick up the dead ducks that fall around him; he pays all his attention to those which are full of life, and are only wounded, and may perhaps get away. He can pick up the dead ones at any time. Even so, when Satan sees that a man's soul is wounded, and yet that it has a measure of spiritual life, he bends his strength in that direction, in the hope of securing that poor bleeding spirit. It is grace that attracts his malicious eye and his diabolical arrows. He would not sift if there were no wheat, nor break into the house if there were no treasure within. It is no ill proof, therefore, when you find yourself tempted of Satan; his assaults are no sign of a want of grace, but rather a token of the presence of it.

But can a good man be tempted to use bad language? Ah, that he can! The purest mind is sometimes most of all assaulted by insinuations of the filthiest thoughts and most horrible words. I was brought up, as a child, with such care that I knew but very little of foul or profane language, having scarcely ever heard a man swear. Yet do I remember times, in my earliest Christian days, when there came into my mind thoughts so evil that I clapped my hand to my mouth for fear I should be led to give utterance to them. This is one way in which Satan tortures those whom God has delivered out of his hand. Many of the choicest saints have been thus molested. Beloved, think it not strange concerning this fiery trial when it comes upon you, for no new thing is happening unto you but such as is common to godly men.

What is to be done, then, in the case of one who is beaten down and harassed by fierce temptation? If I were the writer of this letter, I suppose I should do as he does; but if I acted rightly, I would go and tell the Lord Jesus Christ all about the devil's suggestions, and beg him to interfere, and restrain the evil one. It is his office to bruise the serpent's head, and he can and will do it. We need not fear that our poor cries and tears will be in vain. Jesus is very faithful, and will come to our rescue. 'That great Shepherd of the sheep' will not allow the wolf to worry his lambs to death.

In addition to spreading his case before the Lord, it may be helpful to the tempted one to write down his trouble. Very much of perturbation of mind arises out of absolute confusion of thought, and a written statement may help to clear away the cobwebs. Luther threw an inkstand at the devil's head at the Wartburg, and the example may be wisely followed; for, often, when you see your misty thought condensed in black and white before your own eyes, it will not exercise over you one-half the power which it possessed before, and often there will be an end of it altogether. I have told you, before, of the poor woman who complained to her minister that she did not love the Saviour. So the pastor went to the window, and with his pencil wrote on a piece of paper, 'I do not Love the Lord Jesus Christ.' Taking it to the good woman, he said, 'Now, Sarah, will you put your name to the bottom of that?' Her horror was most manifest, and she cried, 'Oh, no, sir! I could not do it; I would die first.' 'But you said so.' 'Yes I did, but I will not write it. I love the Lord Jesus too much to sign any such a document.' Is there not wisdom in my advice to write down your temptation?

Still, the main remedy is to keep on going to the Saviour as each new blasphemy is injected, and as each fresh sin is suggested, for he will send the Holy Spirit, the Comforter, to deliver you. If Satan sees a soul constantly driven to Christ by his temptations, he is too crafty to continue them. He will say to himself, 'These attacks of mine accomplish nothing; for, every time that I tempt him, he runs to his Saviour, and so becomes stronger and holier. I will let him alone, and perhaps he will then go to sleep, and so I shall do him greater mischief by my quietness than by roaring at him.' The devil is a cowardly spirit, and fears to meet the courageous in heart. Stretch out your hand, and lay hold upon the sword of the Spirit, and give him a believing thrust, and he will spread his dragon wings in dastard flight. A man had better go a hundred miles roundabout, over hedge and ditch, rather than meet the archenemy; yet, if any of you must meet him, be not dismayed, but face it out with him. Resist the devil, and he will flee from you. May we, in all our conflicts with him, fight the good fight so bravely that, when a memorial is set up to record the conflict, it may bear those lines of honest John Bunyan:

> The man so bravely played the man
> he made the fiend to fly;
> Whereof a monument I stand,
> The same to testify.

May the brother, whose letter I have read, find the Lord to be his strong helper, and speedily come forth out of darkness into marvellous light!

40

'We Shall Get Home; We Shall Get Home'

Conversing, just now, with an elder of the church, I remarked that he must be somewhere about seventy-five, and he replied, 'I am eighty-two.' 'That,' I replied, 'is a good old age.' 'Yes,' said he, 'it is', and then he cheerfully nodded his head, and added, 'We shall get home; we shall get home.' And so we shall, brothers; so we shall, sisters. In chorus we will take up our brother's word, and say, 'We shall get home; we shall get home.'

'We shall get home.' There is music in that simple sentence: a soft melody, as of the evening bell. Early in life, its sound may be more stirring and trumpet-like, nerving our youth to energy, and making us cry, 'Excelsior'; but, as our years increase, and the sun descends, its note is sweet and soothing, and we love to listen to it in our quiet moods, for each word has a silvery tone, 'We shall get home; we shall get home.' This is our great comfort: however long the way, we shall get home. We may live to be eighty-two, or even ninety-nine; but we shall get home in due time. We may not doubt that blessed truth, for the Lord has taught us to sing in the song of Moses, his servant, 'Thou shalt bring them in, and plant them in the mountain of thine inheritance.' The way may be rough, but it is the King's highway, and no brigands can drag us off from it; we shall by this road get home to the Father's own house above. Some of us are not nearing threescore years as yet, and perhaps we have many long leagues to traverse, but we shall get home; glory be to God!

his love has fixed the happy day
When the last tears will wet our eyes,
And God shall wipe those dews away,

> And fill us with divine surprise,
> To be at home, and see his face,
> And feel his infinite embrace.

One reason why I feel sure that we shall get home is this, that we are found in the road which leads there. This is a great wonder: in fact, a greater wonder than our getting home will be. When we were far astray, with our backs to the Father's house, fond of riotous living, the Lord in his infinite mercy visited us, made us long to return to him, and set our feet upon the way of life. This is a miracle of grace, and I am never tired of thinking of it; and because of all that it includes, I feel quite at ease about getting home. 'For if, when we were enemies, we were reconciled to God by the death of his Son, much more, being reconciled, we shall be saved by his life.' The love which plucked us out of the fire will assuredly keep us from falling back into it. God does not begin a work without intending to finish it.

Besides, my brethren, we have already come far on the road, and therefore we shall get home. Considering our many temptations and trials, and the evil of our nature, we are bound to praise the Lord with our whole hearts because we have been preserved unto this day. Our life in the future can hardly be more full of miracle than the past has been; why should we suppose that the Lord will stay his hand? Nothing but omnipotent grace could have brought us thus far, and that grace is quite sufficient to preserve us through all the rest of the way. We shall get home; for 'the Lord hath been mindful of us: he will bless us'. Even in the hour of death, fear shall not overshadow us. You know how quaintly John Mason puts it:

> I have a God that changeth not:
> Why should I be perplext?
> My God, that owns me in this world,
> Will own me in the next.
>
> Go fearless then, my soul, with God
> Into another room:
> Thou who has walked with him here,
> Go, see thy God at home:

I am persuaded we shall get home because, oftentimes, we receive messages from the Father himself, and these love-words assure us that he remembers us; and if he remembers us, he will not let us perish. Moreover, we receive substantial help from him, and comforts by the way both by day and by night. If he meant to cast us off at last, he would not so often have cheered our spirits by his gracious visits and love-tokens on the road. As the land-birds, which light upon the rigging of his vessel, assure the voyager that he is nearing the shore, which as yet he sees not, so heavenly blessings without number flying to our succour tell us that the glory-land is nigh. We shall soon cast anchor in the Fair Havens.

We shall get home, for others have done so who were once at our side travelling the same path. We asked them, as they departed from us, how they hoped to reach their journey's end, and they told us that all their hope rested upon sovereign grace: what less or what more do we rest in? That grace, which has secured to them a safe journey, will secure the like to us; why should it not? It is true that we do not deserve it, nor did they; it was to them a matter of grace, as it certainly will be to us. But that grace is true and constant. All who sail with Jesus shall be saved from the yawning deep. Yes, even though it should be on boards and broken pieces of the ship, we shall get safe to land!

We shall get home; for, oh, if we do not, what a lament there will be in heaven! Think of that. If the children do not come home, what mourning for the lost ones will be heard in the mansions above! Neither God nor good men could see the divine family broken, and yet be happy. Every angel in heaven would feel a disappointment if one child of God was absent at the reading of the muster roll. Did they not once rejoice over each one of us as a sinner repenting? Their sympathetic mirth was premature in our cases if we perish by the way. But angels are not doomed to find their hopes frustrated, neither will the great Father find that he himself was glad too soon. Heaven would be a desolate place if at its banquets some David's seat was empty! We cannot endure to imagine some member of the sacred family missing, lost for ever, cast into hell! It must not be, for in that land of absolute perfectness there is

No missing heir, no harp that lies unstrung
No vacant place those hallowed halls among.

We shall get home, for the great Father himself will never rest until we do; and he that bought us with his precious blood will never be satisfied till all his redeemed shall stand around him girt in their snow-white robes. If we had been on pilgrimage with our families, and we had reached home ourselves, and then missed a dear child, what a stir there would be! I appeal to every father's heart; would you sleep with a child lost? Would you not tramp back every step of the road to seek your dear stray lamb? You would cry everywhere, 'Saw ye him whom my soul loveth?' Well can I imagine our good Shepherd using the same words concerning any one of us if we did not get home, and asking everywhere, 'Saw ye him whom my soul loveth?' He would not rest until he had found his chosen, his heart's delight. Did he rest, the first time, till he brought us home on his shoulders rejoicing? Would he rest, a second time, till he had folded us in glory? No, he can never have full joy in his heart until all his ransomed are in the place where the many mansions be.

Brothers, we shall get home, I am sure we shall; and what a joy it will be! Think of the bliss of seeing our Father, our home, our Saviour and all those who are dear to us for Jesus' sake. A venerable sister, who saw me very busy, the other day, remarked that we shall have plenty of time to talk to each other in eternity. I do not quite see how there can be time when time shall be no more; but no doubt there will be space and opportunity for the fullest communion with each other, and for much fellowship of united delight in the adorable person of our blessed Lord. I anticipate much felicity from fellowship with perfect saints above, since I have had so much pleasure in the society of imperfect saints below. Many have gone home from us of late, and we are getting older; but let us not regret the fact, since the home above is being filled, and a perfect society is being formed which will last for ever.

I remember a remark of my dear friend, John Edwards, before he left us for the Fatherland above. I said to him, one day, 'Our brother So-and-so is gone home', and he replied, 'Where else should he go?' Just so. When evening draws nigh, home is the fit place for each one of us, and we instinctively turn to it. We think badly of people who do not care to go home when their work is done. Some workmen make long hours, and stay late at work; but nobody envies them on that account: most persons think the sooner they are home the better. Do not you think so? Do you not long for the home-going? It is best to have no impatience about it, but to fill up the whole day with holy service, and then consider going home as the crown of it all. Even this poor world can be made very homelike if we have the true childlike spirit. 'Where is your home?' said one to a little girl. The reply was, 'my home is where mother is'. Even so, our home is where Jesus is; and if he wills for us to tarry out of heaven for awhile, we will feel at home in the desert in his sweet company.

Here, however, comes in a word of caution; it will be wise to ask ourselves, 'Where is our home?' Somebody said, 'It is well to go home if we have a good home to go to.' That point is worthy of deep thought. Every creature goes to its own place: the fox to its hole, the bird to its nest, the lion to its den and man to his home. The righteous will rise to the light that is sown for them; but as for the ungodly, where will they go? Where must they go? You may judge of their place by their pleasures. What are their pleasures? Vanity, sin, self. There are none of these things in heaven; and, therefore, those who love them cannot enter there. If they have found their pleasure in the ways of Satan, there shall they find their endless portion.

We may judge men by their company. Like will to like. What sort of company do you prefer? The man who sings the drunkard's song, the man who pours forth loose talk, is he your companion and friend? Then you shall be gathered to him, and to such as he, in the assembly of the dead. I remember a good woman saying to me, on her dying bed, 'I am sure the Lord will not cause me to dwell for ever with the ungodly and the profane, for I have never loved such society. I think he will let me go to my own company.' Yes, that he will. Those who are your companions here will be your companions hereafter.

You may also foretell your future abode from your present character, for your eternal destiny will be the ripe fruit of your character in time. If you are numbered amongst the ungodly when the Lord comes to judgement, you must have your portion far off from God. The false, the foul, the prayerless cannot find a home among the true, the pure, the holy. Oh, you who are unrenewed, I pray you think over those words of the psalmist, 'If I make any bed in hell.' What a bed! But as you make it, you will have to lie upon it. If you find rest in sin, you will make your bed in hell. O my beloved, do not one of you run the risk of such a doom! We have loved each other here; let us not be divided. Let us go together along the way of holiness. Together let us follow Jesus, and then we shall all get home to the same Father's house. My joy, my crown, my second heaven shall be to meet you all there in that sweet, sweet home, where danger shall be ended, where sorrow shall be banished, and sin excluded. Our Father will receive us, our elder Brother will joy in us and the Spirit of God will be glad over us. The dear ones, whom we wept as lost, will meet us; and all the rest of the company redeemed by blood will welcome us. Do not our souls joyfully anticipate that grandest of all family gatherings? Is it not a jubilee to our hearts to think of the general assembly and church of the first-born, whose names are written in heaven?

WE SHALL GET HOME;
WE SHALL GET HOME.

C H Spurgeon's Hymn for an Early Morning Prayer Meeting

Sweetly the holy hymn
Breaks on the morning air;
Before the world with smoke is dim
We meet to offer prayer.

While flowers are wet with dews,
Dew of our souls descend;
Ere yet the sun the day renews;
O Lord, thy Spirit send!

Upon the battle field
Before the fight begins,
We seek, O Lord, thy sheltering shield,
To guard us from our sins!

Ere yet our vessel sails
Upon the stream of day,
We plead, O Lord, for heavenly gales
To speed us on our way!

On the lone mountain side,
Before the morning's light,
The Man of sorrows wept and cried,
And rose refresh'd with might.

Oh, hear us then, for we
Are very weak and frail!
We make the Saviour's name our plea,
And surely must prevail.

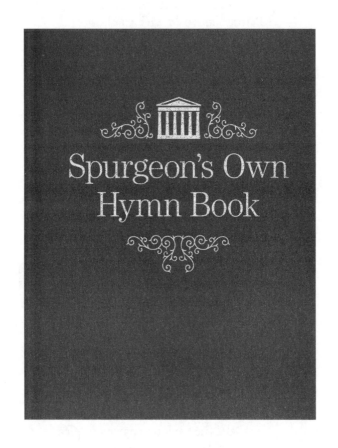

Spurgeon's Own
Hymn Book

978-1-5271-0442-6

Spurgeon's Own Hymn Book

C. H. Spurgeon

Charles Haddon Spurgeon was passionate about congregational worship. Arising from devout affection, the frustration he found while using the the compilations of hymns available in his day, spurred him to compile this selection of hymns for use in his congregation. Over 1,000 psalms, hymns and spiritual songs include not only direct praise, but doctrine, experience and exhortation, enabling the saints to edify one another in their singing. Cross-references to Spurgeon's other works ensure that this will be a valuable addition to any library.

This beautiful gift edition includes

- a foreword by Spurgeon scholar Tom Nettles
- added Spurgeon essay 'How Shall We Sing?'
- elegant hardback cloth bound cover

Persons frequently ask me how to get started reading poetry. Reading the rich texts found in this hymnal is a pretty good way to learn how to read and enjoy poetry, but it is an even better way to feed your soul with these beautiful Psalms and hymns.

Jim Scott Orrick
Professor of Literature and Culture, Southern Baptist Theological
Seminary, Louisville, Kentucky

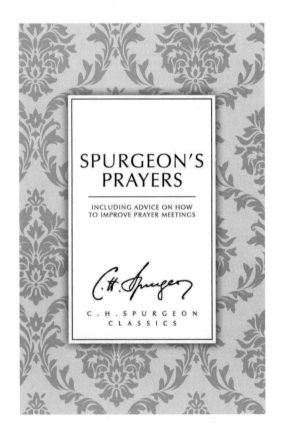

SPURGEON'S PRAYERS

INCLUDING ADVICE ON HOW
TO IMPROVE PRAYER MEETINGS

C.H. SPURGEON
CLASSICS

978-1-5271-0118-0

Spurgeon's Prayers

C. H. Spurgeon

Listening to someone else pray gives you an insight into their mind – their hopes, concerns, and understanding of their relationship with God. Spurgeon thought that prayer was a measure of the vitality of the church – he once ushered some visitors into the prayer meeting at his church with the words 'would you like to see the church's power plant?' These are Spurgeon's prayers taken down as he prayed them. You can learn a lot about how to pray by studying their structure and content. Each short prayer shows you the knowledge of the Bible he had and his understanding of human needs.

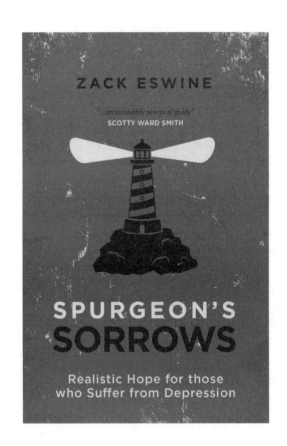

ZACK ESWINE

"...an incredibly practical guide"
SCOTTY WARD SMITH

SPURGEON'S
SORROWS

Realistic Hope for those
who Suffer from Depression

978-1-7819-1538-7

Spurgeon's Sorrows

Realistic Hope for those who Suffer from Depression

Zach Eswine

Christians should have the answers, shouldn't they? Depression affects many people both personally and through the ones we love. Here Zack Eswine draws from C.H Spurgeon, 'the Prince of Preachers' experience to encourage us. What Spurgeon found in his darkness can serve as a light in our own darkness. Zack Eswine brings you here, not a self–help guide, rather 'a handwritten note of one who wishes you well.'

You can almost taste Spurgeon's tears in this book... Eswine's gentle, poetic, unmasking of Spurgeon's inner turmoil may become a soothing balm for your soul. It may not heal you, but a healthy empathy emerges when you read about the struggles of a man who has walked down the same dark alleys you stumble along, and somehow found God in the valley of despair. If you don't struggle with depression yourself, it will help you love those who do!

Jeremy McQuoid
Teaching Pastor, Deeside Christian Fellowship, Aberdeen, Scotland
Chair of Council, Keswick Ministries

Eswine's work demonstrates the value of reading biographies, old books, and sermons. Interacting with godly men and women from church history can be a vital aid to Christian maturity. He handles Spurgeon carefully, yet provoca-tively at points, and produces a volume that promises to help pastors and lay-people confront the sad terror of the dark night of the soul.

The Gospel Coalition

Christian Focus Publications

Our mission statement –

STAYING FAITHFUL

In dependence upon God we seek to impact the world through literature faithful to His infallible Word, the Bible. Our aim is to ensure that the Lord Jesus Christ is presented as the only hope to obtain forgiveness of sin, live a useful life and look forward to heaven with Him.

Our books are published in four imprints:

CHRISTIAN
FOCUS

Popular works including biographies, commentaries, basic doc-trine and Christian living.

CHRISTIAN
HERITAGE

Books representing some of the best material from the rich heritage of the church.

MENTOR

Books written at a level suitable for Bible College and seminary students, pastors, and other serious readers. The imprint includes commentaries, doctrinal studies, examination of current issues and church history.

CF4•K

Children's books for quality Bible teaching and for all age groups: Sunday school curriculum, puzzle and activity books; personal and family devotional titles, biographies and inspirational stories – because you are never too young to know Jesus!

Christian Focus Publications Ltd,
Geanies House, Fearn, Ross-shire,
IV20 1TW, Scotland, United Kingdom.
www.christianfocus.com